H. P. BLAVATSKY
and the
THEOSOPHICAL MOVEMENT

H. P. BLAVATSKY
and the
THEOSOPHICAL MOVEMENT

A Brief Historical Sketch

CHARLES J. RYAN

Second and Revised Edition

Edited by
GRACE F. KNOCHE

THEOSOPHICAL UNIVERSITY PRESS
PASADENA, CALIFORNIA

THEOSOPHICAL UNIVERSITY PRESS
PASADENA, CALIFORNIA
91109

First edition published in 1937

Library of Congress Catalog Card No. 75-4433

Manufactured in the United States of America

CONTENTS

ILLUSTRATIONS

PREFATORY NOTE
to the Second and Revised Edition

"TIME DISCOVERS TRUTH," wrote Seneca as the Graeco-Roman influence, spiritual and political, was ebbing under the influx of the new cycle of thought taking hold. Who and what H. P. Blavatsky was and the purport of her teaching have been the earnest concern of thinkers and writers for a hundred years now, and while the public in general comprehends neither the fullness nor the majesty of her sacrifice, time is her advocate.

To attempt to chronicle the life story of H.P.B. and of the Society she founded in 1875 demands a rare combination of qualities: perception of values, devotion to the theosophic ideals, a sense of history and, above all, an identification with the ageless purpose behind the sending of a messenger. For this is just what H.P.B. was, the sower of the messianic seed for the coming age (the Aquarian) and the restorer of confidence in the validity of the Way.

Charles J. Ryan's *H. P. Blavatsky and the Theosophical Movement* makes no pretense to being a definitive biography of H. P. Blavatsky – much less of H.P.B. – or of the movement she inspired. Nonetheless, it is a product of exhaustive research into the early history and documents of the Society, hostile and friendly, so that the end result is a faithful portrait of the Founder and her life work. The narrative is disarming in its simplicity, but one soon becomes aware of the author's rich reserve of knowledge and grasp of essentials.

Yet why reissue a book, however authentic, that was written back in 1937, now that fuller archival and biographic material is to hand? Data alone do not suffice. The history of any movement, especially one of spiritual origin, is best authored by a protagonist, by one who is convinced of the worthiness of his theme. Unless the writer himself has profoundly experienced the reality of its inner purpose, how can he render a verdict that will pass the test of time?

Not only did Charles J. Ryan have the advantage of having been deeply committed since youth to the cause of human betterment, but he likewise lived close to the flame; he himself never met Madame Blavatsky, but he had as lifelong friends and associates some of her pupils who carried with them until their death the atmosphere of their teacher's heroic dedication. A near eyewitness, and one who during the stormy years of the '90s staunchly defended the principles for which she had given her life, may have something to offer that later historians cannot so easily provide, however much they may benefit from the perspective of years.

A native of Halifax, England, Charles James was born on August 31, 1865, to an English mother from Manchester and an Irish father, descended from the Ryans of Idrone, Tipperary. An artist by profession, he served as principal of the government School of Art in Ventnor, Isle of Wight, succeeding to the post after the death of his father, also an artist, with whom he exhibited at the Royal Academy in London. But C.J.R. was more than an artist and headmaster. A wide reader with an insatiable curiosity, there was no subject in astronomy, archaeology, philosophy or the arts to which he was a stranger. When rather suddenly he was called to California in 1900, to help with Katherine Tingley's new school just opened at the Point Loma theosophical headquarters, his colleagues were at a loss how to do honor to this quiet, self-effacing yet industrious gentleman who not only had exercised a power for good on the several institutions which he had served, but had touched each of their lives in a most intimate way.

Professor Ryan had joined the theosophic scene several years earlier, in January 1894, when the Society was in the throes of controversy and divided loyalties. He himself had been reared in the rationalistic Free-thought atmosphere of the day when anything approaching dogma or authoritarianism in religious matters was suspect. His first exposure to theosophy, he tells us, was "somewhat unpromising," this being the spate of articles that appeared in the British press after H.P.B.'s death in 1891, most of them uncomplimentary, but he had been repelled by the prejudice and ignorance of the "self-styled judges" of the Society for Psychical Research. When later he read A. P. Sinnett's books, he "found his sincerity impressive"; he was not averse to believing there were great teachers who possessed "a more profound knowledge of spiritual and even physico-intellectual man than our modern psychologists, anatomists or theologians." Still, he held back, until one day he met a devoted pupil and friend of H.P.B., a member of the London headquarters staff. "I immediately joined the Theosophical Society – the wisest act of my life" – and helped found the Portsmouth Lodge. In the fateful division of the Parent Society in April 1895, he chose to support William Q. Judge – a decision that was personally painful to him, for it had been Annie Besant's conversion from rank materialism to theosophy that had strongly affected him.

For fifty-five years, Charles J. Ryan gave unqualified devotion to Masters' work, and from 1900 until his death in

Covina on December 24, 1949, contributed his remarkable literary and scientific talents to the theosophical world.

The careful student will be grateful for the inclusion in this second and revised edition of precise references to quotations cited in the text where these were lacking, and for the correction and clarification of a considerable number of minor but significant points of fact. For these we are indebted, first to the author whose personal copy turned over by him to Arthur Conger in 1946 is marked throughout with his editorial changes, omissions and additions; second, to those who worked with me in preparing this edition; and third, to Kirby Van Mater, archivist, for his tireless labor in searching out obscure sources of historic data in the early letters, pamphlets, and original documents preserved in the Archives of the Theosophical Society (Pasadena) – sources which were not readily available to the author at the time of writing. Moreover, Professor Ryan had extended his chronological listing of developments up to 1946, but there seems no call to continue the record beyond that year, over and above the notation (in square brackets) of the sequential changes in administrative responsibility respectively of the two main branches of the movement. Also included are a new bibliography and enlarged index.

Assuredly, the author has accomplished his objective: to give a concise outline of theosophic history and, more importantly, to present H. P. Blavatsky "in such a true light that the reader will see that it was impossible for such a being – the *real* H.P.B. – to be anything but genuine."

GRACE F. KNOCHE

Pasadena, California
June 21, 1975

FOREWORD TO THE FIRST EDITION

RUNNING through the record of the Theosophical Society from its inception to the present day is one unbroken line of underlying purpose to provide a rational solution for the great problems which face humanity. From the first the Society stated that its main object was to disseminate Ideas which would, if put into practice, change the hearts and minds of men to better and higher things. Theosophy, the philosophy of life that has come down the ages, can do this work of spiritual and intellectual alchemy by giving light by which the peoples of the earth can live as high-minded and large-hearted men and women.

Theosophy can set a new current of thought in the world so that brotherhood in thought and act will bring peace on earth and heaven into our midst. This is no visionary dream, it is intensely practical, but we must begin upon ourselves, we must correct ourselves, we must live what we preach. No readjustments of conditions, however drastic, can ever permanently do away with our troubles; we must readjust ourselves and cease to identify ourselves with the material body; we must explore within and find what true living means.

The Theosophical Movement had, and has, if it live true to its purposes and ideals, the backing of certain wise men of the East who possess the light and who are ever ready to help. But even they must abide the time when men are seeking for more light. So in 1875 they sent their messenger,

H. P. Blavatsky, that "strange woman" whose occasional unparliamentary language and outward uncouthness in manner were deliberately assumed to shock men out of their conventional judgments and to arouse their intuition.

Strange indeed she was, but true as steel, and by far the best qualified then available to "break the molds of mind," and to sow the seeds which would germinate in the coming centuries. She began in America, with the simplest teaching about the ethereal forces behind the veil of matter, using the only convenient tool at hand, the well-known phenomena of spiritualism. She discountenanced mediumship, but proclaimed the existence of great Adepts in wisdom and trained knowledge of nature's hidden laws – Rosicrucians, as she called them among other names – and of the lofty possibilities of adeptship latent in every man, a startling concept in the Western world. To scholars she interpreted the deeper meaning of the traditional Qabbālāh in its bearing upon the Christian scriptures, and showed that the Qabbālāh, freed from its corruptions, contained the secret wisdom possessed by the true Rosicrucian or Theosophical societies in past ages under whatever name these societies were called. In her first book, *Isis Unveiled,* she touched on the so-called magical forces in nature and man, repudiated in the nineteenth century, and yet so perfectly natural to those who were spiritually qualified to use them wisely.

H. P. Blavatsky also indicated to a limited degree the other features of her later teachings, such as reincarnation, karma, the complex nature of man, and the cycles of evolution.

Leaving the seeds of the Great Purpose to germinate in the West, she turned toward the Orient, one of the ancient fountains of inner knowledge still existing. Here she strove to arouse the "dreamy Aryans" to study and profit by the unique treasures of truth in their keeping, the wisdom which would not only reflect honor upon India in the critical eyes of the restless West but bring the whole world much needed help. In spite of age-long and ingrained conservatism, proud Brahmans of high caste recognized the authenticity of the messenger and of her message, and joined hands with the theosophists.

H. P. Blavatsky saw that the essential truths in all the great religions had been deeply honeycombed with error, and that for this reason religion had become an element of contention and division in the world. A return to an understanding of the ancient wisdom-religion – theosophy – the spiritual center from which the rival faiths all diverged, is the only way to produce harmony among their followers, and thereby to take an immense step toward universal brotherhood. In the words of G. de Purucker:

> She saw how humanity had been drifting through the ages unaware of its birthright and unconscious of its dignity; how the indefiniteness of modern ideas had confused the minds of the people and engendered everywhere uncertainty and helpless doubt . . . and she left for posterity a body of teachings with power in them to change the whole world, and as it were to raise from the dead the Immortal Part of man.
> – *The Theosophical Path,* XXXVI, 398, Aug. 1929

The underlying current of the original purpose having reached the Orient, its real birthplace, the messenger moved to Europe where she finished her masterpiece, *The Secret Doctrine,* and wrote other theosophical classics. Though an intellectual response came from matter-of-fact Europe, its almost complete failure to understand the "chela-spirit" of devotion was disappointing. Nevertheless, the lionhearted Blavatsky never gave up and, at last, against all odds, she aroused in "the few" a deeper comprehension of her mission. She was then able to take the first steps in the revival of the forgotten schools of the Mysteries, and at the opportune moment she produced a devotional gem from the Orient in an exquisite Western setting of her fashioning, *The Voice of the Silence*, a guide for students who aspire to tread the path of spiritual wisdom.

When the time came for the teacher to depart, no crisis occurred, although the cynics vainly imagined that the Movement would perish forthwith. On the contrary, its influence has increased and widened steadily, in spite of external opposition and internal difficulties in some quarters. It is now the privilege as well as the duty of devoted theosophists to keep alive the torch she placed in their hands, but it can burn brightly only in an atmosphere of kindness, brotherhood, and magnanimity. If some reasonable cooperation is not established between the groups which claim to follow the precepts and the example of the founder of their movement, the progress of theosophy and the world's advancement on spiritual lines will be far more seriously delayed than by all the attacks of the detractors.

While assuredly the best way to understand the heart and mind of Helena P. Blavatsky is to study her writings, yet there is much of great value to learn from the story of her life of toil and renunciation, of self-sacrifice and voluntary martyrdom, for she was in essentials a lofty example of what she taught. So many attempts have been made by misguided persons to misrepresent her in the eyes of the ill-informed that a brief but authentic account in handy form of the chief incidents of her life, her ideals, and her methods, such as has not hitherto been available, may not be out of place at this time when recent attacks have aroused widespread attention to theosophy, and when world conditions demonstrate the crying need for its constructive ideas.

This book also presents an outline of the more striking landmarks in the historical background of the Theosophical Society during the lifetime of its chief founder, and touches more lightly upon some of the outstanding events that have occurred since her passing, especially in regard to the protective and sustaining efforts of her most trusted friend and disciple, William Q. Judge, to carry the work and teaching on in accordance with what H. P. Blavatsky called the "Original Plan of the Masters."

The limited space at disposal has compelled the omission of much interesting matter, and the selection of the most important highlights has been no easy task. The administrative affairs of the Society, the establishment of lodges and national sections, the erection or purchase of buildings, the numerous conventions, and the details about the rise of theosophy into the "luminous zone" and its wide recognition by thinkers, while interesting to close students of theosophical history, can only be referred to in general terms. Even the numerous confirmations of H. P. Blavatsky's scientific teachings now being made, and her time-honored methods of training aspirants to chelaship, important as they are, demand far more room than can be spared for adequate treatment.

It is to be regretted that owing to lack of space it is impossible to do justice to, or even mention, most of the devoted Fellows of the Theosophical Society who have unselfishly given their time, money, and work to the Movement, often under very trying conditions, and at great personal sacrifice. If a small number of the more prominent were named the selection might be considered inadequate or ill-advised by some, and so only those persons who have a special relationship with H. P. Blavatsky or with important events in later history have been mentioned.

While it is the duty and the privilege of theosophists to express their gratitude for the spiritual and intellectual illumination received from their teacher by defending her honor and exposing the falsity and hollowness of the foolish and malevolent charges from which she suffered, the aim of this volume is not controversial per se, though it contains information useful in her defense. The writer, who has never hesitated to break a lance with her critics when the opportunity offered, feels that a fair and dispassionate statement of the facts of her career and of the motives underlying her actions is sufficient to satisfy any unprejudiced mind that she was justified in her claim that she was sent by her Masters to bring the ancient wisdom, theosophy, once more to the world at a critical period in its history.

To regard her as a charlatan is to reduce her life history to an incomprehensible jumble of absurdities. One or two controversial matters in regard to theosophical events about which there may still be differences of opinion have had to be discussed because they touch very closely on fundamentals, but they have been treated as impersonally as possible and we hope in such a way as not to give offense.

CHARLES J. RYAN

Point Loma, California
November 17, 1937

H. P. BLAVATSKY
and the
THEOSOPHICAL MOVEMENT

Now bend thy head and listen well, O Bodhisattva – Compassion speaks and saith: "Can there be bliss when all that lives must suffer? Shalt thou be saved and hear the whole world cry?"

– *The Voice of the Silence*, 71

I

INTRODUCTORY

I produce myself among creatures . . . whenever there is a decline of virtue and an insurrection of vice and injustice in the world; and thus I incarnate from age to age for the preservation of the just, the destruction of the wicked, and the establishment of righteousness.
— *Bhagavad-Gītā*

THE THEOSOPHICAL SOCIETY was organized in 1875 by Helena Petrovna Blavatsky, Henry Steel Olcott, William Quan Judge, and others, under the authority of certain Mahatmas or Masters of wisdom belonging to the highest Lodge of Adepts, as an agent or instrument through which the influence of the Theosophical Movement could reach humanity. The primary object of the movement is to bring about a universal brotherhood based upon the essential divinity of man.

The movement is greater than any society, for it includes and employs many organizations and agents, but if they become fossilized in dogma or betray their original purpose, the spirit of theosophy can no longer use them. As William Q. Judge says, the theosophical movement is moral, ethical, spiritual, universal, invisible save in effect, and continuous; while a society formed for theosophical work is a visible organization, a machine for conserving energy and putting it to use, though its unique and comprehensive scope is not easy to express.

Theosophy may be defined as a formulation of the nature and operation of the universe, including, of course, the nature of man, his origin and destiny. It is incomparably more comprehensive than what is generally known in the West as Eastern yoga, and it includes the problems of practical, everyday life in its scope. To quote the opening words of *The Ocean of Theosophy*, by W. Q. Judge:

> Theosophy is that ocean of knowledge which spreads from shore to shore of the evolution of sentient beings; unfathomable in its deepest parts, it gives the greatest minds their fullest scope, yet, shallow enough at its shores, it will not overwhelm the understanding of a child. . . . Embracing both the scientific and the religious, Theosophy is a scientific religion and a religious science.

Theosophical literature contains, therefore, only a very partial presentation of a cosmic scheme which is far beyond ordinary human comprehension. There are, however, a few very highly evolved men who have penetrated more deeply behind the veil of nature and have realized, through initiation into the Mysteries, a far greater understanding of *theosophia*, the divine wisdom. Such men are called Mahatmas or Rishis in India, and those of the highest grade are believed to have attained the most sublime wisdom and knowledge that is possible for humanity in this stage of evolution. The Mahatmas must not be confused with minor adepts, lamas, yogis, or hermits in India or Tibet, such as are described by ancient and modern travelers who have met them on rare occasions. The Masters, as they are frequently called, stand far higher in spiritual and intellectual knowledge. The highest grade of Adepts have passed beyond the need of physical imbodiment, though their superior spiritual and intellectual wisdom is devoted to the welfare of mankind.

The theosophical ideal of brotherhood is neither visionary nor impracticable, though it will, of course, take a long time to realize. It is not limited to philanthropic, intellectual, or economic endeavor as commonly understood. Though it includes these activities, it implies something deeper. The form of brotherhood which it was hoped would spread gradually till it covers the earth must begin with the work and example of a body of men and women who have a profound desire to benefit humanity by giving out *ideas* which will change men's minds by changing their hearts, ideas based on the belief that this world is not an accident, that men are not creatures of chance with no past and no future, but that law and order reign in nature. In brief, to live in brotherly union is the only way to become truly human, because it is the fundamental basis on which the universe is built, and man is an indissoluble part of the universe. Brotherhood – interdependence – as a universal principle in nature is not a mere sentiment, and theosophy is not a sentimental or emotional system, but strictly scientific, as well as religious and philosophical. The universal tradition of a Golden Age is perhaps only a dream of the past, but it is the reality of the future; and if the constructive ideals of theosophy, the ancient wisdom, were universally practiced it would be here today.

The epoch in which the Theosophical Society appeared was one of confusion of ideas in the West, when the mental field was being plowed in preparation for the new cycle of transition in nearly every aspect of life. A few learned scholars in the West had begun to study and translate Oriental literature; a few liberal thinkers were courageously suggesting that the ancient philosophies of India and China were something better than "heathen foolishness"; Emerson was diffusing some of the light from the East. But few except specialists knew anything about the Eastern wisdom, and still fewer attached any importance to its spiritual significance. Hinduism was regarded as rank superstition and Buddhism as pure materialism or at best agnosticism. Max Müller was teaching that nirvāna was annihilation!

Reincarnation was practically unheard-of in the West, or was misinterpreted as transmigration into animals. The law of karma (cause and effect) which makes a man responsible for his own destiny by challenging him "to work out his own salvation" had long been obscured by misleading notions like the vicarious atonement and the remission of sins by priestly mediation.

Science, in its heyday of materialism and self-exaltation, while quite properly breaking down medieval superstitions and illogical dogmas, was also, unfortunately, undermining the belief in the reality of man's spiritual nature. Darwinian evolution was replacing the Christian theory of the creation of man in the image of God by the mechanistic natural selection and survival of the fittest hypothesis. Thoughtful minds who were trying to harmonize the hard facts of science with spiritual interpretations of the universe were in difficulties. Even in India the established creeds were threatened.

Fortunately, however, freedom of thought was no longer prohibited, and new ideas were allowed a hearing. Therefore, when scientific materialism seemed on the eve of triumph, an audacious challenge was thrown by spiritualism. It at least demonstrated the existence of invisible and ethereal planes of substance and of life, other than the physical plane to which materialistic science then limited its universe, built of "hard billiard-ball atoms."

Several distinguished scientists, such as Crookes and Hare the chemists, Wallace the biologist, Wagner the geologist, Flammarion the astronomer, and a few others, with rare courage dared to look into psychic research and to satisfy themselves that some truth lay behind the claims of the spiritualists. The latter, however, offered no adequate philosophy or scientific analysis of their phenomena and, like their contemporaries in other fields, they never dreamed that the subject had already been thoroughly explored in past ages by advanced and fearless Oriental thinkers and other ancient researchers who had found that the phenomena fitted into a legitimate place in the scheme of natural law.

Even in the domain of the arts there was hardly any rational appreciation of the extraordinary greatness and the subtle spiritual background of Oriental accomplishment in that field, which is now so much more intelligently understood in the West.

Amid this welter of contending elements the Theosophical Society made its appearance, a strange meteor from an unseen source destined to make a far greater stir than its first modest proceedings suggested. As the famous French Orientalist, Burnouf, remarked, Theosophy was one of the three most important movements of the age. It fulfilled Schopenhauer's prediction that the most significant event of the nineteenth century would be, in the judgment of posterity, the introduction of the religious philosophy of the East to the notice of the West.

While scholars were mostly studying the technical side of Sanskrit literature, the theosophical movement brought the higher spiritual interpretation of it to the Western world.

A "New Order of Ages"* was at hand, and the Theosophical Society brought one entirely new idea, hitherto obscured, to the West: the actual existence on earth of perfected men, masters of life, elder brothers of mankind. Though many, or perhaps most, of these advanced Intelligences live and work on planes of being invisible to ordinary sight, they are not spirits in the ordinary sense, nor supernatural, though they are superhuman. They are the natural products of human evolution, though they have outdistanced their fellow men. Not only did theosophy proclaim their existence as facts and ideals, but it said that at certain cyclic periods they sent messengers to the world to revive its waning spirituality, and to strike the note of universal brotherhood anew. Furthermore, the unseen helpers, the "Guardian Wall" of humanity, were prepared to share a portion of their knowledge of the hidden laws of the universe with those whose lives proved that they were worthy and well qualified to receive it. Above all, theosophy brought the good tidings that the

*In *The Theosophist*, V, 17, Oct. 1883, W. Q. Judge wrote in regard to the design for the unused side of the Seal of the United States, that it was intended to symbolize the building and firm foundation of "The New Order of Ages" (the motto on the Seal). Only one side – the one with the eagle – has been in use, and Judge said: "When the other side [with the motto and the truncated pyramid beneath the blazing eye] is cut and used, will not the new order of ages have actually been established? . . . the Theosophical Adepts . . . watch the progress of man and help him on in his halting flight up the steep plane of progress. They hovered over Washington, Jefferson . . . who dared to found a free Government in the West, which could be pure from the dross of dogmatism, they cleared their minds, inspired their pens and left upon the great seal of this mighty nation the memorial of their presence." The hitherto unused design of the seal has just (1935) been placed on the dollar bill.

Mahatmas are nothing more than what every one of us may become in time *if he will.*

H. P. Blavatsky challenged the Western world with a formulated plan in which the universe was shown as a cosmos of order and of conscious activity, not an unreasoning or unreasoned chaos, and that man is, and always has been, an inseparable part of the universe, no accidental visitor here today and gone tomorrow. She showed that while the archaic wisdom, preserved and handed down by the Guardians of the human race, is found hidden under worldwide symbol, allegory and legend, it was plainly though secretly taught in the schools of the Mysteries, whose portals even today will open to earnest and unselfish workers who give the right knock.

The history of the Theosophical Society is intimately interwoven with that of a few prominent men and women who have in various ways helped or hindered its progress. By far the most important personality is, of course, the founder of the Society, but the limitations of this brief outline do not permit a detailed and exhaustive study of her personal history. The simple facts about her life and character, however, stated and considered just as they are found, are a sufficient refutation of the unfounded libels and misrepresentations by which unthinking and occasionally vindictive writers from her time to our own have attempted to belittle if not destroy both her reputation and her life work.

Photo by Beardsley

H. P. Blavatsky, 1875, Ithaca, New York

2

HELENA PETROVNA BLAVATSKY

MANY students of modern thought, not connected with the theosophical movement, have called H. P. Blavatsky the most remarkable woman known in the nineteenth century, a most unusual genius. So unusual, so careless of worldly honors, so regardless of her own welfare throughout a career devoted to that of others, so impersonal and yet so intensely vital, was this extraordinary being, that she was bound to be misunderstood by those who interpret the actions of the great in soul by the common self-centered motives that govern those of the multitude.

She brought a great hope to the world — theosophy — at the critical time when the old cycle was evidently passing and the fate of the new one hung in the balance. With the unaffected humility of true greatness which dared to be misunderstood when called upon to lead, she abandoned everything the world holds dear to wage an incessant warfare against the forces of darkness and ignorance. She was a mystery in her very simplicity, like a great mountain or the ocean. She was called the Sphinx of the nineteenth century; but she is better understood in the twentieth. She asked no reward but the joy of rendering service to a world "perishing from spiritual starvation." She brought back the neglected idea of man's responsibility for his own acts and for their consequences which had been so long obscured by theological dogmas. She taught that the true way to happiness, peace, and power, was to find the divine nature within ourselves.

The theosophical movement in the nineteenth century was not the first effort of the kind. Tsong-kha-pa, the great Tibetan Adept and reformer of the fourteenth century A.D., is responsible for the initiation of attempts to help the world spiritually at certain cyclic periods. Similar avatāric leaders and efforts are part of world history, past, present, and future. H. P. Blavatsky writes:

> Among the commandments of Tsong-Kha-pa there is one that enjoins the Rahats (Arhats) to make an attempt to enlighten the world, including the "white barbarians," every century, at a certain specified period of the cycle. Up to the present day none of these attempts has been very successful. Failure has followed failure.
>
> – "S.D. III," 412

Thanks, however, to her courage and self-sacrifice, the movement has not failed this time, though every effort has been made to destroy it, both by traitors and the unthinking within, as well as by open enemies without. For the first time on record, it has been carried safely from one century to the next.

Born at Ekaterinoslav, in Russia, about midnight between August 11 and 12, 1831, Helena P. Blavatsky had every advantage that wealth, culture, and high social position can bestow. Her father was descended from the Counts von Hahn of Mecklenburg, and her mother was the daughter of Privy Councillor Andrey Fadeyeff and Princess Helena Dolgorouky. The latter traced her ancestry to the Grand Duke Rurik, the first actual ruler of Russia. Her mother was an accomplished writer; but of all the Hahns or the Dolgoroukys, brilliant as they were, there never was another like H.P.B. – as most of her theosophical friends generally called her.

From her earliest childhood H. P. Blavatsky displayed unusual qualities. Though exceedingly kindhearted and affectionate, her unconventional ways made her the despair of her governesses, for she was impetuous and daring to recklessness. Her indomitable self-will and inherent rebellion against the conventional restraints of the earlier part of the nineteenth century – traits which were not wisely handled by her adoring relatives – were afterwards the cause of much of the trouble she suffered at the hands of the blind critics who never thought of looking beneath the surface and finding the true gold underneath. And, indeed, the gold of her nature rang true. Intractable to control by force, she was always amenable to reason and kindness, and she would passionately protest against injustice and cruelty to others. When very young her eager sympathy and compassion were deeply aroused by the heartrending scenes of misery and despair she saw among the exiles who were driven in weary files past her father's magnificent estate, on their terrible journey to Siberia. She never forgot those horrible sights, and when the time came she vowed to do her utmost to reduce the awful toll of worldwide human suffering in general *by attacking the causes* and not merely by remedying the effects. Her love of nature was great; everything – the rocks, the trees, the birds – spoke to her; and she soon distinguished between the artificial and hypocritical life of man and the glorious world of reality which is shut out from us only by our selfish limitations.

Unfortunately, she lost her mother when very young, and her education was not well ordered, though her natural abilities were excellent. She spent five years with her grandparents at Saratoff where her grandfather was civil governor, and where she had the advantage of using his enormous library, in which she read extensively if not very systematically. About this time, in 1844 and again in 1845, her father took her abroad, and in France, Germany, Italy, and England she was introduced to the larger world of art and culture. During this period she took lessons from the famous German composer and pianist, Ignaz Moscheles.

According to Olcott, although Helena was so young, her great musical ability qualified her to appear in a concert in London, where she took part in a trio for three pianos, in which the other performers were Clara Schumann and Arabella Goddard. Shortly before she came to America, in 1873, she made some concert tours in Russia and Italy under the pseudonym Madame Laura. Later in life, on the rare occasions when she touched the piano, she made a profound impression by the spiritual power and beauty of her playing. Olcott often heard her in New York. He says:

> She was a splendid pianist, playing with a touch and expression that were simply superb. . . . There were times . . . when her playing was indescribably grand. She would sit in the dusk sometimes, with nobody else in the room besides myself, and strike from the sweet-toned instrument improvisations that might well make one fancy he was listing to the Gandharvas, or heavenly choristers. It was the harmony of heaven. —*Old Diary Leaves,* I, 458–9

After further travel in England, France, Germany, and Russia, she and her father returned home. Though she was more docile with him than with anyone else, she says: "He blessed his stars when we went home," and she was safely lodged in the seclusion of southeastern Russia!

The day on which she was born was regarded by the simple serfs and domestics of her childhood as being very significant. Persons born at that time were said in Russia to have control over the elementals, the goblins with which Russian folklore is well supplied, and her career, even in youth, gives reason to believe that this was certainly true in her case. Her clairvoyant, clairaudient, and telepathic powers were remarkably developed at the age of four, and for many years they were the marvel of the neighborhood – a phenomenon indeed in such a thoroughly conventional, Orthodox Church and patrician family as hers! Yet, as is well known, if the royal and noble families of Europe permitted their secret archives to be published, many startling 'occult' events would be revealed.

Although H. P. Blavatsky's psychic faculties had to be allowed to run wild, so to speak, for a while, and the course of training in which they became disciplined did not begin till about womanhood, she was visibly (to her) under the guardianship of her Master, an Indian Rajput, the Mahatma Morya or, as he is generally called, the Master M. At first he was unknown to her as a living man, but when she met him afterwards in bodily form he was no stranger. More than once her life was saved in a mysterious way by him. She told her family that this guardian, whom of course they could not see, was not a spirit of the departed; and she insisted that wise men, great sages, existed on earth, who knew the greatest secrets of nature but who revealed themselves only to those who deserved help.

An aged man who lived in a forest near her birthplace – a benevolent magician, according to popular belief – told her sisters that "this little lady is quite different from all of you. There are great events lying in wait for her in the future. I feel sorry in thinking that I will not live to see my predictions of her verified; but *they will all come to pass!*"* They certainly did, and to the great profit of the world, though she paid a heavy price for the gifts she brought. All this, and far more of fascinating interest, is related by her Orthodox Church relatives who had no sympathy with her theosophical 'heresies' and activities.

At a later date, a high ecclesiastic had the intuition to recognize that H. P. Blavatsky's occult powers were perfectly genuine and that they could be put to the service of mankind. This broad-minded priest was the Metropolitan Isidore, one of the three 'popes' of the Russian Church, and an old friend of the Hahn family. In 1860, during a visit that H.P.B. and her sister paid to the Metropolitan, many phenomena took place in his presence. Mme. Jelihovsky writes, in her "Personal and Family Reminiscences":

> When bidding good-bye to us, the venerable old man blessed the travellers, and turning to Mme. Blavatsky, addressed to her these parting words:—
>
> "As for you, let not your heart be troubled by the gift you are possessed of, nor let it become a source of misery to you hereafter, for it was surely given to you for some purpose, and you could not be held responsible for it. Quite the reverse! for if you but use it with discrimination, you will be enabled to do much good to your fellow-creatures." —*Incidents*, 137

In 1848, when barely seventeen, the young girl hastily accepted an offer of marriage from the man whose name she afterward bore. N. V. Blavatsky, Councillor of State, vice-governor of the province of Erivan, was in the worldly sense

**Incidents in the Life of Madame Blavatsky*, by A. P. Sinnett, 43.

an excellent match, even though he was more than twice as old as the motherless girl who married him in a fit of bravado. Her governess had taunted her high-spirited pupil by saying that no one would marry her, not even old Blavatsky, whom she had laughed at so much. When she realized what a rash step she had taken, and what were the implications of matrimony, she left her nominal husband without, as her relatives have explained, giving him the opportunity of ever thinking of her as his wife. Soon after this madcap experience, she set forth upon those years of wandering and search during which her indomitable will, natural genius, and the usually unseen protection of her Master, carried her safely through strange countries and stranger experiences.

It was part of her training to review, personally, a cross section of human life, in order to acquire firsthand knowledge to be used later in her work. Her experiences included not only the grand and the beautiful but also much that was weird and occult, oftentimes in isolated and dangerous places. All this prepared her to speak with authority as an eyewitness when she discussed the rationale of many extraordinary happenings which she recorded in her first major work, *Isis Unveiled*, and elsewhere.

The pursuit of a course so unusual for a young girl of her sheltered class not unnaturally aroused comment in those early days of the nineteenth century when women had little freedom; and vague reports of irregular doings of various women of the same name were slanderously attributed by venomous tongues to H. P. Blavatsky. Her father, Colonel Hahn, kept up a regular correspondence with her and supplied her with money, and when the spiteful gossips pretended that she was leading a gay life in Paris or Berlin or Vienna, she was either traveling in some distant continent in pursuit of her investigations, or living quietly at home during the rare intervals when she needed rest and longed for the companionship of her family circle, to which she was greatly attached. Years afterwards, these calumnies were used as poisoned weapons by which bigotry in more than one form tried to destroy the message by reviling the messenger – the old, old story of persecution by the forces of darkness.

As she never kept a diary and her memory for dates was uncertain, it is impossible to be sure about the exact period of some of her journeys, but the general outline and a few precise dates of the period between 1848 and 1873 are properly established. For a while she traveled with a Russian countess in Turkey, Egypt, and other parts of the Levant. In Cairo she studied under a Copt, a remarkable occultist and, probably at this time, she joined the secret lodge of the Druses of Mt. Lebanon. In 1851 she met her Master for the first time in his physical body, though she had frequently seen him clairvoyantly. The day she met "the Master of her dreams" was her twentieth birthday, as she writes in her private *Scrap-Book.* The first Great International Exhibition was held in London in that year, and the Master was there in the suite of the famous statesman, Sir Jung Bahadur of Nepal, who, from being a ruthless despot, became a wise and beneficent ruler after his return home – a most remarkable transformation. Master M. now outlined a plan for H. P. Blavatsky's future, and showed her how to prepare for the work for which she had been chosen.

The Masters had seen that the long-separated East and

West were being brought into close communication on prosaic commercial, economic, and political lines, and that the East would become dazzled by the brilliant materialism of Western progress. They saw that the hour had struck to anticipate the danger of the coming interchange of materialistic thought and ideals with the psychic lure of the acquirement of the lower yoga powers – a contact on lower lines fraught with disaster for both sides. To counteract this danger, they planned to strike a strong keynote on the higher lines of human welfare. They started their unique work by training H. P. Blavatsky, as a European, to bring the Western initiative and energy to awaken the East from its spiritual lethargy and to share with the world some of the buried treasures of the ancient wisdom. To prepare for a society which should be a nucleus of a universal brotherhood, she took her long and adventurous journeys in distant lands in order to gain necessary experience and knowledge of human life. Traveling under the occult supervision of her Master, she found her way to places and had the entrée to sources of secret lore which were not open even to accredited explorers or to learned researchers.

In Canada she came in touch with the American Indians, and learned something of the secrets of their medicine men. In New Orleans, where she investigated Voodoo rites, she was in great danger and had to be warned by her Master to leave quickly. She then proceeded to Texas where she met an old French Canadian, Père Jacques, who took care of her for some time and saved her from serious perils. As her knowledge of English was limited, a protector with whom she could speak freely must have been very helpful. Mexico was the scene of her next adventures, and here she met a Hindu chela of her Master, whose protection was quite necessary in that unsettled country. Accompanied by this chela and another student of mystical subjects, whom she had arranged to meet in the West Indies, she sailed for India. Here she made an abortive attempt to enter Tibet, for she was turned back by the British officer commanding a frontier district. Many years after, in India, the account of her failure was confirmed to Colonel Olcott by the officer himself, Major-General Murray, who said that H.P.B. had to be detained a month in his house in his wife's company (*O. D. L.*, I, 265).

Leaving India, she visited Singapore and Java, and finally reached England. Finding that preparations were being made for the Crimean War involving England, France, and Russia, she, being a Russian subject, departed for the United States (1854), landing in New York and then went to Chicago. Crossing the Rocky Mountains with emigrants' caravans she reached San Francisco, where it is said that she met her Master again. Witnesses have declared that the local newspapers mentioned her name, and published stories of an unusually tall and distinguished Hindu who attracted great attention when he appeared in public. Unfortunately documentary evidence is lacking, because the great San Francisco fire destroyed the files of the papers, and inquiry has, so far, failed to discover a single copy elsewhere.

Once more she set forth for the Orient, and in 1855 she reached India again, where she met a German friend of her father, an ex-Lutheran minister named Külwein. A party was organized with the object of penetrating into Tibet, but H. P. Blavatsky was the only member of it who succeeded. Little is known of her experiences in Tibet on this occasion, except what is so interestingly described in *Isis Unveiled.* After surmounting many difficulties and having many adventures, she was finally rescued from a most critical position and conducted back to the Indian frontier. She tells of the advanced telepathic methods by which the shaman who was her guide called for assistance:

> We had directed the Shaman's inner *ego* to the same friend heretofore mentioned in this chapter, the Kutchi of Lha-Ssa, who travels constantly to British India and back. *We know* that he was apprised of our critical situation in the desert; for a few hours later came help, and we were rescued by a party of twenty-five horsemen who had been directed by their chief to find us at the place where we were, which no living man endowed with common powers could have known. The chief of this escort was a Shaberon, an "adept" whom we had never seen before, nor did we after that, for he never left his *soumay* (lamasery), and we could have no access to it. But *he was a personal friend of the Kutchi.* —*Isis Unveiled,* II, 628

H. P. Blavatsky adds that the above will of course provoke nothing but incredulity in the reader, but it is only an example of the "illimitable powers and possibilities of the human astral soul." Today, when we have innumerable evidences of highly advanced telepathy among so-called primitive races, such as the American Indians, African peoples, Australian aborigines, Eskimos, etc., she would not have to face the ridicule and abuse she then suffered for daring to fly in the face of conventional public opinion. The increasing number of sensitives in every part of the world is so noticeable today that disbelief in telepathy and clairvoyance is becoming absurd and a sign of ignorance.

3

TRAINING IN CHELASHIP

IT SHOULD not be overlooked that during her years of wandering, study, and adventure, H.P.B. was always supplied with funds by her father, who sent money to places where she could find it waiting for her. At times she was hard pressed for cash to meet the day's expenses, and at others she had so much that she spent it lavishly, or gave it away with the impulsive generosity so characteristic of her.

While in America in the fifties, she received a legacy of 80,000 rubles from a relative, but she quickly used it all. After her beloved father's death in 1873, she spent most of her heritage from him in buying land and starting a farming enterprise on Long Island, New York, but, as she had no experience in that direction, it naturally failed. Her pen was the true instrument of her genius, and when she began writing for the Russian journals, her work rapidly became highly successful under the pseudonym of Radda Bai.

After further travel in India she was warned by her Master to leave, and so she safely escaped the troubles of the Indian mutiny of 1857. He sent her to attend to some business of his in Java where she met two other chelas. It was possibly immediately after this that she visited South America in 1857 and gained the archaeological information she describes in *Isis Unveiled.* Anyway, she had returned to Europe before 1860, and after spending some time in France and Germany, she suddenly appeared in a dramatic manner at a family wedding at Pskoff. She remained in Russia for several years before resuming her foreign travels.

When living with her relatives in Russia, great development took place in her inner nature: it was a period of intensive training, though not in any outward or visible esoteric school; that came later, in Tibet. About this time she had several mysterious illnesses during which she seemed, as she said, to lead a double life. Particulars of this strange and significant interlude in her life will be found in Sinnett's *Incidents in the Life of Madame Blavatsky*. It seems more than probable that she was receiving an occult training at those times, when, as she said, she became "somebody else" and found herself in a far-off country having no connection with her waking life. When these periods of inner instruction are added to the time spent in Tibet, Egypt, and Syria with various Adepts, it is easy to understand what she meant when she spoke of having had "seven years of training." This was misunderstood by Mr. Sinnett to mean that she studied *in Tibet* for seven years and so published by him. She wrote to him in 1886 about "weeks and months I passed with the Masters, in Egypt or in Tibet."* Earlier than this she wrote, in 1878:

> I belong to the secret sect of the Druzes of the Mount Lebanon and passed a long life [time?] among dervishes, Persian mullahs, and mystics of all sort. — *Theos.*, LII, 628, Aug. 1931

After these illnesses, sporadic phenomena produced by certain elementals independently of her command diminished and finally ceased. She was nearing the end of her 'apprenticeship.' Her sister, Mme. Jelihovsky, writes:

**The Letters of H. P. Blavatsky to A. P. Sinnett*, 145.

At Pskoff and Rougodevo, it happened very often that she could not control, nor even stop its manifestations. After that she appeared to master it [the occult force] more fully every day, until after her extraordinary and protracted illness at Tiflis she seemed to defy and subject it entirely to her will. This was proved by her stopping any such phenomena at her will, and by previous arrangement for days and weeks at a time. Then, when the term was over, she could produce them at her command, and leaving the choice of what should happen to those present. In short, as already said, it is the firm belief of all that *there where a less strong nature would have been surely wrecked in the struggle, her indomitable will found somehow or other the means of subjecting the world of the invisibles — to the denizens of which she has ever refused the name of "spirits" and souls — to her own control.* —*Incidents*, 153

The "means" that she found to control the invisibles was the spiritual will of her higher self, and the protection and help were called forth by her impersonal motive. She still, however, had a further initiation to pass through before being quite free from her "shell," as she called her lower personality. This happened in America more than ten years later.

Her health being restored, she left home in 1863 and traveled in various parts of Europe, Russia, and possibly Asia, until the end of 1867, when another call came from her Master. Her movements between 1864 and 1866 are lost in considerable obscurity, but there is some reason to believe that she spent part of that time in Tibet training for future work under the Master M. She may have been in Tibet in 1865, and the vagueness of her statements may have been intended to baffle undue curiosity about occult matters, but she explicitly says that she did not meet the Master K.H. in his physical body until 1868, when she went to Tibet for a long stay at Shigatse with his sister and her child.

During the sixties she had become an enthusiastic admirer of Garibaldi's efforts to liberate Italy, and she was actually present at the battle of Mentana, near Rome, on November 2, 1867, in company with a large number of other women sympathizers. Little is known about this incident except that she was almost mortally wounded and that she carried the marks till her death. Her recovery must have been extremely rapid, probably owing to help given by her Master, for early in 1868 she started from Constantinople with him on the long journey to Tibet. Her relatives heard nothing from her during her almost three years' residence in Tibet, and they gave her up for dead. Great was their joy, therefore, when a letter arrived at Odessa on November 7, 1870, saying that she was well and that she would return "before eighteen new moons shall have risen." The letter was in French and unsigned, but it is in the characteristic handwriting of K.H., which became familiar eleven years later when he carried on a long correspondence with A. P. Sinnett and others in India.

This is the first known letter to be delivered in a phenomenal manner, for the bearer, an Oriental, appeared mysteriously at Odessa in the room of Madame Fadeyeff, H. P. Blavatsky's beloved aunt, handed her the letter, and, as she herself writes, "disappeared before my very eyes." The orthodox Madame Fadeyeff was greatly opposed to her niece's "heretical" views and assumed that the letter was brought by a spirit. She was greatly disturbed by the phenomenon, and was not fully reassured when H. P. Blavatsky, on her return to Russia, told her that the occult messenger was a living man who had the power of appearing at will in what is called in the Orient the *māyāvi-rūpa,* or illusion body (thought-body).

This incident has two implications especially important in refutation of the charge that H. P. Blavatsky fabricated and delivered letters which she falsely attributed to the Mahatmas. Madame Fadeyeff's intensely rigid orthodoxy caused her to condemn any kind of 'supernatural' phenomena outside the pale of her church; she would be a most unwilling witness to their existence. H.P.B. writes:

> When she got the proofs that they were living men she regarded them as devils or *sold to Satan.* . . . She is the shyest, the kindest, the meekest individual. All her life her money and all is for others. Touch her religion and she becomes like a fury. I never speak with her about Masters. —*Blavatsky Letters,* 154

She would naturally be expected to suppress the story of the letter which she had phenomenally received, when she found that it supported her niece's heretical theories. Yet, when requested by Colonel Olcott to verify its truth, she courteously forwarded the original letter to him, accompanied by a clear account of the 'miraculous' way in which it appeared when H. P. Blavatsky was thousands of miles away. Richard Hodgson, the agent of the London Society for Psychical Research, of whose charges against her more will be heard later in these pages, fatuously suggested that as Madame Fadeyeff was a Russian and a relative of H. P. Blavatsky it is probable that she was a liar, and was bearing false witness in order to support her niece's "political motives" (in plain language the old "spy" accusation which he revived to explain her career). As H.P.B.'s worst enemies have abandoned the absurd theory that she was a Russian spy, we may leave them to find some other equally stupid excuse for disbelieving the Fadeyeff letter-incident, if they can.

Further significance of this especially convincing phenomenon lies in the support it gives to the claim that trained occultists can transmit material objects such as letters by "astral mail" over long distances with extreme rapidity. In the seventies this possibility was unknown in the West, although familiar to the lamas of Tibet and some Indian yogis. Spiritualism and Christian legends of the saints present instances of similar transmission, but they are always ascribed to the supernatural.

In connection with the letters of the Master K.H., certain critics of H. P. Blavatsky who pretend that she fabricated them and that no Mahatmas exist, have asserted that the earlier letters attributed to K.H. are in a more vigorous style of handwriting than those of a later period when, they claim, H. P. Blavatsky was getting old and ill, and her failing powers were reflected in the handwriting of the "so-called Mahatma Letters." The falsity of this is proved by a comparison between the letter written to Madame Fadeyeff by K.H. and another written by him nearly *sixteen years* later. Photographic reproductions of both letters are given in *Did Madame Blavatsky Forge the Mahatma Letters?* by C. Jinarājadāsa, which show no difference whatever between the two handwritings. The later communication was found written diagonally across a blank page in a letter from a devoted member, Tookaram Tatya, mailed at Bombay, June 5, 1886, to Colonel Olcott, and received by him at Adyar two days later. H.P.B., who was at that time living in Germany, could not, of course, have been connected with this phenomenon. The facts are thoroughly authenticated, and have never been explained away. They have only been ignored by the biased critics.

The intensive training H. P. Blavatsky had received in Tibet, where she lived with the sister and nephew of K.H. at Shigatse, being completed, she returned to Europe. After a short visit to Cyprus and Greece, during which she met the Greek Master Illarion, she embarked probably for Egypt, but the vessel, which contained a cargo of gunpowder, blew up near Spezzia* and she was one of the very few passengers saved. As the survivors had lost everything, the Greek government provided free transportation. H.P.B. finally landed in Egypt where she had to wait without any resources until remittances came from her Russian relatives.

She stayed in Cairo for about four months, and it was during this period that she made her first attempt to bring some of her knowledge of the hidden side of nature to the world, by gathering a few interested inquirers to investigate the phenomena of mediumship and the inadequate but well-known reincarnation theory of Allan Kardec. Conditions in Cairo were very bad for her purpose; therefore she sent to France and England for supposedly reputable mediums. Unfortunately they failed to appear, and the little group had to make the best of some very poor local specimens. H. P. Blavatsky appears to have done some phenomena herself in order to help out, for she was regarded by the members as a

*[This is Sinnett's spelling (*Incidents*, 154) of what undoubtedly is the island of Spétsai in the Gulf of Argolis, Greece. H.P.B. refers to this experience in her letter (LXI) to A.P.S. as "Speggia in view of which we were blown up" (*Blavatsky Letters*, 153). —ED.]

kind of medium. She paid no attention to this error, saying: "They know no better, and it does me no harm – for I will very soon show them the difference between a passive medium and an active doer" (*Incidents*, 158). This statement occurs in one of her letters to her Russian relatives, and a little later she told them, in regard to the Cairo mediums:

> "They steal the society's money" . . . "they drink like sponges, and I now caught them cheating most shamefully our members. . . . So I ordered them out. . . . The *Société Spirite* has not lasted a fortnight – it is a heap of ruins – majestic, but as suggestive as those of the Pharaoh's tombs. . . . To wind up the comedy with a drama, I got nearly shot by a madman – a Greek who had been present at the only two public séances we held, and got possessed, I suppose, by some vile spook."
>
> – *Incidents*, 159

Here is seen the definite mention of the difference between an occultist with trained powers, and a helpless, passive medium who is exposed to the danger of possession by unknown and undesirable entities of the lower astral plane. The experience she had in Cairo must have been of service when writing in *Isis* upon the dangers of mediumship.

This tentative effort to reveal some of the teachings of theosophy by throwing light on the rationale of psychic phenomena having failed, she spent some months in the Levant before returning to Russia. While in Egypt she passed a night alone, it is said, in the King's Chamber in the Great Pyramid, where she had some remarkable experiences – not the only seer who has had such in that ancient chamber of initiation.

4

FROM APPRENTICESHIP TO DUTY

IN July, 1872, H. P. Blavatsky arrived in Odessa where her relatives were then living. Exactly "eighteen moons" had risen since her aunt had received the occult letter. She remained there for about nine months and then went to Paris, where a cousin was living. On July 7, 1873, she arrived at New York, having been directed by her Master, under whose orders she was working, to begin the great effort of the nineteenth century in that modern center of energy. She remained in the United States for more than five years, mostly residing in New York, and became a naturalized citizen in 1878.

Colonel Olcott quotes an interesting confirmation of H.P.B.'s statements to him about her journeyings. Miss Anna Ballard, a veteran journalist, wrote to him in 1892 in answer to his request, in part:

". . . I met her in July, 1873, at New York, not more than a week after she landed. I was then a reporter on the staff of the *New York Sun*, and had been detailed to write an article upon a Russian subject. In the course of my search after facts the arrival of this Russian lady was reported to me by a friend, and I called upon her; thus beginning an acquaintance that lasted several years. At our first interview she told me she had had no idea of leaving Paris for America until the very evening before she sailed, but why she came or who hurried her off she did not say. I remember perfectly well her saying with an air of exultation, 'I have been in Tibet.' Why she should think that a great matter, more remarkable than any other of the travels in Egypt, India, and other countries she told me about, I could not make out, but she said it with special emphasis and animation. I now know, of course, what it means." —*O. D. L.*, I, 21

An incident occurring during H. P. Blavatsky's journey to America displays the kindness of heart which was one of her leading characteristics. At Havre she saw a woman with two children in great distress, and on inquiry learned that the woman was going to her husband in America, but had been cheated out of all her money by the purchase of counterfeit tickets and was left utterly destitute and friendless. H.P.B., being short of cash, instantly exchanged her first-class ticket for steerage tickets for herself and the unfortunate family. How many persons of refined instincts would have chosen the steerage with its overcrowded and unsavory conditions, as it was in those days, in order to rescue a total stranger from distress?

When she reached New York she found no funds awaiting her, for her father had just died and her remittances were not forthcoming because of the ensuing legal delays. The Russian consul saw no way to advance any money to her, and for some months she suffered serious privation, having to live in one of the poorest quarters of the city and supporting herself by making cravats.

At last, in October 1874, the time came for action, and she was instructed to go to the village of Chittenden, Vermont, where the two Eddy brothers of then spiritualist fame were holding their historic séances. Henry Steel Olcott, afterwards president of the Theosophical Society, was investigating and reporting them for the *New York Daily Graphic*, and her remarkable face with its impress of power and knowledge attracted him at once. She recognized that this was no accidental meeting; here was the man she needed to help her in the work she was sent to do. At that time she had almost forgotten how to speak English, though she could read fairly well, and Colonel Olcott noticed that she was speaking Parisian French to a Canadian lady friend. As he had a good knowledge of that language, he found an excuse to address her and a friendship quickly sprang up between them. It was indeed no accidental meeting and the Mahatma Morya told Mr. Sinnett several years later how it was brought about.

Some of the Masters, having realized that another of the cyclic opportunities had arrived when the "occult doctrine" might get a hearing, finally decided to make the trial. The higher "chiefs" were not over sanguine, but they raised no objection. The Master M. writes in 1882:

> It was stipulated, however, that the experiment should be made independently of our personal management; that there should be no abnormal interference by ourselves. So casting about we found in America the man to stand as leader – a man of great moral courage, unselfish, and having other good qualities. He was far from being the best, but (as Mr. Hume speaks in H. P. B.'s case) – he was the best one available. With him we associated a woman of most exceptional and wonderful endowments. Combined with them she had strong personal defects, but just as she was, there was no second to her living fit for this work. We sent her to America, brought them together – and the trial began.
>
> – *The Mahatma Letters to A. P. Sinnett*, 263

Two years later, when Mr. Sinnett was approaching a critical period which was brought about by his lack of spiritual understanding and intuition, K.H. felt it necessary to repeat the tribute to H.P.B. and Olcott just quoted:

> Those two are, say, far from perfect – in some respects, quite the

> opposite. But they have that in them (pardon the eternal repetition but it is being as constantly overlooked) which we have but too rarely found elsewhere — UNSELFISHNESS, and an eager readiness for self-sacrifice for the good of others; what a "multitude of sins" does not this cover! It is but a truism, yet I say it, that in adversity alone can we discover the real man. . . . One who would have higher instruction given to him has to be a *true* theosophist in heart and soul, not merely in appearance. — Ibid., 370

Colonel Olcott was a lawyer with a successful practice which he abandoned within a few years after he began to devote himself heart and soul to theosophy. He had a fine record as a soldier in the Civil War, and later as a Special Commissioner of the War Department in which he rendered such valuable service that he was given official tributes of the highest appreciation when he left America to reside in India. His book, *People from the Other World,* a narrative, among other things, of his experiences at the Eddy farmhouse where he met H. P. Blavatsky, created a strong impression among persons interested in psychic research.

This sketch is too brief to permit an adequate study of the mystery of H. P. Blavatsky — the very unconventional Russian personality on one side and, on the other, the complete spiritual Intelligence that the Masters refer to on several occasions as "our Brother H.P.B." In view of the slanders directed against her a few words in defense may be in place here.

In regard to the extraordinary complexity of her nature and its apparent inconsistencies, a valuable hint was given to Sinnett in 1881, and if he had realized its profound significance much misunderstanding on his part would have been avoided. The Master K.H. wrote to him:

Notwithstanding that the time is not quite ripe to let you entirely into the secret; . . . owing to the great injustice and wrong done, I am empowered to allow you a glimpse behind the veil. This state of hers [excitability, lack of reserve, etc.] is intimately connected with her occult training in Tibet, and due to her being sent out alone into the world to gradually prepare the way for others. . . . Please then, remember, what she tried to explain, . . . namely the fact of the *seven* principles in the *complete* human being. Now, no man or woman, unless he be an initiate of the "fifth circle," can leave the precincts of *Bod-Las* and return back into the world in his integral whole – if I may use the expression. *One*, at least of his seven satellites has to remain behind for two reasons: the first to form the necessary connecting link, the wire of transmission – the second as the safest warranter that certain things will never be divulged. She is no exception to the rule, and you have seen another exemplar – a highly intellectual man – who had to leave one of his skins behind; hence, is considered highly eccentric. The bearing and status of the remaining *six* depend upon the inherent qualities, the psycho-physiological peculiarities of the person, especially upon the idiosyncrasies transmitted by what modern science calls "atavism." Acting in accordance with my wishes, my brother M. made to you through her a certain offer, if you remember. You had but to accept it, and at any time you liked, you would have had for an hour or more, the real *baitchooly* [true, complete individual] to converse with, instead of the psychological cripple you generally have to deal with now.

– *Mahatma Letters,* 203–4

In his *Old Diary Leaves* (I, 18), Colonel Olcott makes a curious remark which may possibly refer to this change and psychological 'crippling' in H. P. Blavatsky:

. . . when a certain wonderful psycho-physiological change happened to H. P. B. that I am not at liberty to speak about, and that nobody has up to the present suspected, although enjoying her intimacy and full confidence.

Olcott had probably not seen the Master's letter to Sinnett in which he tells of the crippling from which she suffered and which handicapped her, but, of course, the change Olcott mentions may have been something else. It is an interesting record, in any case, but the speculations published by various writers on the subject are not evidential.

H. P. Blavatsky was no thick-skinned, unfeeling cynic, but an intensely generous and warmhearted soul, instantly moved to give what help she could when she heard of a case of distress. Instances were known where she even bore the blame of the foolish actions of others in order to save innocent people from scandal. To excuse the shortcomings of others, she would say that she might have made worse mistakes in their place, and that she would be more to blame because her training had been better. No charge was ever made against her of showing the least desire for revenge against even those who lied about her and treated her with the meanest treachery. In spite of her volcanic temperament and sudden explosions of wrath against Olcott and others when provoked by their "flapdoodles," as she half-humorously called their lapses, the deep down, serene impersonality of her real Self is undeniable. Olcott once asked why a permanent control was not put upon her fiery temper, and was told by a Master, as Olcott reports:

> . . . such a course would inevitably lead to her death from apoplexy; the body was vitalised by a fiery and imperious spirit, one which from childhood brooked no restraint, and if vent were not allowed for the excessive corporeal energy, the result must be fatal. . . . The only persons she actually reverenced were the Masters, yet even towards them, she was occasionally so combative that, as above said, in certain of her moods the gentler ones could not, or did not approach her. To get herself into the frame of mind when she could

have open intercourse with them had — as she had pathetically assured me — cost her years of the most desperate self-restraint.

— *O. D. L.*, I, 258

K.H. himself refers to the difficulty he had in approaching her during a certain crisis, as mentioned in her *Letters* to A. P. Sinnett (p. 7). Her Russian princely ancestors, the Dolgoroukys, were distinguished by extraordinary courage and a passionate love of personal independence, and one of them successfully defied the Tsar Peter the Great in the Senate, a most desperate proceeding.

Although handicapped by her heredity in some ways, and by the psychological 'crippling' explained above, when it became a question of the great mission she had to fulfill, her extraordinary personality, self-willed, impulsive, erratic in many ways, became absolutely subject to the will and purpose of her higher nature. This 'complex' produced many of the paradoxical events of her career which aroused criticism. Her detractors failed to appreciate the importance of the fact that the great, self-sacrificing and devoted Being "H.P.B." was not always visible through the "H.P. Blavatsky" personality.

Trying to explain this to A. P. Sinnett, she commented:

Do you believe that, because you have fathomed — as you think — my physical crust and brain; that shrewd analyst of *human* nature though you be — you have ever penetrated even beneath the first cuticles of my *Real Self?* You would gravely err, if you did. . . . What I say is this: you *do not know* me; for whatever there is *inside* it ["that unprepossessing rock"], is *not what you think* it is. . . . *I*, (the inner real "I") am in prison and cannot show myself as I am with all the desire I may have to. Why then, should I, because speaking for myself *as I am* and feel myself to be, why should I be held responsible for the *outward* jail-door and *its* appearance, when I have neither built nor yet decorated it? — *Mahatma Letters,* 465–6

Rather later, in 1885, trusting to Mrs. Patience Sinnett's intuitive understanding of her, she wrote:

The world is divided into the millions *who do not know* me, . . . but who have heard *of* me; and what they did hear, even in the palmy days of Theosophy, when it was nearly becoming a fashion, could never prepossess them *in my favour;* and among those millions — a few hundreds — say thousands — who have seen me personally, i.e. the very rough personality in her "black bag," and of unrefined talk. Those who *do* know me and have had a glimpse of the *inner* creature — are a few dozens. — *Blavatsky Letters,* 102

In the first year of the Society, the Egyptian Master Serapis (called the "Mahā-Sahib") wrote to Olcott, who was evidently puzzled by some of her ways:

O poor, poor Sister! Chaste and pure Soul — pearl shut inside an outwardly coarse nature. Help her to throw off that appearance of assumed roughness, and any one might well be dazzled by the divine Light concealed under such a bark.
— *Letters from the Masters of the Wisdom,* II, 36–7

Dr. G. de Purucker sums up the greater side of that "strange woman," H.P.B.:

. . . that wondrous Thing . . . that wondrous being, which was in H. P. Blavatsky and worked through her, came from Śambhala — came from this hierarchy. I do not here refer merely to the woman, to the physical body; no, nor even to the personality born in Russia; but to that wonderful Thing who incarnated in that body, and who left part of "herself" behind there and who went forth into the world crippled psychically, obeying in this respect an archaic law, which was the cause of so much misunderstanding about her. This Entity did its work in the world at the proper cyclic time for its appearance among men: the opening of a new "Messianic Cycle."

— *Fundamentals of the Esoteric Philosophy*, 361

Elsewhere Dr. de Purucker writes:

Does anyone think that H.P.B., that the Russian body which most people call H.P.B., was the Messenger from the Lodge? How absurd! Not even her leonine character, her great and noble soul, which all who really knew her love her and revere her for having — not even these were the Messenger; but that avatāric Something, that occasionally incarnating Spirit-Soul which used her and which worked through her, precisely because she was so great, precisely because she was a chela, precisely because she was the willing and self-chosen sacrificial victim, giving herself as a willing instrument for a sublime purpose and end.

I write these words hoping that they will remain, and be on record as a warning to those who will live in the opening years of the last quarter of this century not to be carried away by merely outward appearances, nor by their human prejudices; and also as a plea to them of the future to be ready and alert, ready to recognize the spirit, the inner grandeur, of the Worker for 1975 and thereafter.

— *The Theosophical Forum*, V, 234, April 1934

Some of the idiosyncrasies of her outward personality often irritated strangers, and to those whose insincerity or selfish egotism was like an open book to her she not infrequently spoke in unguarded language, thereby earning their bitter resentment. But she never had any real ill-feeling towards even her most unscrupulous persecutors; it was admitted even by her critics that if her worst enemy came to her for assistance (as some actually did!) she would help him in any way in her power. The Master M. told Sinnett that she would have saved herself much trouble if she had been more diplomatic in speech:

. . . were she more of a natural born *liar* — she might be happier and won her day long since by this time. But that's just where the shoe pinches, Sahib. She is *too truthful, too outspoken, too incapable* of *dissimulation:* and now she is being daily crucified for it. . . . Martyrdom is pleasant to look at and criticise, but harder to suffer. There never was a woman more unjustly abused than H.B.

— *Mahatma Letters,* 272–3

To awaken a student to a realization of his failings, she did not hesitate to castigate him severely — if she saw a promise of better things — and those who had the sense to recognize her earnest desire to help were deeply grateful for her outspoken courage. The *real* teacher aims to invoke the inner, diviner self, regardless of likes or dislikes on the part of the disciple, while the false one flatters the lower personality in order to gain power or popularity. The former will frequently turn away his face for a while, or he may even display an unattractive appearance, in order that the disciple will follow the truth he teaches for its own sake and not for any personal inducement such as the favor or the commendation of the teacher. Mme. David-Neel and the few others who have penetrated even a little way behind the veil in Tibet and India, bear witness that the higher yogis or lamas adopt drastic methods in training their most promising pupils, methods which are almost incomprehensible in the West. The discipline practiced by the Zen Buddhists in Japan, for the development of impersonality, is framed on a similar principle.

Colonel Olcott, whose personal contact with so many Orientals confirms all this, wrote:

. . . nothing is so weakening, as the encouragement of the spirit of dependence upon another, upon another's wisdom, upon another's righteousness. It is a most pernicious thing and paralyzes all effort. Now a method that is pursued in schools of Yoga in India and in Tibet is this: the Master gives at first no encouragement whatever to the would-be pupil, perhaps he will not even look at him, and frequently persons attach themselves to a Yogī as chelas, despite his trying to drive them away, perhaps with blows, or, at any rate, despite their being apparently scorned and put upon in every possible way by the Yogī. — *O. D. L.*, IV, 311–12

Instructive stories are told of H. P. Blavatsky's efforts to provide her serious students with opportunities for the self-eradication of vanity (a deep-rooted source of trouble), ill-temper, envy, and all the *apparently* minor faults which must be overcome on the first steps of the Path. One student candidly confessed that on one occasion she tried his temper by a seeming injustice and harsh treatment so severely that he finally "saw red" and broke out in bitter complaint, demanding an explanation or an apology. She immediately became perfectly calm and looked searchingly at him, saying: "And *you* want to be an Occultist!" He instantly realized the meaning of her strange conduct, and saw that he had failed in one of the simplest tests. But he was grateful for the opportunity and profited by it.

In contrast to this, the tragic story of the Russian novelist, V. Solovyoff, is an example of complete failure. This is outlined on a later page.

The true path, the occult path, is defined by H. P. Blavatsky as leading:

. . . to the knowledge of what is good to do, as to the right discrimination of good from evil; a path which also leads a man to that power through which he can do the good he desires, often without even apparently lifting a finger. — *Lucifer*, II, 150, April 1888

. . . Occultism differs from Magic and other secret Sciences as the glorious sun does from a rush-light, as the immutable and immortal Spirit of Man – the reflection of the absolute, causeless and unknowable ALL – differs from the mortal clay – the human body.

– *Lucifer,* II, 174, May 1888

[To those who are not "passion-proof" and who are "deaf to the voice of Humanity"] the golden gate of Wisdom may get transformed into the wide gate and the broad way "that leadeth unto destruction," and therefore "many be they that enter in thereby." This is the Gate of the Occult arts, practised for selfish motives and in the absence of the restraining and beneficent influence of ATMA-VIDYA.

– Ibid., 181

5

WORK BEGUN IN AMERICA

UPON H. P. Blavatsky's return from the Eddy Farm at Chittenden to New York, she again met Colonel Olcott, who, at her request, introduced his friend, William Quan Judge, a young attorney of Irish birth, who was just starting to practice law. From her first meeting with Olcott, she tried to open his eyes to the realities hidden behind the phenomena of the spiritualists, and to impress on his mind the rudiments of the theosophical interpretation of those phenomena so far as they were facts. His response was slow, but he ultimately accepted her explanation. She writes:

> I was sent to America on purpose and sent to the Eddies. There I found Olcott in love with spirits, . . . I was ordered to let him know that spiritual phenomena without the philosophy of Occultism were dangerous and misleading. I proved to him that all that mediums could do through spirits others could do at will without any spirits at all; that bells and thought-reading, raps and physical phenomena, could be achieved by anyone who had a faculty of acting in his physical body through the organs of his astral body; and I had that faculty ever since I was four years old, as all my family know. I could make furniture move and objects fly apparently, and my astral arms that supported them remained invisible; all this ever before I knew even of Masters. — *The Path,* X, 369, March 1896

With W. Q. Judge her approach was different. Though interested in occultism and the philosophy of the inner side of nature, he was not "in love with spirits." He quickly recognized her mission, as is shown in the following words from his tribute to her memory:

In 1874, in the City of New York, I first met H. P. B. in this life. . . . It was her eye that attracted me, the eye of one whom I must have known in lives long passed away. She looked at me in recognition at that first hour, and never since has that look changed. Not as a questioner of philosophies did I come before her, . . . but as one who, wandering many periods through the corridors of life, was seeking the friends who could show where the designs for the work had been hidden. And true to the call she responded, revealing the plans once again, and speaking no words to explain, simply pointed them out and went on with the task. . . . it was teacher and pupil, elder brother and younger, both bent on the one single end, but she with the power and the knowledge that belong but to lions and sages.

—*Lucifer,* VIII, 290, June 1891

And of her character he writes:

That she always knew what would be done by the world in the way of slander and abuse I also know, for in 1875 she told me that she was then embarking on a work that would draw upon her unmerited slander, implacable malice, uninterrupted misunderstanding, constant work, and no worldly reward. Yet in the face of this her lion heart carried her on. . . .

Much has been said about her "phenomena," some denying them, others alleging trick and device. Knowing her for so many years so well, and having seen at her hands in private the production of more and more varied phenomena than it has been the good fortune of all others of her friends put together to see, I know for myself that she had control of hidden powerful laws of nature not known to our science, and I also know that she never boasted of her powers, never advertised their possession, never publicly advised anyone to attempt their acquirement, but always turned the eyes of those who could understand her to a life of altruism based on a knowledge of true philosophy. If the world thinks that her days were spent in deluding her followers by pretended phenomena, it is solely because her injudicious friends, against her expressed wish, gave out wonderful stories of "miracles" which can not be proved to a skeptical public and which are not the aim of the Society nor were ever more than mere incidents in the life of H. P. Blavatsky.

Her aim was to elevate the race. Her method was to deal with the mind of the century as she found it, by trying to lead it on step by step; to seek out and educate a few who, appreciating the majesty of the Secret Science and devoted to "the great orphan Humanity," could carry on her work with zeal and wisdom; to found a Society whose efforts – however small itself might be – would inject into the thought of the day the ideas, the doctrines, the nomenclature of the Wisdom Religion, . . . – *The Path*, VI, 67–8, June 1891

An American journalist gives an interesting description of H. P. Blavatsky's appearance and lines of action at this time. To quote a few relevant passages:

In appearance, Mme. Blavatsky, though not at all handsome in the common acceptance of the term, was exceedingly impressive and interesting. Tall and stoutly built, she carried herself with queenly dignity. Her head is large, and under a broad, intellectual brow shone a pair of large, luminous blue eyes whose strange spiritual expression fascinated all . . . She might have been under forty; with the physical vigor and elasticity of youth she possessed the mental maturity of age. . . .

It was in these rooms, afterwards familiarly known as "The Lamasery" (the name given a Buddhist convent in Tibet), that a brilliant crowd of Bohemians were wont to gather of an evening . . . The hostess proved herself a conversationalist of rare magnetic power, and no one ever tired of listening to her fascinating recital of experiences in many lands, her views on life and art, or her exposition of the occultism of the East. She was an accomplished linguist, as most Russians are; and she . . . displayed a deep knowledge of the ancient and modern literature of all countries. She was familiar with German and French philosophy, and commenting upon the work of the great thinkers, expressed many ideas of striking force and originality. Occasionally she entertained her guests with music, and her piano playing was pronounced emphatically that of a great musician.

– Quoted in *World Theosophy*, I, 657–8, Aug. 1931

The journalist then gives a list of notable people who

frequented her receptions, including such names as Professor Weiss of the New York University, Thomas A. Edison (afterwards a Fellow of the Theosophical Society), Dr. Alexander Wilder, the Earl of Dunraven, Edwin Booth, Edward Bierstadt, Laurence Oliphant, the Earl of Dufferin (later Viceroy of India), and many others distinguished in literature, art, and public affairs.

It was rumored that she possessed unusual mystic powers, and yet she was no trance medium. Occasionally she would show a psychical experiment to illustrate a point, but, in contrast to the ordinary mediums, she always retained her personal consciousness even when the Masters spoke through her. She said she stood aside and watched. Her powers were trained and under her own control. At first she only showed her ability to use supernormal faculties to a few friends in private, for she had been directed not to spread too publicly the fact that she could produce phenomena at will. Her drawing-room experiments in occultism were analogous to the curious experiments shown at popular lectures in chemistry, but the serious demonstrations she gave to her two trusted pupils, Olcott and Judge, were mostly for their personal instruction and were more clearly or technically set forth, so to speak. Judge apparently saw more deeply than the older man into the occult aspect of the matter, for he says in regard to certain private manifestations of her powers that he witnessed:

> . . . I do not think they were done just for me, but only that in those early days she was laying down the lines of force all over the land and I, so fortunate, was at the centre of the energy and saw the play of forces in visible phenomena. . . . I shall hold to her own explanation made in advance and never changed. That I have given above.
> —*Lucifer*, VIII, 290–1, June 1891

After a while, H. P. Blavatsky was directed to show some so-called signs and wonders more openly, for the purpose of attracting the attention of the best minds among scientists or philosophers who might recognize something entirely new for study in the deeper nature of man – something entirely different from and infinitely superior to the despised mediumistic phenomena, yet supernormal. Her own explanation of this course is illuminating:

> It was supposed that intelligent people, especially men of science, would, at least, have recognised the existence of a new and deeply interesting field of enquiry and research when they witnessed physical effects produced at will, for which they were not able to account. It was supposed that theologians would have welcomed the proof, of which they stand so sadly in need in these agnostic days, that the soul and the spirit are not mere creations of their fancy, due to ignorance of the physical constitution of man, but entities quite as real as the body, and much more important. These expectations were not realized. The phenomena were misunderstood and misrepresented, both as regards their nature and their purpose.
>
> . . . It was believed that this manipulation of forces of nature which lie below the surface . . . would have led to enquiry into the nature and the laws of those forces, unknown to science, but perfectly known to occultism. . . .
>
> Never were the phenomena presented in any other character than that of instances of a power *over perfectly natural though unrecognised forces,* and incidentally over matter, possessed by certain individuals who have attained to a larger and higher knowledge of the Universe than has been reached by scientists and theologians, or can ever be reached by them, by the roads they are now respectively pursuing. Yet this power is latent in all men, and could, in time, be wielded by anyone who would cultivate the knowledge and conform to the conditions necessary for its development. . . .
>
> An occultist can produce phenomena, but he cannot supply the world with brains, nor with the intelligence and good faith necessary to understand and appreciate them. Therefore, it is hardly to be

wondered at, that *word* came to abandon phenomena and let the ideas of Theosophy stand on their own intrinsic merits.

—*Lucifer,* I, 504, 506, Feb. 1888

In the seventies little or nothing was known about Eastern yoga or genuine magic, subjects which are now so well recognized that innumerable counterfeits have sprung up everywhere. H.P.B.'s preliminary work in America was intended to turn the attention of the spiritualists away from mere phenomenalism to a higher form of thought, to a true spiritualism, "only not on the modern American fashion, but on that of ancient Alexandria, with its Theodidaktoi, Hypatias, and Porphyries" (*Incidents,* 180); in other words, to theosophy, which includes the *phenomena* of modern spiritualism as a fraction of an infinitely larger field. She wrote: "I was sent from Paris to America on purpose to prove the phenomena and their reality, and show the fallacy of the spiritualistic theory of spirits" (*O. D. L.,* I, 13).

She naturally admired the courage of the spiritualists in standing firmly by their belief in psychic phenomena, and hoped they would welcome the new teaching she brought from the East, which did not deny their phenomena but explained them in the light of larger knowledge. Her public work began by participation in the newspaper battle raging between the spiritualists and the skeptics. She vigorously defended the possibility of the phenomena and the honesty of some mediums, while exposing notorious frauds. The spiritualists felt that they had received a valuable ally, though, unfortunately, many repudiated her and her teachings when she began to criticize their hypothesis of "spirit return," and still more vehemently when she began to teach reincarnation in plain language.

Some of the most prominent spiritualists in America and England, such as Mrs. E. Hardinge Britten, Henry J. Newton, C. C. Massey, Dr. Carter Blake, Mrs. Hollis Billing, etc., did good work in helping to start the Theosophical Society, and others became warm sympathizers, including the noted scholar and medium, the Rev. Stainton Moses (widely known as M. A. Oxon), a high-minded man of irreproachable reputation, editor of *Light* and a member of the staff of University College, London. He was a lifelong friend of H.P.B. and Colonel Olcott, though he did not accept all the teachings of theosophy. Much is written about him in the *Mahatma Letters*.

One spiritualist who promised to be a valuable helper was young Elbridge Gerry Brown, editor of *The Spiritual Scientist*, a paper devoted more to the philosophical possibilities underlying psychic manifestation than to the phenomena themselves. For instance we read in the issue for May, 1875:

> It is rumoured that one or more Oriental Spiritualists of high rank have just arrived in this country. They are said to possess a profound knowledge of the mysteries of illumination, and it is not impossible that they will establish relations with those whom we are accustomed to regard as the leaders in Spiritualistic affairs. If the report be true, their coming may be regarded as a great blessing; for, after a quarter century of phenomena, we are almost without a philosophy to account for them or to control their occurrence.
>
> — *Theos.*, LIV, 328–9, Dec. 1932

H. P. Blavatsky wrote on the margin, "At[rya] and Ill-[arion] passed through New York and Boston; thence thro' California and Japan back. M ∴ appearing in Kama Rupa daily." Atrya and Illarion are the names of two of the high Adepts; M ∴ is the Mahatma Morya, her personal teacher.

Brown was given by the Masters the special privilege of working side by side with H.P.B. and Olcott, but unfortunately he did not prove ready to take advantage of this unusual opportunity. First-class literary contributions were obtained for his struggling journal, money was given for expenses, but to no avail. He disappears from our ken in 1876. H.P.B. makes the pungent remark:

> Several hundred dollars out of our pockets were spent on behalf of the Editor, and he was made to pass through a minor "diksha" [initiation]. This proving of no avail – the Theosophical Society was established. . . . The man might have become a POWER, he preferred to remain an ASS. *De gustibus non disputandum est.* – Ibid., 332

6

FOUNDATION OF THE THEOSOPHICAL SOCIETY

THE time had now come when it was necessary to speak plainly about the real interpretation of the spiritualistic manifestations. H. P. Blavatsky had gained the attention of the public by her brilliant intelligence, the charm of her striking personality, and her slashing attacks on materialism and other evils. Her voice would now be listened to and recognized as speaking with authority. She writes in her *Scrap-Book* in May, 1875:

> Ordered to begin telling the public the *truth* about the phenomena and their mediums. And *now* my martyrdom will begin! I will have all the Spiritualists against me in addition to the Christians and the Skeptics. Thy Will, O, M ∴, be done! H.P.B.
>
> — *Theos.*, LIV, 330–1, Dec. 1932

On receipt of this order H.P.B. set Colonel Olcott to work to form a group of students into a society to discuss psychic subjects, which he rather disrespectfully called a "Miracle Club." This proving a failure, a few weeks later urgent orders were received by H.P.B. from her Master to try again and enlarge the scope of the work. She writes:

> *Orders* received from India direct to establish a philosophico-religious Society and choose a name for it, — also to choose Olcott. July 1875.
>
> — Ibid., 332

This shows the definite object for which the Masters

started the Society—a center of spiritual energy which would be both philosophic and religious and, it might be said, scientific. It was not intended to be a mere "psychical research" association, however glorified. H.P.B. knew this perfectly, as can be seen from her letters to her friend Professor Corson of Cornell University, but it was not so obvious to others until some time after the Theosophical Society was established.

H. P. Blavatsky was the *immediate agent* of the Masters from the inception of the Society until her death, and every other associate was subordinate in real authority. But she received help and instruction from other Adepts as well as from M. and K.H. The words "from India direct," which she uses in the memorandum just quoted, are significant as they evidently mean that the orders came from her personal Master, M. In her New York period she was largely under the protection of a Section of the Great Lodge which has its center in Egypt, and whose Chief was then privately spoken of as Serapis Bey. In several places Olcott makes interesting references to this occult group under the name of "The Brotherhood of Luxor," and K.H. also mentions them in the *Mahatma Letters* (p. 116), but less is said about them than about the Tibetan Brotherhood.

A curious incident is recorded by Colonel Olcott in this connection. When E. Gerry Brown was struggling with financial difficulties the Masters wished to help his progressive journal, and Olcott drew up an attractive circular to advertise it. H. P. Blavatsky told him the Masters wished it signed: "*For the Committee of Seven*, BROTHERHOOD OF LUXOR." She did not dictate any of it, or see it until it was printed, but then she pointed out, to Olcott's astonishment, that the initials of the six paragraphs spelt the name of the Egyptian Adept, Tuitit, under whom he was then working through H. P. Blavatsky (*O. D. L.*, I, 72–6).

Ten years later, in 1886, this same Egyptian Adept is again referred to. In one of the Colonel's letters to H.P.B. he asks her to request Tuitit Bey or one of his colleagues to arrange an exchange of studies between someone in Cairo and Subba Row in India (*Blavatsky Letters*, 326). K.H. also speaks of his Egyptian and Druse colleagues and their special duty in Egypt during the armed rising under Arabi Pasha in 1882 (*Mahatma Letters*, 116).

A brief outline of the formation of the Theosophical Society (the "philosophico-religious Society") is all that is necessary here. It was first suggested in public on September 7, 1875, in H. P. Blavatsky's rooms at 46 Irving Place, New York, after a lecture to an invited audience, on "The Lost Canon of Proportion of the Egyptians" by G. H. Felt. He was an original thinker whose studies had convinced him that the ancient Egyptians were adepts in magical science – a belief that was far more unorthodox in 1875 than it is now, when more than one distinguished Egyptologist is on record as taking Egyptian magic seriously, and responsible investigators report meeting adepts in Egypt of more or less advancement.

H. P. Blavatsky must have been especially interested in Felt's remarks because he had knowledge of the existence in nature of elementals or nonhuman 'spirits,' an important factor in her teachings which the spiritualists at that time repudiated and ridiculed. Today their attitude is entirely different. But H.P.B. knew the danger of ignorantly arousing these elemental forces, and soon had to take action to protect the infant Theosophical Society from becoming an Arcadia for elementals!*

The company were evidently much impressed by Felt's address, for Olcott writes:

> . . . an animated discussion followed. In the course of this, the idea occurred to me that it would be a good thing to form a society to pursue and promote such occult research, and, after turning it over in my mind, I wrote on a scrap of paper the following:
>
> "*Would it not be a good thing to form a Society for this kind of study?*"
>
> – and gave it to Mr. Judge, . . . to pass over to her [H. P. Blavatsky]. She read it and nodded assent. – *O. D. L.*, I, 117–18

Olcott seems not to have known of the Master's order directing the formation of a "philosophico-religious Society," received by H. P. Blavatsky in the previous July; it is not mentioned in his voluminous writings. He says that even

---

*Mr. Felt's researches into the meaning of the Egyptian symbolic representations of the zodiacal constellations, etc., in animal forms and their possible connection with elementals or nature spirits of various orders, led him to the discovery of certain purely theosophical principles. Quoting from one of his letters:

> "As a result I have become satisfied that these Zodiacal and other drawings are representations of types in this invisible creation delineated in a more or less precise manner, and interspersed with images of natural objects more or less conventionally drawn.
>
> ". . . they formed a series of creatures in a system of evolution running from inanimate nature . . . to man, its highest development; that there were intelligences capable of being more or less perfectly controlled, as man was more or less thoroughly acquainted with them, . . . or as he was more or less in harmony with nature or nature's works. . . . Purity of mind and body, I found to be very powerful, . . .
>
> "I satisfied myself that the Egyptians had used these appearances in their initiations; . . ." – *O. D. L.*, I, 128–9

In this letter Mr. Felt describes the strange effect which his work

"the Brotherhood plank in the Society's future platform was, therefore, not thought of"– nor the "philosophico-religious" one, it would seem! Not by him, of course, but one can imagine H. P. Blavatsky's quiet smile when she nodded her head, knowing well the deep significance of the proceedings. Although the Society was not established by the Masters for the pursuit of psychic research, Olcott's suggestion was well adapted to attract independent minds and, once a working organization was established, the real teaching could begin.

His proposition was received with enthusiasm and, after several conferences, the name, the Theosophical Society, was chosen, officers elected and bylaws adopted. H. S. Olcott was appointed President and W. Q. Judge, Counsel. H. P. Blavatsky chose the modest title of Corresponding Secretary. The Society was legally constituted on October 30, and on

---

with certain Egyptian symbols had upon his cat and dog. He says that on a certain occasion, at an open meeting of the Society, when he was lecturing on the subject, H. P. Blavatsky "who had seen unpleasant effects follow" indiscriminate concentration on such matters, requested him to put aside his drawings and change the subject. He soon realized the absolute necessity of confining such studies to those only who were properly prepared morally and spiritually, and strongly supported the organization of different degrees in the T. S. In this he was, of course, well advised, and H. P. Blavatsky never stopped till she had taken the first steps to establish a real school of the Mysteries where earnest students could be taught the way to self-knowledge in preparation for effective work for the benefit of humanity. Her esoteric teachings were never directed to the development of psychic powers, and her suppression of Mr. Felt's attempt to exhibit his occult experiments to unqualified persons, mere intellectual curiosity-seekers, of which his audience largely consisted, shows that even in the earliest days of the Theosophical Society she discouraged psychic practices within the Society and directed its course to spiritual and philosophical lines.

November 17, 1875, the president's Inaugural Address was delivered at the Mott Memorial Hall, 64 Madison Avenue, New York. The latter date has by many been accepted as the official birthday of the Society. In regard to the name Theosophical it was said that the choice was the result of the casual finding of the word theosophy in a dictionary when the subject was discussed. This, however, may not have been a fortuitous happening, for in one of her letters to Professor Hiram Corson H.P.B. writes in February 1875:

> I am here in this country sent by my Lodge on behalf of Truth in modern spiritualism, and it is my most sacred duty to unveil what is, and expose what is not. . . .
>
> My belief . . . springs out from the same source of information that was used by Raymond Lully, Picus della Mirandola, Cornelius Agrippa, Robert Fludd, Henry More, et cetera, etc., all of whom have ever been searching for a system that should disclose to them the "deepest depths" of the Divine nature, . . . I found at last, and many years ago, the cravings of my mind satisfied by this theosophy taught by the Angels and communicated by them that the protoplast might know it for the aid of the human destiny.
>
> —*Some Unpublished Letters of Helena Petrovna Blavatsky*, 127–8

Here we find her employing the unusual word theosophy in referring to the teaching which her "philosophico-religious Society" was soon to promulgate, more than six months after writing this letter, and which she had tried to introduce to the world when she started the unlucky *Société Spirite* at Cairo. In the "Hiraf" letter, described in the next chapter, she uses the word Theosophists, months before the Theosophical Society was started.

A metropolitan paper in reporting the foundation of the Theosophical Society summarizes what Colonel Olcott had in mind at the time:

"One movement of great importance has just been inaugurated in New York, under the lead of Colonel Henry S. Olcott, in the organization of a society, to be known as the Theosophical Society. . . . The company included several persons of great learning and some of wide personal influence. [Here follow names and descriptions.] . . . Col. Olcott . . . proposed to form a nucleus around which might gather all the enlightened and brave souls who are willing to work together for the collection and diffusion of knowledge. His plan was to organise a society of Occultists and begin at once to collect a library and to diffuse information concerning those secret laws of Nature which were so familiar to the Chaldeans and Egyptians, but are totally unknown by our modern world of science."

— *O. D. L.*, I, 118–20

Among the early Fellows were Dr. Alexander Wilder, the well-known physician, scholar, and Platonist; Major-General Abner W. Doubleday of Gettysburg fame, also a distinguished inventor and the founder of baseball; Thomas Alva Edison; Dr. Seth Pancoast, learned Kabbalist; and other notable people. The purpose of the Society was briefly defined in the second bylaw, and it covers an immense field, spiritual, ethical, and physical; it reads:

The objects of the society are to collect and diffuse a knowledge of the laws which govern the universe.

Properly understood this includes a sincere effort on the part of the Fellows of the Society to gain a true understanding of the laws of life so that their conduct may become harmonious with them. A body of unselfish men and women thinking and acting in this light would indeed be a nucleus of universal brotherhood. When the Rules were revised in India in 1879–1880, the principle of brotherhood was emphasized, but it had never been far from the mind of H.P.B.

During the formative period of the movement in New York the publication of two circulars was authorized. The one displaying the name of the Egyptian Adept, Tuitit, in the form of an acrostic, has already been mentioned. The second one, not dated, but said to have been issued in 1878, is of greater importance because it is the first detailed statement for inquirers about the conditions of membership and, above all, of the chief object of the Society, brotherhood. It runs in part:

> Its Fellowship is divided into three Sections, and each Section into three Degrees. All candidates for active fellowship are required to enter as probationers, in the Third Degree of the Third Section, and no fixed time is specified in which the new Fellow can advance from any lower to a higher degree; all depends upon merit. To be admitted into the highest degree, of the first section, the Theosophist must have become freed of every leaning toward any one form of religion in preference to another. . . . He must be ready to lay down his life, if necessary, for the good of Humanity, and of a brother Fellow of whatever race, color or ostensible creed. . . . Those who have not yet wholly disenthralled themselves from religious prejudice, and other forms of selfishness, but have made a certain progress towards self-mastery and enlightenment, belong in the Second Section. The Third Section is probationary; . . .
>
> The objects of the Society are various. . . . The Society teaches and expects its fellows to personally exemplify the highest morality and religious aspiration; to oppose the materialism of science and every form of dogmatic theology, especially the Christian, which the Chiefs of the Society regard as particularly pernicious; . . . to disseminate a knowledge of the sublime teachings of that pure esoteric system of the archaic period, . . . finally, and chiefly, to aid in the institution of a Brotherhood of Humanity, . . .
>
> — The Theosophical Society: *Its Origin, Plan and Aims* (Circular from Doubleday Notebook, no. 7).

The remark about Christian dogmatic theology refers,

of course, to the outmoded creeds and crude literal interpretations of the Bible, and not in the least to the teachings of Christ, of which H. P. Blavatsky always spoke with profound respect, affirming that in their esoteric meaning they were identical with the ancient wisdom taught in schools of the Mysteries. From the first, the Society has been absolutely unsectarian and nonpolitical. The belief in brotherhood and the sincere desire to promote it in every legitimate way is the only prerequisite of Fellowship. The study of theosophy is held to be the best means of discovering the true nature of man and therefore of finding the remedies for man's troubles, but theosophy is not presented as a creed or a dogma.

The course of events in the presentation of this philosophy was not haphazard. "To collect and diffuse a knowledge of the laws which govern the universe" was a highly condensed expression of a very wide-reaching program, which was not fully revealed at first, but among the principal teachings of theosophy there is one that runs through the entire cycle of H. P. Blavatsky's guidance. This, the most important of all, is that of the inner divinity in man and of the possibility of becoming united with it. This is the fundamental basis of universal brotherhood. H.P.B. had realized this mystical illumination in a high degree, and was therefore qualified to point the way to others. She speaks of

> my inner Self which but for His [her Master Morya] calling it out, awakening it from its slumber, would have never come to conscious being – not in *this* life, at all events; . . . –*Blavatsky Letters,* 104

Writing to Dr. Franz Hartmann in 1885 or 1886, she quotes "the Chinese Alchemist" who speaks of the necessity of a living teacher, saying:

"If you covet the precious things of Heaven you must reject the treasures of the earth. You must kindle the fire that springs from the water and evolve the Om contained within the Tong: One word from a wise Master and you possess a draught of the golden water."

– *The Path,* X, 367, March 1896

H.P.B. continues: "I got my drop from my Master (the living one) . . . He is a Saviour, he who leads you to finding the Master within yourself."

H. P. BLAVATSKY'S PERSONAL SEAL

THE SEAL OF THE THEOSOPHICAL SOCIETY

The symbolic seal shown on the left is the one H.P.B. always used on her stationery. A modification of it was adopted as the public corporate seal of the Theosophical Society. When this was done, early in 1876, the coronet of nobility, the upper signs of Leo and Virgo, and the lower kabbalistic ones were removed, and her monogram in the center was replaced by the ansated cross, the Egyptian tau.

In its original and its present form, the Society design contains a synthesis of the basic teachings of theosophy. It represents the universe expanding into manifestation, or evolution, from the central heart, and comprised within the serpent of time and space. The white triangle represents wisdom concealed and the black one wisdom revealed, as well as other things. The tau not only stands for the regenerated man but for life, and the circle hovering over the cosmic cross is the golden germ which will expand into future glory as the neophyte or 'embryo' develops into the grown-up being. The swastika in the small circle may be taken for the great mill of the gods, the cycle of transformation, the "Wheel of the Law." The broken ends of the swastika may turn either way without changing the symbolism.

7

"ISIS UNVEILED"

IN ORDER to bring the ancient wisdom to the Western world, which had lost it, the initial effort was made with those who had some conception that invisible worlds and intelligences exist behind the veil of the seeming, i.e., the spiritualists. They were challenged on their own ground to broaden their outlook. *Isis Unveiled*, H. P. Blavatsky's first book, while not neglecting the consideration and criticism of materialistic science and dogmatic theology, gave special attention to the hidden side of nature, and to the control of occult forces by trained Adepts. In this way the idea that man is far greater than he seems was suggested to the unprepared audience of the seventies. Occult phenomena, including those of the séance room as well as what is commonly called magic, were removed from the domain of the supernatural and shown to be subject to scientific laws known to a few highly evolved human beings – Adepts. *Isis* also contained a sketchy outline of the teachings of cosmic and human evolution. These were further developed in succeeding years and still more fully explained in *The Secret Doctrine*.

Although *Isis Unveiled* was H. P. Blavatsky's first book, it was not her first effort to unveil some of the teachings of the ancient wisdom. She fired what she called her "first occult shot" in E. Gerry Brown's *The Spiritual Scientist*, in July 1875, in "A Few Questions to 'Hiraf'" (*H. P. Blavatsky: Collected Writings*, I, 101–19), written about two years before *Isis* appeared. This article is remarkable not only for its own sake, but as being the first revelation of teachings that were fully explained in that book. It refutes the charge that she "invented" her philosophy and her teachings about the existence of the Mahatmas in later years, when she reached India. She speaks of occultism as standing in relation to spiritualism as the infinite to the finite; of the great Oriental mother-root from which the Kabbalists and other mystic bodies have spread throughout the world; of Christ and Buddha, the divinely wise and spiritual Illuminati; of the "living mystery" of Count Saint-Germain, and of other Adepts; of the seven globes of the planetary chain of which "our planet comes fourth," and even of "the modern doctrine of Re-incarnation, perhaps." She calls herself a "practical follower of Eastern Spiritualism." One striking passage in her "Hiraf" letter about the Mahatmas, her teachers, should be quoted in full:

> Heirs to the early heavenly wisdom of their first forefathers, they [the "Oriental Rosicrucians," as she called the Mahatmas at that time] keep the keys which unlock the most guarded of Nature's secrets, and impart them only gradually and with the greatest caution. But still they *do* impart sometimes. — Ibid., I, 108

Isis Unveiled was begun almost simultaneously with the birth of the Theosophical Society, and it was published in 1877. It provided the only 'textbook' of theosophy available for several years; but it was far from being a complete outline of the philosophy, for the more definite teachings were reserved until students were better prepared to understand them. Described as "A Master-Key to the Mysteries of Ancient and Modern Science and Theology," it quickly became a classic in occult literature, though it only turned the key a little way. Two large editions of this really "epoch-making" work were sold immediately, and new editions have been appearing ever since. Her sympathy for the suffering prompted H.P.B. to send the first payments to Russia in aid of the relief work during the Russo-Turkish war then raging.

Isis was a phenomenon in itself, for the author was not equipped with the technical scholarship or the literary training apparently indispensable for such a task, and with the exception of the learned Dr. Alexander Wilder, who rendered her valuable service, her few helpers were not qualified to give her the editorial assistance she most needed. H.P.B. disregarded all recognized literary canons, of which she knew nothing, and the book contains palpable errors of the printer and a few other slips which could not be corrected later because it was electrotyped. Although she could read and understand English when she landed in New York, she had almost forgotten how to speak it. She says that when she started to write a work which gradually developed into a two-volume book of 1,320 pages, she had "no more idea than the man in the moon what would become of it." She had, however, the inestimable advantage of having the direct inspiration of the Mahatmas, who were making their first effort to "break the molds of mind" in preparation for the bold undertaking: to build "a new continent of thought," and "to invite the elect of mankind to co-operate . . . and help in his turn enlighten superstitious man" (*Mahatma Letters*, 51).

Isis Unveiled was a preparatory sketch, fragmentary by the deliberate intention of its inspirers, yet nearly all the subsequent teachings can be found in its pages, more or less plainly expressed or suggested. The method adopted was that of genuine Mystery schools which develop the intuition of the disciples in the early stages by merely giving hints or seemingly disconnected facts. *The Secret Doctrine,* her most important work, which appeared eleven years later, filled many of the gaps, but it also left much to be elucidated by the intuition of the reader.

The Master K.H. says:

> "Isis" was *not* unveiled but rents sufficiently large were made to afford flitting glances to be completed by the student's own intuition. In this curry of quotations from various philosophic and esoteric truths purposely veiled, behold our doctrine, which is now [1881, four years later] being partially taught to Europeans for the first time.
>
> The Occult Science is *not* one, in which secrets can be communicated of a sudden, by a written or even verbal communication. If so, all the "Brothers" [the name by which the Masters were first spoken of] should have to do, would be to publish a *Hand-book* of the art which might be taught in schools as grammar is. It is the common mistake of people that we willingly wrap ourselves and our powers in mystery — that we wish to keep our knowledge to ourselves, and of our own will refuse . . . to communicate it. The truth is that till the neophyte attains to the condition necessary for that degree of Illumination to which, and for which, he is entitled and fitted, most *if not all* of the Secrets are *incommunicable*. The receptivity must be equal to the desire to instruct. The illumination *must come from within.*
>
> — Ibid., 121, 282–3

It is an error to think that H.P.B. denied the principle of reincarnation in *Isis,* as some have said. She denied the misleading view of it held by the Allan Kardec school of spiritualism, then popular in France, which claimed that the human *personality* regularly and quickly returned to earth-life. She touched lightly on the subject, as it seemed to be too soon for the full exposition of it in view of the unpreparedness of the Western mind, which in general regarded reincarnation as "heathen foolishness." In order to understand the process of reincarnation properly a study of the complex nature of man is necessary – of the seven (or four) aspects of his nature, according to the subdivisions given in Indian psychology – the so-called seven principles of man. As the Masters found it was almost impossible for the audience H. P. Blavatsky was then addressing to understand even three principles – "body, soul or astral monad, and the immortal spirit" – the full exposition of reincarnation was postponed until a few years later, when it was more easily assimilated. This is explained by the Master K.H. in one of his letters to A. P. Sinnett (page 289).

Today, after years of continuous work by the Society, it has become widely accepted in the West, even by many spiritualists. Periodical reincarnation of the *higher ego* on earth is only one example of the universal law of rhythm or periodicity – the "habit of Nature," reimbodiment.

The apparent denial of reincarnation in *Isis* relates only to the lower mundane personality which H.P.B. called the "astral monad," never to the true spirit, the higher ego, as can be seen in volume I, pages 348–9, and volume II, pages 145, 277, 279, 280, and 320. She speaks of "a series of births and deaths" and makes plain the difference between the "immortal Ego," the spirit, and the "soul," the ephemeral personality of each life. She even declares that the conditions of each incarnation depend upon the karma of the previous acts and deeds:

> Nirvana means the certitude of personal immortality in *Spirit*, not in *Soul*, which, as a finite emanation, must certainly disintegrate its particles a compound of human sensations, passions, . . . before the immortal spirit of the *Ego* is quite freed, and henceforth secure against

further transmigration in any form. And how can man ever reach this state so long as the *Upadāna*, that state of longing for *life*, more life, does not disappear . . . Thus the disembodied *Ego*, through this sole undying desire in him, unconsciously furnishes the conditions of his successive self-procreations in various forms, which depend on his mental state and *Karma*, the good or bad deeds of his preceding existence, . . . —*Isis Unveiled*, II, 320

The teaching, even in its most occult form, could hardly be more plainly suggested without going into the detailed exposition that was deliberately avoided as being premature.

H. P. Blavatsky said she suffered intensely for years from the errors that crept into *Isis Unveiled*, unwittingly by her, and too late to be remedied. One specially unfortunate mistake has caused much controversy, and as her opponents seized the opportunity to charge her with denying reincarnation in the New York days, it is necessary finally to clear up this point by presenting a conclusive point in rebuttal which could not be brought forward till lately.

The 'difficult' passages usually cited against her occur in the first volume of *Isis*. On page 346 this sentence is found: "This is what the Hindu dreads above all things—*transmigration* and *reincarnation;* only on other and inferior planets, never on this one." And on page 347: ". . . this *former life* believed in by the Buddhists, is not a life *on this* planet, for, more than any other people, the Buddhistical philosopher appreciated the great doctrine of cycles."

H.P.B. deals with these passages in *Lucifer*, III, 527–8, February 1889, and in *Lucifer*, VIII, May 1891 ("My Books"), as well as in *The Path*, November 1886 ("Theories about Reincarnation and Spirits"). In regard to the first sentence, she points out that she had written on the same page: "Thus, like the revolutions of a wheel, there is a regular succession of death and birth, the moral cause of which is the cleaving to existing objects . . ." and that without some rational explanation the whole thing "reads like the raving of a lunatic, and a jumble of contradictory statements" (*Lucifer*, III, 528).

She continues:

> Since 1882 when the mistake was first found out in "Isis Unveiled," it has been repeatedly stated in the *Theosophist*, and last year in the *Path* that the word "planet" was a mistake and that "cycle" was meant, *i.e.*, the "cycle of Devachanic rest." . . . The same and a worse mistake occurs on pages 346 and 347 (Vol. I). For on the former it is stated that the Hindus dread *reincarnation* "only on other and inferior planets," instead of what is the case, that Hindus dread reincarnation *in other and inferior bodies*, of brutes and animals or *transmigration*, while on page 347 the said error of putting "planet" instead of "cycle" and "personality," shows the author . . . speaking as though Buddha had never taught the doctrine of reincarnation!!
>
> —Ibid., III, 527, Feb. 1889

Now, H. P. Blavatsky was no lunatic, and as in several places in *Isis* she definitely teaches reincarnation, the explanation obviously lies in her statement that this confusion (and other obscurities) was caused by faulty proofreading by well-meaning persons on whom she had to depend, owing to her imperfect knowledge of English, and who were entirely ignorant of the problems in question. Not wishing to give offense, she guardedly says the trouble was largely due to the fact that "one of the literary editors" was "ignorant of Buddhism and Hinduism."

Today, however, it has been revealed why H.P.B. had to suffer vilification in this matter, especially for the statements quoted above from pages 346–7. According to a footnote in the *Mahatma Letters*, page 77, by the Master K.H., the "literary editor" responsible for the errors (innocently, of course) was Colonel Olcott: "By-the-bye, I'll re-write for you pages 345 to 357, Vol. I., of *Isis* – much jumbled, and confused by Olcott, who thought he was improving it!" These are the very pages on which the enemies of H. P. Blavatsky have depended for their unfair attack.

More than a passing reference to the conditions under which *Isis* was written cannot be made here. H.P.B. herself had no idea of writing a book until the urge came from the Master. Olcott says:

> One day in the Summer of 1875, H.P.B. showed me some sheets of manuscript which she had written, and said: "I wrote this last night 'by order,' but what the deuce it is to be I don't know. Perhaps it is for a newspaper article, perhaps for a book, perhaps for nothing: anyhow, I did as I was ordered." And she put it away in a drawer, and nothing more was said about it for some time. But in the month of September – if my memory serves – she went to Syracuse [Ithaca] (N.Y.), on a visit to her new friends, Professor and Mrs. Corson, of Cornell University, and the work went on. She wrote me that it was to be a book on the history and philosophy of the Eastern Schools and their relations with those of our own times. She said she was writing about things she had never studied and making quotations from books she had never read in all her life: that, to test her accuracy, Prof. Corson had compared her quotations with classical works in the University Library, and had found her to be right. – *O. D. L.*, I, 202–3

Colonel Olcott, in his semi-autobiographical work above quoted, and W. Q. Judge, in various magazine articles, describe her methods of work on *Isis*. She was constantly helped by telepathic dictation from the Masters K.H. and M., and also from other Adepts in the Orient. The various kinds of occult phenomena produced by her during the time she was being helped with *Isis* by Olcott and Judge were not intended to satisfy their curiosity, but to serve strictly practical purposes. To her, and even to them, they were not prodigies but natural events in her busy day's work.

After its establishment in 1875 the small Society slowly felt its way, holding private meetings and giving occasional public lectures. Very soon signs and passwords were adopted, and in 1878 degrees of membership were introduced. To the grief of the wonder-seekers H.P.B. declined to produce any occult phenomena at the Society's meetings, and few of the spiritualists retained their interest when they found that philosophies rather than phenomena were the main subjects of study, and that she discouraged attempts to evoke the shades of the departed. She took this course, not only from her knowledge of the misleading nature of information received from the astral world, but from the possible hindrance to the normal progress of the communicating entities in the afterlife, and also on account of the dangers to which the mediums exposed themselves in their ignorance of occult laws. She wrote to her sister as early as 1875:

> "The more I see of spiritist séances in this cradle and hotbed of Spiritism and mediums [America], the more clearly I see how dangerous they are for humanity. Poets speak of a *thin partition* between the two worlds. There is *no* partition whatever. Blind people have imagined obstacles of this kind because coarse organs of hearing, sight, and feeling do not allow the majority of people to penetrate the *difference* of being. Besides, Mother-Nature has done well in endowing us with *coarse* senses, for otherwise the individuality and personality of man would become impossible, because the dead would be continually mixing with the living, and the living would assimilate themselves with the dead." – *The Path*, IX, 379–80, Feb. 1895

The Master K.H. explains that:

> . . . it is not against *true* Spiritualism that we set ourselves, but only against indiscriminate mediumship and — physical manifestations, — materializations and trance-*possessions* especially. . . . it is the Occultists and the Theosophists who are true Spiritualists, while the modern sect of that name is composed simply of *materialistic* phenomenalists.
>
> — *Mahatma Letters*, 113–14

Isis Unveiled boldly challenged the theological, the scientific, and the spiritualistic worlds, and while H. P. Blavatsky knew that the two former would try to discredit her and her work, she hoped that the broader-minded spiritualists would welcome her exposition of the "Higher Spiritualism," the true science of man, which she brought from the archaic teachings of the mystic East. Unfortunately, the spiritualists in general did not respond to her efforts, and her lifelong martyrdom began (as she had foreseen and told W. Q. Judge), during which she was treated by the unthinking as some kind of criminal instead of the benefactor she really was.

The prevailing belief among spiritualists when *Isis* was written (largely for their instruction) was that occult phenomena were produced only by disimbodied human spirits. Nothing was known about the complex nature of man or the existence of the astral body; *soul* and *spirit* were mere undefined words. The astral light, well known to the ancient philosophers, was ignored, the elementals or nature spirits were flatly denied and the very word *occultism* was declared by prominent spiritualists to be an invention of the theosophists. These and other concepts, although hoary with age, when presented by H.P.B. in *Isis* and elsewhere, aroused bitter opposition and even persecution, which were not diminished by her claim to be able to produce occult phenomena by her trained will, and not by passive mediumship.

In contrast to the antagonism her teachings received in the seventies, we find them seriously discussed and many of her interpretations accepted in the spiritualistic journals today. For instance, in regard to the transformation that takes place after death, during which the reincarnating ego is liberated from the lower principles – a theosophical teaching formerly denounced as fabulous – there appeared the following editorial in one of the best spiritualistic journals:

> We know that identity persists beyond death – we have proved it innumerable times – but we more than suspect that spirit-personality is a very much less limited and arbitrary thing than personality as we know it on earth, where it is closely bound up with the idea of some particular face and form, character, manner and cognomen. All these must needs change as the soul progresses. Thus a communicator, instead of saying, for example: "I am John Smith" might more truthfully say: "On earth I was John Smith, but though my identity is unchanged I am no longer the John Smith I was." We think, in short, that much of the skepticism regarding personality at the back of phenomena arises from a lack of a clear perception of what personality really stands for. And that is a very large question indeed.
>
> – *Light*, July 31, 1931 (London)

The trend of modern spiritualism suggests that it is approaching the true teaching of the ancient "Spiritualism of Alexandria, the Theodidaktoi, etc.," which H. P. Blavatsky offered the spiritualists in New York, only to have it rejected without proper study. Even reincarnation is no longer a bugbear. Spiritualistic journals and speakers give sympathetic attention to its possibilities, and many of their best minds are putting forward the theosophical arguments for it.

When *Isis Unveiled* proved such a brilliant success, the publisher offered H.P.B. $5,000 for a one-volume continuation in which still more should be 'unveiled,' and which would be sold for $100 per copy. Poor as she was, she refused, saying it was not permissible to give out any further teachings *at that time*. Olcott says that enough additional MSS. to make a third volume had actually been written, but they were destroyed before she left America. Throughout her whole career she never let pecuniary advantages swerve her from the strict lines of conduct inculcated in the esoteric schools in regard to the presentation of occult information.

In the summer of 1875, just as H.P.B. was beginning to write *Isis*, she passed through one of the formidable trials which must be faced by those indomitable souls who are being prepared to solve the great problems of secret nature in order to become efficient helpers of humanity. This ordeal was within herself; she never mentioned it, and little would be known of it but from certain private letters of advice received by Colonel Olcott from the Egyptian Adepts, who called upon him to give her his strongest support and encouragement. She seems to have seen few if any of these particular letters, though she must of course have been in close touch with the writers. Her outward life proceeded as usual during this crisis. A few passages from the letters give a sufficient idea of the conditions behind the scenes:

> The *Dweller* is watching closely and will never lose his opportunity, if our Sister's courage fails. This is to be one of her hardest trials . . . how dangerous for her will be the achievement of her duty and how likely to expect for both of you [Olcott and Gerry Brown] to lose a sister and a — Providence on earth. . . .
>
> She must encounter once more and face to face the dreaded one she thought she would behold no more. She must either conquer — or die . . . solitary, unprotected but still *dauntless* she will have to face all the great perils, and unknown mysterious dangers she *must* en-

counter . . . Brother mine, I can do naught for our poor Sister. She has placed herself under the stern law of the Lodge and these laws can be softened for none. As an Ellorian she must win her right . . .
— *Letters from the Masters of the Wisdom*, II, 42 et seq.

She succeeded in her inner battle and, as can be seen in the *Blavatsky Letters*, page 187, she could boldly defy the dreaded "Dweller on the Threshold" more than ten years afterward, though others—unprepared by self-discipline, such as Babaji — were not so fortunate. From all this it is seen that she not only challenged the opposition of the representatives of materialistic science and of traditional ecclesiasticism, but also the most powerful and malignant intelligent forces on the invisible planes of being. The average man is totally ignorant of these forces, which are extremely dangerous to all who are not perfectly pure in heart and impersonal. A few mystics, such as the earnest seeker, Stainton Moses, appear to have encountered them, and to have suffered thereby. A reference is made in the *Mahatma Letters* (p. 42) to his trying experience, and to H.P.B.'s desperate attempts to rescue him.

While living in Philadelphia, to Olcott's astonishment, she decided to marry M. C. Betanelly, a man who was not her equal in mentality or station in life. She was forty-three years old and the marriage was contracted on unusual terms. The suitor professed the greatest admiration and respect for her, and she finally agreed to his offer on the understanding that the marriage was to be purely nominal, and merely one of friendly companionship and complete independence on her part. She even retained her name Blavatsky. But the alliance lasted a very short time, for the husband, if he can be so called, soon repented of his contract and became a passionate lover. As she rejected his overtures with horror, the "phantom marriage," as it was called, was in 1878 dissolved in court, Mr. Judge being her counsel. Colonel Olcott said she told him that the affair was the effect of karmic complications in past lives, and that, while it seemed very unfortunate and strange, it was a necessary experience as a final corrective for certain temperamental weaknesses which troubled her real Self.

About the same time, another cause of anxiety arose. Colonel Olcott says:

> She fell dangerously ill in June [1875] from a bruise on one knee caused by a fall the previous winter in New York upon the stone flagging of a sidewalk, which ended in violent inflammation of the periosteum and partial mortification of the leg; and as soon as she got better (which she did in one night, by one of her quasi-miraculous cures, after an eminent surgeon [Dr. Seth Pancoast] had declared that she would die unless the leg was instantly amputated), she left him [the second husband] and would not go back. —*O. D. L.*, I, 57

This was only one of several remarkable and sudden restorations to health when physicians declared her condition critical. She attributed them to the direct intervention of her Master because she was needed to continue her work. Unfortunately, she neglected to rest her limb, as instructed by the Master, and in consequence she was not really well for several months.

In 1876, considerable attention was focused on the Theosophical Society by the cremation of a certain Baron de Palm, to whom Colonel Olcott had been very kind during his last illness. This was the first public cremation in America in a crematorium. In the two previous cases, open-air funeral pyres were prepared. Colonel Olcott arranged and conducted a funeral service in the New York Masonic Temple which was attended by an enormous crowd, mostly curiosity-seekers not sympathetic with theosophy or cremation. What promised to be a serious disturbance was avoided by Colonel Olcott's tactful handling of the situation, and the impressive ceremony gave the audience a new conception of the theosophical interpretation of death.

Intense opposition had been displayed against cremation, but the successful disposal of the body of de Palm greatly helped in breaking down the ignorant prejudice against this sanitary and reverent disposition of the worn-out vehicle of the soul. The baron bequeathed his supposedly valuable property to Colonel Olcott, who arranged to hand it over to the Society. But when the will was probated and inquiries were made about the property, it appeared that it would not even cover the cost of probate and funeral! De Palm was a ne'er-do-well Bavarian baron with a past. He had no means, but plenty of debts. He had no literary interests or scholarship, and he displayed only a purely superficial fancy for psychical phenomena. It is necessary to mention these unfortunate matters because unscrupulous persons, especially the French Kabbalist Encausse (Papus), have spread the calumny that *Isis* was "a compilation from the manuscripts of Baron de Palm, and without acknowledgment." In his *Old Diary Leaves*, Colonel Olcott gives documented particulars of de Palm's career, legally certified. This slander presents a typical illustration of the depth of mendacity to which apparently decent human beings can descend when they are determined to besmirch the character of H. P. Blavatsky. It is significant that the baser side of human nature is instinctively aroused to opposition whenever it comes within the radius of the revealing light of Truth.

The publication of *Isis Unveiled* brought immense correspondence, and branches of the Society began to be thought of, a group of students in London being the first officially to form themselves into an organized branch of the T. S. Another group, who seem to have had a deeper understanding of theosophy than many of the original London members, existed in Liverpool from an early date but saw no reason to organize into an official lodge until much later. The Liverpool Lodge became a strong center of theosophy. Another group, in Corfu, Greece, also delayed organizing until after the London members formed the first chartered T. S. branch, "The British Theosophical Society," in June 1878. In the circular of the London Society the primary importance of brotherhood is plainly stated. After enumerating some of the objects of its existence, which include self-study and self-development, it concludes: "and chiefly to aid in the institution of a Brotherhood of Humanity."

Early in 1878 an alliance was made between the Theosophical Society and the Ārya Samāj, an Indian reform movement established by Swami Dayānand Saraswatī, a learned pandit and a famous yogi, at that time having genuine occult relations with representatives of the Great Lodge, and "endowed some years back with great powers and a knowledge he has since forfeited, . . . this truly great man, whom we all knew and placed our hopes in," as K.H. said in 1882 (*Mahatma Letters*, 309). The aims and methods of the two societies seemed almost identical, and the name of the T. S. was even changed for a while to "The Theosophical Society of the Ārya Samāj."

Unfortunately, Dayānand's views proved narrower than was at first apparent, and his Samāj turned out to be little more than a reformed Hindu sect. Dayānand protested bitterly against the friendly attitude of the theosophists toward Buddhism, Zoroastrianism, and other faiths, "false religions," as he called them. Finally, in 1882, following a period of troubled relationship which culminated after the theosophical headquarters was established in India, the working alliance was severed and each society went its own way. It is impossible for the Theosophical Society to be identified in any way with any kind of sectarian organization or belief, even the most progressive, for that would destroy its neutrality and its strictly nondogmatic character, which is essential in the effort to establish a *universal* brotherhood.

The seeds of theosophy having been planted in the West, orders came from the Masters in 1878 to begin work in the Orient, and H. P. Blavatsky prepared to leave for India; this time, however, not as an unknown traveler but as the writer of a widely read book and the chief representative of what was becoming known as a new development in thought and action.

Colonel Olcott was directed to accompany her, and he quickly wound up his business and personal affairs to devote his life to theosophy in strange lands where the future was veiled in darkness and mystery. This successful, American, matter-of-fact man of affairs must have had a magnificent trust in H. P. Blavatsky's mission and in the support of the Masters, for, although he obtained high testimonials and a special passport from the United States government, and received a commission to report to the government on the commercial conditions in the East, no definite business opportunity was awaiting him. He was sacrificing all that ordinary men hold dear.

The prospect, however, was not altogether a surprise to him, because some years before he had been prepared by the Master M. for a drastic change. Late one night, in New York, after he and H.P.B. had ended their day's work on *Isis*, he was sitting alone in his own room with the door locked, when to his great surprise the Master M. appeared suddenly and conversed with him, offering him the opportunity of taking part in a great work for humanity, and telling him of the mysterious tie between H. P. B. and himself (Olcott), which could never be broken though it might be greatly strained. The Master disappeared as strangely as he had arrived, leaving his turban as a proof of the reality of the interview. Colonel Olcott was greatly impressed by this experience, and many years after he declared that it had helped him to stand firm and unshaken during many serious crises. He describes it in detail in *Old Diary Leaves*.

8

EARLY DAYS IN INDIA

HELENA PETROVNA BLAVATSKY and H. S. Olcott traveled to India in the ostensible capacity of a "Committee" of the Society to "visit foreign countries and report," which obviously meant to study the opportunities for spreading theosophy, and to do all they could to promote it in whatever way seemed best. They sailed for England on December 18, 1878, and as they departed H.P.B. wrote in Olcott's "Diary," "All dark – but tranquil."

In no way were their hands tied. In anticipation of unknown possibilities, Colonel Olcott, as president, had been given practically autocratic power by the Council of the Theosophical Society by resolutions passed on July 18 and August 27, 1878, at New York. He was authorized to transfer the headquarters of the Society to any foreign country, to admit new members and, still more comprehensively, to

> have full power and discretion to make such rules and regulations, and do such things as he may consider necessary for the welfare of the Society, and the accomplishment of the objects which it represents.
>
> All Bye-Laws inconsistent with the above are *hereby repealed*.
>
> – *Historical Retrospect*, 5

All these resolutions were ostensibly passed under the understanding that they applied to a *temporary* residence abroad, but conditions arose which made the temporary visit a permanent one and, under what Olcott took to be complete freedom of action given him by the resolutions, he made and authorized many administrative changes without consulting the mother-group in New York. There is no record that either H. P. Blavatsky or anyone else disapproved of his point of view in the matter when the changes were made. His first presidential "Order," dated January 17th, 1879, was sent out from London, on his way to India. It appointed Major-General Abner Doubleday, U.S.A., "President ad-interim," and made two other appointments. William Q. Judge was already recording secretary; and, for a while, all diplomas, even though issued in India, were sent to New York for his signature. Many other changes were soon authorized by Colonel Olcott, an important one being the adoption of the "Revised Objects, Rules, and Regulations" by a Convention of the Theosophical Society at Bombay early in 1880.

General Doubleday and W. Q. Judge were absolutely devoted to the Cause, but the activities of the general membership in New York gradually diminished after a few years, largely, no doubt, because of the absence of the inspiring and powerful personality of the foundress, but also on account of the dissatisfaction of the psychic researchers when they found that the Society was not intended to be a "Miracle Club." General Doubleday, the president pro tem in New York, was an earnest and trusted theosophist who understood the real objects of the movement and who remained faithful till his death in 1893. Judge, who was being trained personally by H.P.B., was at that time deeply immersed in the difficulties of a young married man struggling to gain a foothold at the bar. For long periods his law business took him away from New York and even to foreign countries.

What attention he was able to give to theosophical work required the greatest self-sacrifice. He wrote to Olcott in 1883:

> Anyway I can never [go] back. If I were to back out, I could not exist. Each day makes me stronger. You no doubt say, Why don't you *act?* Well, I have up to date acted so that my temporal concerns are not good for five cents, all through Theosophy.
>
> – *Theos.*, LIII, 68, Oct. 1931

It was not until a few years later, when his financial position became secure, that he was able to give the needed attention to the spread of theosophy; and then, by means of his administrative ability and, above all, by the general recognition of his unique combination of practical common sense with spiritual wisdom, the lodges quickly spread from coast to coast.

The journey of H. P. Blavatsky and Colonel Olcott to India was uneventful, though not agreeable on account of severe storms at sea. A short stay was made in London where work was done among the members of the British Theosophical Society (afterwards the London Lodge) who were mostly psychically-minded and included among other persons of some note, the Rev. Stainton Moses, C. C. Massey, and the distinguished biologist Alfred Russel Wallace. One of the Masters was seen by Olcott walking in Cannon Street. This Master later called at the house of Mrs. Hollis Billing where H.P.B. was staying, and had a conversation with the latter. Mrs. Billing was a medium of an unusual type who became a faithful supporter of H.P.B. Much is written about her in the Masters' letters and those of H. P. Blavatsky, and W. Q. Judge mentions her with appreciation. Two English members, Miss Rosa Bates and Mr. E. Wimbridge, were added to the party of travelers, but they soon lost interest and resigned not long after they arrived in India.

Bombay was reached on February 16, 1879, where a deputation of the local theosophists greeted them with much enthusiasm. A suitable house was taken in Bombay for temporary headquarters and active work began, at first among learned Hindus, Parsis, and a few Europeans. The Indians were astonished; here was something new – Westerners coming to India, not to scoff at its ancient teachings or to investigate them as quaint heathen survivals, or even to study them academically, but to revive the grandeur and spiritual value of Sanskrit literature and Oriental philosophy, and to encourage the Orient to resist scientific materialism on one hand and foreign dogmatic theology on the other!

Alliances or friendly associations were formed with various native Indian progressive bodies. One of these was the "Hindu Sabhā," a broad-minded society of southern India which aimed "to promote unity and good-will amongst the sects and castes of India, to encourage marriage of girls after reaching puberty, and the re-marriage of child-widows," etc. The caste rule was modified so that "a Hindu may associate with a Theosophist at meals," a most radical innovation. The editor of *The Theosophist* writes:

> This is the first time that our quasi-national relation with the Hindus has been officially affirmed, though we have on several occasions dined with even Brahmins. – *Theos.*, II, May 1881, Suppl. 3

In another way the native residents were aroused to enthusiasm. Here were people from America and England who, instead of identifying themselves in the usual way with the people of their own race, were associating on equal terms with the native Indians, and largely ignoring the Anglo-Indians. However, the theosophists came with the main purpose of bringing theosophy to the Indian people, and incidentally to others. If the Anglo-Indians became interested and were willing to help, so much the better, but there must be no racial distinction. H. P. B. despised the haughtiness which looked with contempt on fellow human beings of another kind, whether the difference was in color or, as among native Indians, between castes.

Long before Gandhi began his work among the pariahs, "those helpless outcastes or rather creatures of no caste, rejected by all their fellow-men," as H. P. Blavatsky said, she strove to arouse them to stand on their own feet, declaring "You are Divine, children of the One Father, and members of the great brotherhood of mankind." When she started her first magazine, *The Theosophist,* in 1879, she opened its columns to articles espousing their cause. She also made strenuous efforts to abolish child-marriage (now illegal), to ameliorate the lot of the unhappy child-widows, and to help Hindu women to regain the freedom they formerly enjoyed in ancient Āryāvarta. All races were the same to her, for universal brotherhood embraces all mankind. In April 1882, she established "The Ladies' Theosophical Society" at Calcutta, composed of native women – an innovation indeed at that time in India, but the Master K.H. had "always felt the need of enrolling women" in the work of spreading theosophy (*Mahatma Letters,* 251).

Wherever she and Colonel Olcott went, they emphasized the need of a fraternization among religious bodies in which the only rivalry would be in good works. Much good was done in this way, and the motto of the Theosophical Society,

"There is no Religion Higher than Truth," adopted from the family motto of the Maharajas of Benares, aroused favorable comment. Under the auspices of the Theosophical Society, as the work expanded, Hindus, Parsis, Buddhists, Jews, Mohammedans and Europeans of various beliefs met together in friendly intercourse, an unprecedented sight in the East. Nothing, except the radical modification in outlook brought about by one of the fundamental teachings of theosophy, which is that the esoteric basis of all the great religions is identical – the ancient wisdom-religion of the archaic ages – could have produced this result.

Olcott, on his part, had a sympathetic understanding of the Oriental mentality, and his tact, straightforward dealing, and obvious devotion to humanity, earned the love and confidence of the Asiatics among whom he worked with indefatigable energy for so many years. His simple but practical lectures on the needs of India, material and spiritual, always attracted large audiences.

H. P. Blavatsky created intense interest among the Hindus by her bold affirmation that the great sages of India (Rishis or Mahatmas) had not withdrawn from contact with the world, as so many feared. She not only declared her personal knowledge that the Adept Fraternity existed, but also that she herself was their messenger and a chela of a high Hindu Mahatma.

Even before the T. S. was started H.P.B. frequently mentioned the Adepts in her letters to various journals but often under the name of Rosicrucians, and it was not until she settled in India that the words Mahatmas or Masters were used. Writing to Dr. Hartmann, she says:

I said to him [Olcott] that I had known Adepts, the "Brothers,"

not only in India and beyond Ladakh, but in Egypt and Syria, – for there are "Brothers" there to this day. . . . That, whether they were called Rosicrucians, Kabalists, or Yogis – Adepts were everywhere Adepts – silent, secret, retiring, and who would never divulge themselves entirely to anyone, unless one did as I did – passed seven and ten years probation[*] and given proofs of absolute devotion, and that he, or she, would keep silent even before a prospect and a threat of death. . . . All I was allowed to say was – the truth: There is beyond the Himalayas a nucleus of Adepts, of various nationalities; and the Teschu Lama knows them, and they act together, and some of them are with him and yet remain unknown in their true character even to the average lamas . . . My Master and K.H. and several others I know personally are there, coming and going, and they are all in communication with Adepts in Egypt and Syria, and even Europe.
– *The Path*, X, 369–70, March 1896

An interesting corroboration of the reality of H.P.B.'s teachers is found in an experience related by Prince Emil von Sayn-Wittgenstein, F.T.S., a Russian officer and an old childhood friend of hers. Writing to *The Spiritualist* (London) on June 18, 1878, in order to criticize the infallibility of "spirit predictions," he said that he had been warned several times by the spirits to avoid service in the Russo-Turkish war as it would be fatal to him. H.P.B. learned of this prediction and, he writes, told him that her Master would protect him and that he would be perfectly safe. The prince continues:

"The fact is, that during the whole campaign I did not see one shot explode near me, and that, so far as danger was concerned, I could just as well have remained at Vevey [Switzerland]. . . . Whenever I was near a scene of action the enemy's fire ceased."

---

*Probation for chelaship can be passed anywhere.

He made many efforts to get near the firing line, but:

> "As long as I was there, the scene was quiet as in the times of peace, and the firing recommenced as soon as I had left the place. . . .
>
> "I cannot believe all this to be the sole result of chance. It was too regular, too positive to be explained thus. It is, I am sure of it, magic, — the more so as the person who protected me thus efficaciously is one of the most powerful masters of the occult science professed by the theosophists."

The letter is given in full in *The Theosophist*, March 1883, and in Sinnett's *Incidents*, page 209. The protection exerted in favor of the prince was an exceptional though not a unique exercise of occult power on that line by the Masters, and must have been given for some special reason.

The Mahatmas are greatly opposed to their personalities being exploited or their places of residence known, and they have taken pains to throw a veil over such matters, and to create doubts about their very existence except with the few to whom such information is necessary. Several emphatic passages occur to this effect in the *Mahatma Letters.* Let the details of their retreats and their activities be proclaimed for the satisfaction of the curious and

> not only will sceptical society derive no great good but our privacy would be constantly endangered and have to be continually guarded at an unreasonable cost of power. — Ibid., 227

Again on page 337 a Master writes:

> But I have never undertaken to convince any of them [Fellows of the British T. S.] of the extent of our powers nor even of our personal existence. . . . Too much, or too little was said and proved of us as M.A. (Oxon) justly remarked. *We are ordered* to set ourselves to work to sweep away the few vestiges . . . and the more our actual existence be doubted — the better.

Again:

> For the present we offer our knowledge – some portions of it at least – to be either accepted or rejected on its own merits independently – entirely so – from the source from which it emanates.
>
> – Ibid., 417

H. P. Blavatsky declares in "The Original Programme of The Theosophical Society" that

> They had to oppose in the strongest manner possible anything approaching *dogmatic faith and fanaticism* – belief in the *infallibility* of the Masters, or even in the very existence of our invisible Teachers, having to be checked from the first. – *Theos.*, LII, 564, Aug. 1931

They have no desire to start a new superstitious worship of saints or godlings.

Owing to misconception of a statement by the Master K.H. that he could not endure "the stifling magnetism" of even his own countrymen for any length of time and was obliged to return to Tibet (*Mahatma Letters*, 12), it was suggested that no Adepts remained in India. Apparently in order to correct this, H.P.B. wrote the following explanation of the real conditions:

> European and even Hindu students of Occultism are often deploring and even wondering, why all the "Initiates" or "adepts" seem to have died out in India? They have not "died" out, nor, is their absence due to "Kali Yug" as popularly yet erroneously supposed. The "adepts" have simply and gradually if not altogether forsaken India, at least retired from its public populated portions, keeping their knowledge and often their very existence as secret as they can. Many of them are gone beyond the Himalayas. Some yet remain – especially in Southern India, but few are the privileged ones who know of them; still fewer those who could point out their places of retreat.
>
> – *Theos.*, III, 135, Feb. 1882

One of these southern Indian Adepts was the Master Narāyan, who telepathically dictated parts of *Isis Unveiled* when H.P.B. was in New York, and later, some of the very valuable "Replies to an English F.T.S." brought out in *The Theosophist* in 1883 and republished in *Five Years of Theosophy* (see *O. D. L.*, I, 249). He also contributed to *The Theosophist* under the pseudonym "One of the Original Founders of the T. S." An important and interesting article exposing the self-contradictions of the Swami Dayānand when the T. S. had to withdraw from association with his Ārya Samāj is printed in *The Theosophist* for June 1882. The Master Narāyan lived at Tiruvallum, a retired spot in southern India, a landed proprietor to all appearance, and it is reported that Subba Row once had the privilege of visiting him (see *Blavatsky Letters*, 63). Subba Row himself writes:

> Southern India has always produced the greatest Aryan philosophers. Madhavāchārya came from Southern India, and Sankarāchārya was born in Malabar; and at the present day there are high adepts and schools of occultism in Southern India.
>
> – *Theos.*, X, 228, Jan. 1889

A reproduction of one of Narāyan's letters is given in C. Jinarājadāsa's *Did H. P. Blavatsky Forge the Mahatma Letters?*

It may not be an accidental concurrence, if true, as some modern writers on Indian mysticism declare, that there is far more spirituality on the whole in southern India than in other parts of the country. However this may be, the "Holy Man of Benares," Swami Bhaskarānanda Saraswatī, a chela of one of H.P.B.'s Masters, and later known to Katherine Tingley who visited him in his āśrama, lived in more northern parts. He was a noble and learned representative of the highest class of yogis working openly, but even such outstanding men as he are only on the way to the spiritual altitudes of the fully initiated Mahatmas who inspired the theosophical movement, and whose work and lives are consecrated to the whole of humanity.

How, then, are such helpers to be found? They put it plainly thus:

> . . . *nothing* draws us to any outsider save his evolving spirituality. He may be a Bacon or an Aristotle in knowledge, and still not even make his current felt a feather's weight by us, if his power is confined to the *Manas.* The supreme energy resides in the *Buddhi;* latent – when wedded to *Atman* alone, active and irresistible when galvanized by the *essence* of "Manas" and when none of the dross of the latter commingles with that pure essence to weigh it down by its finite nature. *Manas,* pure and simple, is of a lower degree, and of the earth earthly: and so your greatest men count but as nonentities in the arena where greatness is measured by the standard of spiritual development.
>
> – *Mahatma Letters,* 341–2

> I can come nearer to you, but you must draw me by a purified heart and a gradually developing will. Like the needle the adept follows his attractions. . . .
>
> If you hear seldom from me, never feel disappointed, my Brother, but say – "It is my fault." . . . your thought *will find me* if projected by a pure impulse, . . . Like the light in the sombre valley seen by the mountaineer from his peaks, every bright thought in your mind, my Brother, will sparkle and attract the attention of your distant friend and correspondent. If thus we discover our natural Allies in the *Shadow*-world – your world and ours outside the precincts – and it is our law to approach every such an one if even there be but the feeblest glimmer of the true "Tathāgata" light within him – then how far easier for you to attract us. Understand this and the admission into the Society of persons often distasteful to you will no longer amaze you. – Ibid., 266–8

The revelation to the West that the occult Fraternity of

Adepts still exists has been increasingly profaned and their teachings perverted of late years by vulgar charlatans who exploit sacred things for money or to get a personal following. H.P.B.'s frank admissions that she was not faultless or infallible, and her poignant regret for errors when her enthusiasm outran her judgment, are in significant contrast to the sorry metaphysical mountebanks who brazenly claim to be in intimate touch with the secret Lodge, and even in some cases to be "Masters" themselves. In those early days Subba Row and other sincere disciples evidently had a prevision of such abominations. A heavy responsibility rests on theosophists to keep the movement, with its austere, simple dignity, free from contamination so that the difference between the true and the false teachers will be unmistakable.

The authenticity and intrinsic value of H.P.B.'s teachings in their appeal to the loftiest aspirations of the heart and mind, stand out in vivid contrast to the specious as well as to the crude counterfeits which have sprung up like poisonous toadstools. Unscrupulous charlatans, false prophets indeed, are misleading thousands of simpleminded victims with alluring prospects of acquiring psychic powers, etc., of worldly "success," "personal magnetism and *control of others*" for personal ends, by so-called occult means. Some even promise initiation, or recognition by Masters for cash!

On a higher plane, many persons, even some Western scholars, have been attracted by the misleading Tibetan tantric yoga in its modern form, with its subtle enticement for a certain class of intellects. The Master said that about four hundred years ago it took the wrong path. In the lower lamaistic or tantric or semi-tantric system a superficial resemblance in part to the genuine spiritual yoga may be observed, but the two methods are fundamentally opposed in purpose. The noble Mahāyāna Buddhism so eloquently set forth by H.P.B. in her *Voice of the Silence* reveals the only real path to emancipation.

While at this time the efforts of the Masters were largely concentrated upon India, they had a much larger field in view. Oriental philosophy had to be brought to the Western peoples in a more popular way than by its academic presentation by the learned European Sanskrit scholars in a few universities, and the Theosophical Society was their instrument for this important work. The result is plainly seen today, and has been admitted by even the severest critics of theosophy. W. Q. Judge, writing in 1891, says:

> See how much the English government and the colleges pay for the work of such men as Max Müller and others, which, although it is good work in its way . . . has made no sensible change in the people by its weak and wavering impact upon their minds. Yet in fifteen short years the efforts of H. P. Blavatsky, Col. Olcott, and others have made the entire world look with longing and respect and hope to the vast stores left to us by the ancient philosophers of the East. And all of this by the few for no pay and for no honor, and in the face of calumny and scorn from the world at large.
>
> — *The Path,* V, 378, March 1891

The Master K.H. pointed out that:

> The present tendency of education is to make them [Hindus] materialistic and root out spirituality. With a proper understanding of what their ancestors meant by their writings and teachings, education would become a blessing, whereas now it is often a curse. . . . old MSS., hitherto buried out of the reach of the Europeans, would again come to light, and with them the key to much of that which was hidden for ages from the popular understanding, for which your skeptical Sanscritists do not care, which your religious missionaries

do not *dare*, to understand. Science would gain much, humanity everything. Under the stimulus of the Anglo-Indian Theosophical Society, we might in time see another golden age of Sanscrit literature.
—*The Occult World*, 6th Amer. ed., 136–7

Realizing the importance of Sanskrit as a factor in the regeneration of India, and in the spread of theosophy, H.P.B. and Olcott made strenuous efforts to revive Sanskrit learning and to establish Sanskrit schools and publications. Under her advice and helped from her slender resources, the Nellore Branch in southern India started a small Sanskrit school in 1882 which has since developed into a residential college. Many other Indian branches followed the same course, and the subject was taken up vigorously in America a few years later by individual theosophists.

In H. P. Blavatsky's Indian period even the academic scholars admired the energetic work done by the Sanskrit revival which she initiated, including the collection and translation of rare manuscripts; but criticism was aroused among many European scholars when it was declared that the texts of the Purānas, Upanishads, etc., concealed hidden meanings, and that the exoteric teachings were trivial in comparison with what could be found beneath the surface when studied with the proper keys. Olcott reports a conversation he had with the eminent Sanskritist, Professor Max Müller, in regard to the educational work of the Theosophical Society in India; he writes:

"You have done nobly," he said, "in helping so much to revive the love for Sanskrit, and the Orientalists have watched the development of your Society with the greatest interest from the commencement. But why will you spoil all this good reputation by pandering to the superstitious fancies of the Hindus, by telling them that there is an esoteric meaning in their Shastras? I know the language perfectly, and I assure you there is no such thing as a Secret Doctrine in it." In reply, I simply told the Professor that every unspoilt (*i.e.*, unwesternized) Pandit throughout all India believed, as we did, in the existence of this hidden meaning; and that, as for the *Siddhis*, I personally knew men who possessed them and whom I had seen exhibit their powers. "Well, then," said my erudite host, "let us change the subject." — *O. D. L.*, III, 177–8

Max Müller's opinion is no longer universal among Orientalists, but it is only very lately that serious investigators have realized that trained yogis can develop the siddhis or occult powers described more or less obscurely in Sanskrit literature. Western Orientalists in general have still to learn that the Mahatmas have advanced much farther in rāja-yoga — true occultism or spiritual development — than even the living higher yogis or lamas whose names and reputation are widely known in India, Tibet, or elsewhere in the East.

H.P.B.'s high regard for Sanskrit is shown in her comment:

The attempt to render in a European tongue the grand panorama of the ever periodically recurring Law . . . is daring, for no human language, save the Sanskrit — which is that *of the Gods* — can do so with any degree of adequacy. — *The Secret Doctrine*, I, 269

In regard to the charges that H. P. Blavatsky had no real knowledge of Oriental philosophies, the records show that she was not only admitted by learned students of the Kabbalah — such as Dr. Seth Pancoast in America, Baron Spedalieri, and other high-ranking Kabbalists in Europe — to be a master in that partial presentation of the ancient wisdom, but in India her profound insight into the meaning of ancient Hindu philosophies was recognized by the most learned Sanskrit students and pandits who gave her many testimonials to that effect.

For example, when Dr. G. Thibaut, a distinguished German Sanskritist, principal of Benares College and a special protégé of Professor Max Müller, had a long discussion with her on the Sānkhya philosophy, and asked her the most searching questions, he declared that she answered them better than Max Müller or any other Orientalist had done. This took place at Benares in December 1879, when she was there to attend a Council meeting of the Society. While she seems to have had difficulty at times in calling forth the knowledge latent in the depths of her consciousness, she could always draw upon it when the occasion justified the effort.

It was not only in India that her erudition was recognized by competent scholars, but also in Japan and Tibet. According to Evans-Wentz, the well-known Tibetan scholar, the Tibetan lama Kazi Dawa-Samdup was of the view that

> . . . despite the adverse criticisms directed against H. P. Blavatsky's works, there is adequate internal evidence in them of their author's intimate acquaintance with the higher *lāmaistic* teachings, into which she claimed to have been initiated.
>
> — *The Tibetan Book of the Dead*, 7

This learned Tibetan Buddhist lama was a member of the staff of the 13th Dalai Lama, and lecturer in Tibetan at the University of Calcutta. He was thoroughly familiar with the deeper Tibetan teachings which are yet only partially revealed to Western scholars, and his opinion outweighs those of a thousand ill-informed and prejudiced critics.

Mrs. Salanave asked Sardar Bahadur S. W. Laden La, of Darjeeling, a well-known and very independent Buddhist scholar of Tibetan ancestry, if he thought that H. P. Blavatsky had real "inside information" about the higher Tibetan Buddhism. He replied that she certainly had, and that *The Voice of the Silence* contained the most profound Tibetan teachings. Mrs. Salanave also quotes Professor D. T. Suzuki, the great Japanese authority on Mahāyāna Buddhism, who said:

> "I saw *The Voice of the Silence* for the first time while at Oxford. I immediately got a copy and sent it to Mrs. Suzuki (then Miss Beatrice Lane, American) at Columbia University, writing to her: 'Here is the real Mahayana Buddhism.' "
>
> – *The Canadian Theosophist,* XIV, 100, June 1933

9

DEVELOPMENT OF THE INDIAN WORK

WHILE Bombay remained the temporary headquarters, H. P. Blavatsky and her colleague were constantly making toilsome journeys to spread the light of theosophy. One day they would be entertained by a raja in his palace, the next day they would have an open-air discussion with a yogi carrying his begging bowl, or they might attend a great public meeting of all classes followed perhaps by a profound debate with the most learned Sanskrit pandits on the inner meaning of the Purānas or the Upanishads.

Some interesting events that happened during these journeys, and while H.P.B. was traveling in India during her earlier visits, sometimes with her Master, were used by her as the groundwork of a picturesque romance of travel written for the *Russian Messenger (Russkiy Vyestnik)* and afterwards published under the title, *From the Caves and Jungles of Hindostan.* Though stated to be a work of imagination in large part, this fascinating narrative contains valuable theosophical teaching and some Indian historical and archaeological information in popular form. These brilliant articles produced a profound impression in Russia, and after their appearance she was besieged with requests for further contributions at her own price.

The general interest in theosophy and the personal correspondence with scholars and inquirers had now so greatly increased that it became imperative to start a journal; and a monthly magazine, *The Theosophist,* saw the light in October

1879, edited by H. P. Blavatsky. The Masters took great interest in it and, according to Colonel Olcott, at least three of them, including the Master M. and the Egyptian Master Serapis, also called the Mahā-Sahib, gave valuable advice, the latter coming to Bombay in his natural body for a long interview with H.P.B. and Olcott on September 15, 1879. In *Old Diary Leaves*, II, Olcott describes a secluded āśrama or rest-house in the suburbs of Bombay where Masters and their chelas sometimes stay when taking their long journeys so frequently referred to by H.P.B. and Olcott.

In the first six volumes of *The Theosophist*, teachings which had only been hinted at in *Isis Unveiled* were gradually expanded. Much was contributed by various Masters, though always under pseudonyms, and by Dāmodar, Subba Row, and other chelas. A remarkable example of the scientific teaching of the Mahatma K.H. will be found in a long article by him (signed "Another Theosophist") beginning on page 319 of Volume III, September 1882, called "What is Matter and What is Force?" The Mahatma M. anonymously contributed many "Answers to Correspondents" to the Supplement of the March number of the same year, and it is interesting to compare the two writings and observe the contrasting literary styles of the two Masters, which are also plainly marked in the *Mahatma Letters*, and which are so different from that of H. P. Blavatsky.

The editor of *The Theosophist* was greatly helped by the learned Hindu, Buddhist, Parsi, and other scholars who took advantage of such a favorable opportunity of presenting the deeper interpretation of their own scriptures to a sympathetic audience. The journal was H.P.B.'s own "child," and it soon made a profit, most of which went to defray some of the heavy expenses of the Society. While her enemies were charging her with making money out of the membership dues, she was actually straining her limited resources to keep the Society solvent, as the published and audited accounts prove. In this way $10,000 was donated to it in the first few years. It is clear that *The Theosophist* had become very popular, not only abroad but in India, for the "Administration Report of the Bombay Government for 1881–2," dealing with "Books Published" says that "the only English periodical which appears to enjoy an extensive circulation among natives is the '*Theosophist*,' which deals in Mesmerism and Spiritualism"[!] (*Theos.*, IV, 152, April 1883).

In addition to her interminable labors as editor, proofreader, writer of the most important articles,* Corresponding Secretary, etc., she had to find time to write popular articles for Russian journals in order to make a living. Colonel Olcott had no available financial resources, but he contributed his splendid enthusiasm, great ability and incessant work on his own particular lines.

In August 1879, just in time to give the special help needed in the production of *The Theosophist*, a most valuable recruit joined the Society – Dāmodar K. Māvalankar, a young Brahman of high standing. When a boy, he had a vision of one of the Masters whom, years later, he recognized as one of H.P.B.'s teachers. Dāmodar was quickly accepted by that Master as one of the limited number of candidates for chelaship, and he soon overcame the first trials of proba-

*[The early volumes of *The Theosophist* are practically unobtainable, but all known articles by H. P. Blavatsky are being reprinted in *H. P. Blavatsky: Collected Writings.* – ED.]

tion. He had no difficulty in recognizing H. P. Blavatsky as a real occultist and teacher, though she was a European – and a woman! Dāmodar's health was poor, but he worked for theosophy to the limit of his strength and capacity with extraordinary devotion. He abandoned his Brahmanical caste and its privileges, and renounced fortune and advantageous worldly prospects to follow what he felt was his duty. He adopted a few simple rules of meditation and regulation of diet, but he absolutely avoided the methods of hatha-yoga. As Olcott says, his method of making progress was by "cultivating a spirit of perfect unselfishness, and by working night and day, to the uttermost limits of his strength, on the duties of the official position I gave him in the Society." In one of her letters to Mr. Sinnett, H.P.B. sharply contrasts his easy life and short hours of work with the incessant labors of Dāmodar and herself under the most trying conditions.

Gradually, and without strain, Dāmodar found inner powers awakening quite naturally and becoming available for use in his increasing responsibilities. Olcott describes this development with appreciation and sympathy. He gives instances showing the increase in Dāmodar's power of communication with the Masters and H.P.B. at great distances, in general clairvoyance, and in other supernormal powers. This young chela was also able at times to make remarkable cures by magnetic healing. By the year 1883, it was possible for the Master to employ him to transmit his messages by "astral mail." As in the case of all advanced souls who have killed out personal egotism and transmuted desire into spiritual energy, the occult powers that emerged into activity were perfectly normal under the conditions. They had not been ambitiously coveted, or sought for personal gratification, and they were never displayed to the mere curiosity seeker, nor exhibited as inducements to join the Society. Such a proceeding is utterly opposed to the principles of theosophy, though:

> If we have had one we certainly have had an hundred intimations from strangers that they were ready to join at once if they could be sure that they would shortly be endowed with *siddhis*, or the power to work occult phenomena.
>
> – "Editorial Notice" in *The Theosophist*, II, 85, Jan. 1881

For those who might doubt the existence of high Adepts living on the physical plane, the evidence of Dāmodar is valuable, because he gives firsthand testimony in writing of several experiences which cannot be explained away. In November 1883, at Lahore, he met the Master K.H., and a little later he spent a few days with the Masters at their āśrama in Kashmir. When in Ceylon with H. P. Blavatsky and Colonel Olcott in 1880, a Master took him to an āśrama on a small island where he had a long conversation with another Adept who was living there. Details of this and other similar events are given in two letters of great interest written by Dāmodar to Mr. Judge, and published in *The Theosophical Forum* for November 1932, and April 1933.

In April 1885, Dāmodar started on the perilous journey to Tibet, going, according to Colonel Olcott, "in the company of an 'Avatari Lama,' a very influential and mysterious Tibetan prelate who *happened* to be within reach, at Sikkim, just at the nick of time." (*Theos.*, LIV, 151, Nov. 1932. Also see *O. D. L.*, III, 253–68.) In *The Theosophist*, July 1886, Olcott and Subba Row issued a signed statement "that he [Dāmodar] has safely reached his destination, and is alive under the guardianship of the friends whom he sought."

Before he reached his occult friends, however, he had, according to a Master, "to undergo the severest trials that a neophyte ever passed through" (*L.M.W.*, I, 77). Colonel Olcott pays Dāmodar a very high tribute:

> A nobler heart never beat in a human breast, and his departure was one of the hardest blows we ever received. As above remarked, he had almost broken down his constitution by incessant official work, . . . Yet, with undaunted courage, he undertook the hard journey across the Himālayas, . . . intent upon reaching the Guru [spiritual Teacher] whom he had first seen in his youth . . . What made him so devotedly attached and unswervingly loyal to H.P.B. was the discovery that this Guru was one of the Adepts behind our movement, . . .
>
> – *O. D. L.*, III, 265–6

The estimation in which Dāmodar was held by H.P.B. is shown in these words from her letter to Judge N. D. Khandalāvala:

> Damodar was ready from his last birth to enter the highest PATH and suspected it. He had been long waiting for the expected permission to go to Tibet before the expiration of the 7 years; . . .
>
> *I was* driven away [from India], by the cowardice of those for whom I had risked my whole life, reputation and honour and he was the only true, devoted friend I had in all India, the *only one* who having the Masters' and my secret, knew the *whole* truth and therefore knew that whatever people thought being blinded by appearance I had never deceived anyone – though I was bound on my oath and pledge to conceal much from everyone, even Olcott.
>
> – *Theos.*, LIII, 623–4, Aug. 1932

Another high caste Brahman, T. Subba Row (or Rao), B.A., B.L., a brilliant lawyer, and a chela of the Master M., became a Fellow of the Society about the same time as Dāmodar. Endowed with a powerful intellect, great learning, and the rare opportunity of obtaining knowledge implied in chelaship, Subba Row was able to contribute valuable articles to *The Theosophist*, some of which have been republished.* In view of the absurd charges still occasionally circulated against H.P.B. and her work, the enthusiastic support of such high-minded and intelligent men as Dāmodar and Subba Row, and of numerous other Hindus of high caliber, should be borne in mind. From the worldly standpoint they had everything to lose, for in "following the gleam" they risked the loss of friends and the estrangement of relatives, and defied Indian public opinion. It was almost incredible to find the proud Brahmans recognizing a European, a *mlechchha* or 'impure foreigner,' and a woman, as a spiritual teacher or guru; but it would have been impossible unless her life and character had been unselfish and stainless. Subba Row wrote from personal knowledge:

> It is not necessary [that] one should be a member of any society to deserve a Guru. But the Occult Fraternities in every part of the world have now made a rule that admission into their ranks must be sought through the "Theosophical Society." I mistake no confidence when I inform you that I know personally of many instances in which those who were Chelas – a very high Chela one of them, before the advent of the Society among us in India, were compelled by their Gurus to join the Society on pain of their being forsaken by them. But joining the Society alone will not help you. You must work, work uphill. What I did, I repeat, is nothing to be admired from my Hindunstand point [Hindu standpoint]. There is not one Hindur [Hindu] Brahmin, who will not do the same a hundred times over.
>
> – *Forum*, VI, 188, Mar. 1935

In December 1879, H. P. Blavatsky met A. P. Sinnett and A. O. Hume, C.B., at Allahabad, and rather later at Simla, the

**Notes on the Bhagavad Gita.*

summer capital of India. These two English gentlemen took an active part in theosophical activities in the earlier years of theosophy in India, and their prominence in political and social life helped to attract considerable attention to the movement from the Anglo-Indians.

Mr. Sinnett was an able writer, the editor of *The Pioneer*, an influential Anglo-Indian newspaper, and he was well equipped to give opportune help. Mr. Hume was a former Secretary of Agriculture to the Indian government, and had scientific standing as an ornithologist. While Sinnett remained connected with theosophy to the end of his life, Hume unfortunately lost his interest and, after giving H.P.B. considerable trouble, left the Society.

He, and even Sinnett, to a degree, wished to have the "Simla Eclectic Theosophical Society" (of which Hume was president for a while) entirely independent of the headquarters, and demanded for it special privileges in regard to the study of occultism under the Masters. As neither Sinnett nor Hume were chelas, nor had they shown any aptitude or desire for chelaship but only an interest in psycho-intellectual studies, their demand was kindly but firmly rejected. Brilliant minds as they were, neither of them was prepared to understand, much less to accept, the very first conditions required for the study of ātma-vidyā, the divine wisdom: absolute devotion to the interest of others and the renunciation of desire for personal gratification. The Master K.H. pointed out to them that their motives were in the deepest sense *selfish*. He said:

> They are selfish because you must be aware that the chief object of the T. S. is not so much to gratify individual aspirations as to serve our fellow men: . . . —*Mahatma Letters*, 7–8

Sinnett was undoubtedly sincere and thoroughly devoted to the ideal of theosophy as he fancied it to be, and he never lost his belief in the real existence of the Masters, but Mr. Hume's attitude was far less satisfactory, and quickly became worse. It is instructive though painful to follow the gradual revelation of certain weaknesses in this undoubtedly able man, as shown in the *Mahatma Letters* and elsewhere. The reader, if at all intuitive, can see almost from the first that his intellectual "pride and unconscious selfishness," mentioned by the Masters, would stand as a barrier to real progress in spite of their patient endeavors to awaken his soul-vision. A glance at their voluminous correspondence with both Sinnett and Hume shows the almost incredible pains the Masters took to explain their teachings, ideals, and methods of training to these men who had such exceptional opportunities of acquiring wisdom, and of becoming agents to pass it on to the West.

Hume's dual nature became well marked as circumstances lifted the veil of polite conventions. For a while he gave valuable help and the Masters were so grateful to him for his kindness to their messenger that they were willing to overlook his lapses. He worked hard for the betterment of the Indian masses and, as the Masters said: "When the spiritual soul is left to guide him, no purer, no better, nor kinder man can be found" (Ibid., 225). But when his intellectual pride was aroused, and he demanded the occult knowledge which cannot be given to the unprepared, it was a different story. The Master K.H. writes to Mr. Sinnett as early as 1881:

I tell you, my good friend, he will *never* be satisfied do what we may! And as, we cannot consent to over flood the world at the risk of drowning them, with a doctrine that has to be cautiously given out, and bit by bit like a too powerful tonic which can kill as well as cure – the result will be a reaction in that insatiable craving of his, and then – well you yourself know the consequences. – Ibid., 245

When the Simla branch was formed, however, everything seemed promising. Many Anglo-Indians joined it, and some remained faithful to the movement. Unfortunately, though perhaps unavoidably, far more inquirers were attracted by H. P. Blavatsky's reputation as a wonder-worker than by the teachings of the ancient wisdom, and much trouble and bitter controversy arose from this cause. Exaggerated reports were spread about the phenomena she occasionally produced in the presence of a few private friends, and she and some of her devoted members had to suffer heavily from false charges. Perhaps unwisely, she took no pains at first to propitiate the Anglo-Indians by conforming to the orthodox conventions of fashionable society which she, though a born aristocrat, regarded as little better than a hypocritical veneer covering the dry rot of selfishness. The independence of character so marked from her childhood, and her ingrained rebellion and contempt for artificial forms made it hard for her friends to protect her against misrepresentations which they knew were cruelly unjust. Her outspoken and blunt remarks were often highly embarrassing to their 'victims,' especially as they were only too true; and they were not calculated to turn enemies into friends. High rank, official position, or wealth were nothing to her. On one occasion, for example, when the aged, white-haired, Parsi Chief Justice of Baroda introduced his wife, *a little girl ten years old*, she told him in plain and decidedly unvarnished language that he was "an old beast" and ought to be thoroughly ashamed of himself. In extreme cases, when H.P.B. wished to arouse the dormant soul in a man or woman she would assume uncouth ways and use rough language, regardless of the consequences to herself, or the almost inevitable misunderstanding that she risked.

In regard to her phenomena, she showed an almost childish naiveté in her method of presenting them, and she was astonished when anyone insisted that the absence of "test conditions" in some cases permitted her critics to suggest the possibility of fraud. The control of the occult forces by her trained will was so perfectly natural to her that she found it hard to understand that her phenomena were bewildering and practically incredible to those unfamiliar with psychic matters. No charlatan would have either spoken or behaved so unceremoniously as she often did to persons whom she hoped to convince of her genuineness. No trickster would have dreamed of presenting fraudulent manifestations in the utterly casual and unmethodical way described by numerous witnesses. All this was part of her complex character which was curiously unsophisticated and childlike in many ways and as far removed from that of a cunning impostor as could be. She is known to have put her trust in the most disappointing people, even after being warned by her Master, though at other times she showed an amazingly keen perception of character.

In justice to the skeptics, it should not be forgotten that to the educated Westerner of the nineteenth century, even the simplest demonstration of the occult, such as telepathy, was received as an insult to his intelligence, and H.P.B. had to suffer from this lack of understanding. That, however, is no excuse for the gross unfairness and lack of common honesty on the part of those who wanted to destroy her reputation before theosophy became too widely spread. For instance, a charge was published in a book on India and in magazine articles by the Rev. Moncure Conway, that she had concocted the name Koot Hoomi (or Kuthumi as it is also spelled) from the names of Olcott and Hume! He claims the support of several Sanskritists in saying that the name "was outside all analogies of any language ever known in India." These 'Sanskritists' were either strangely ignorant of their subject or they deliberately misled Rev. Conway in order to fling a stone at H. P. Blavatsky, for the name is perfectly familiar to real students. For example, see Garrett's *Classical Dictionary of India*, or the well-known *Vishnu-Purāna* (Book III, chap. vi, 60, Wilson's trans., 1866), where the learned sage Kuthumi is mentioned as a teacher of the Sāma Veda and a pupil of Paushyinji (or Paushpinji). It is said to be a fairly common name in India today. Students of theosophy have become used to such perversions of the truth, which are so frequently made to deceive the ignorant in order to discredit H. P. Blavatsky.

Hostile comment was aroused by her "incomprehensible" preference for the society of Hindus, Zoroastrians, or Buddhists, whether independent pandits or scholars, or theosophical students; for in her day little or no social intercourse took place between Europeans and natives of India. Then again, her unorthodox religious views utterly condemned her in the eyes of the intolerant missionaries. This was perhaps the cause of the greatest persecutions she suffered. It is worth noting that one of the leading Christian organizations working in India was sufficiently well-informed in the history of the so-called miraculous as to admit the genuineness of her phenomena and therefore her personal honesty, at the same time putting them down to the cunning work of the Devil!

About this time a situation arose which, although only a temporary misunderstanding, must be mentioned because it was afterwards used most dishonorably against the good name of the movement. In the eighties, exaggerated fears of a Russian invasion of India were rampant, and the most elaborate precautions were taken against espionage. Now, H. P. Blavatsky was a Russian and Colonel Olcott was not British, and their brilliant success in arousing a new patriotic pride in the Hindus and others in India for their national religions and philosophical traditions was a strange phenomenon. Could there be something hidden behind it? Was she a Russian agent? A watch was set on their every movement, but of course there was nothing suspicious to be found. Finally, Colonel Olcott protested directly to the Viceroy's government, explained the nonpolitical and nonsectarian work of the Theosophical Society, and submitted full documentary proof from the United States government of his own high standing and honorable career in America, as well as the official evidence from Russia which established H. P. Blavatsky's reputation and high rank, and her freedom from political interests. The police supervision was at once removed and there was no further trouble. Although H.P.B. had thundered against the chief of the Indian police for his hypercritical attitude in regard to a phenomenon he had seen at Simla, and he could not have been too friendly, he never attempted to bring any charges of fraud against her.

H. P. Blavatsky suffered exquisitely from all these misunderstandings, knowing that every slander raised another obstruction between the Cause and thousands who needed its spiritual help. But a liberating work like hers ever challenges attack and its value might be questioned if all went easily with its pioneers.

In later years Colonel Olcott was occasionally employed by the Madras government to advise on agricultural problems as an expert authority. He also had a standing invitation to attend receptions at Government House.

When H.P.B. and Olcott were in Simla in 1880, A. P. Sinnett was enabled to collect the material for his book, *The Occult World*, which was based largely on his notes of her occult activities, and which made her name widely known, though it contained nothing from her pen. It explained the relation of the Masters of wisdom with the outer world, and described events at Simla which had convinced Sinnett and many others that such advanced Adepts exist who are far ahead in occult and spiritual knowledge and power even of the most celebrated Hindu yogis or Tibetan lamas known to the world. It also contained extracts from letters of the Masters, by whose perusal those who had no connection with them could realize that they were actual human beings, albeit of a superior order, and that each had a well-marked individuality. While the letters are the most valuable portion of the book, the author's straightforward account of the occult phenomena he had personally observed was probably responsible for its enormous sale. Rather unfortunately, as it turned out, *The Occult World* was not seen by the Masters until it was published, although generally approved by them and, as the Master K.H. told Sinnett, if they had read his manuscript many hastily written and obscure passages quoted from personal letters not meant for publication as they stood, would have been corrected or revised. Sinnett found it difficult to present the deeper, spiritual teachings of theosophy because the psycho-intellectual aspect appealed more strongly to his nature. He was warned by the Masters more than once against that one-sidedness of outlook which was ultimately his undoing as an exponent of theosophy. In one of the earliest letters he received, the Master K.H. writes:

> . . . the chief object of the T. S. is not so much to gratify individual aspirations as to serve our fellow men: . . . Yet, you have ever discussed but to put down the idea of a universal Brotherhood, questioned its usefulness, and advised to remodel the T. S. on the principle of a college for the special study of occultism. This, my respected and esteemed friend and Brother – will never do!
>
> The *Chiefs* want a "Brotherhood of Humanity," a real Universal Fraternity started; an institution which would make itself known throughout the world and arrest the attention of the highest minds.
>
> – *Mahatma Letters,* 7–8, 24

But lest there be any misunderstanding, the Mahā-chohan, the great Teacher, the Superior of both the Mahatmas M. and K.H., made it plain:

> Rather perish the T. S. with both its hapless founders than that we should permit it to become no better than an academy of magic and a hall of occultism. That we – the devoted followers of the spirit incarnate of absolute self-sacrifice, of philanthropy, divine kindness, . . . should ever allow the Theosophical Society to represent the *embodiment of selfishness*, the refuge of the few with no thought in them for the many, is a strange idea, my brothers.
>
> . . . Let us understand each other. – *L.M.W.*, I, 10–11

Unfortunately, Sinnett never understood because, as the Master said, his spiritual intuitions were "dim and hazy."

But he did good pioneering work for which he deserves a tribute of gratitude from the theosophical world. His second book, *Esoteric Buddhism*, an outline of some of the main teachings of theosophy, attracted much attention and served as a harbinger of H.P.B.'s monumental work, *The Secret Doctrine*. He also deserves honor for his courage in standing by her in India when so many fainthearted followers fled before the first attacks on her reputation. The good work done by the early pioneers in theosophy must never be forgotten, even though many dropped out by the wayside. How many who enthusiastically praise H. P. Blavatsky at this safe distance of time would have stood staunchly by her under her downright and unflattering methods of training, not to speak of the ridicule and misrepresentation which theosophists suffered from the ignorant and prejudiced in her time!

In regard to Sinnett, certain tributes from the Master K.H. written in 1882 are instructive. After pointing out some of his very serious mistakes which had done great harm to the Society, the Master says:

> Your strivings, perplexities and forebodings are equally noticed, good and faithful friend. In the imperishable RECORD of the Masters *you have written them all.* There are registered your every deed and thought; for, though not a chela, as you say to my Brother Morya, nor even a "protégé" — as you understand the term — still, you have stepped within the circle of our work, . . . Your hidden *Self* has mirrored itself in *our* Akasa; your nature is — yours, your essence is — ours. The flame is distinct from the log of wood which serves it temporarily as fuel; . . . During the past few months, especially, when your weary brain was plunged in the torpor of sleep, your eager soul has often been searching after me, . . . What that "inner Self," impatient, anxious — has longed to bind itself to, the carnal

man, the worldlings' master has not ratified: the ties of life are still as strong as chains of steel. — *Mahatma Letters,* 266–7

It should be well understood that H. P. Blavatsky never received a penny from the enormous sale of Sinnett's *Occult World* and that the accounts of the phenomenal occurrences at Simla upon which its vogue largely depended were the cause of much of the misunderstanding and suffering she had to endure for the rest of her life. She never made the smallest financial profit from her occult powers — such a thing is a crime in occultism. Olcott describes occasions where she was offered large sums to show "even one little phenomenon" to wealthy persons. She invariably rejected such offers, but would often perform one of her occult experiments for the instruction or encouragement of a humble but sincere theosophist, and this, perhaps, immediately after disappointing the rich curiosity-seeker.

The unfortunate notoriety attached to her name by the phenomena became a serious handicap on her work, and she found that the Master K.H. was right when he told Sinnett that occult matters "ought to have been limited to an *inner* and very SECRET circle." But her position was very embarrassing, for Sinnett and others were carried away by their discovery of an occult world behind the veil of nature, and were demanding phenomena and more occult phenomena, and she felt compelled to satisfy their natural curiosity, in order to break down their crude materialistic point of view.

But she sacrificed more than the skeptics or even the theosophists imagined when she produced phenomena of a more elaborate character than the trifling ones such as raps or the "fairy bells," which she called "parlor tricks," yet which were remarkable enough in themselves and equally inexplicable to all but trained occultists. Few, even of the theosophists, realized the great expenditure of vital energy required to precipitate matter out of the atmosphere into an astral matrix formed by the trained imagination and held by an intense act of will, and so apparently to 'create' objects, or to make writing appear on paper. Students of psychic phenomena learn that the vital force required for occult purposes has to be carefully conserved, as it is not free as air, even to the Adept. Thoughtless persons who craved "just one little phenomenon" never suspected how much vital energy every display of her occult power cost her. She may not always have been wise in the presentation of her phenomena, for to many persons they were like a red rag to a bull; but it was no pleasure or diversion for her to produce them for, as the Masters said, it was "killing her inch by inch," and they tried, though not always with success, to induce her to conserve her power. In such matters of personal conduct chelas are left to their own devices and have to take the consequences of mistakes. The chela training is designed to develop strong, self-reliant characters, not marionettes pulled by invisible strings.

The time came, however, when it was no longer necessary for phenomena to be shown, because they had served their purpose. H.P.B. had proved that an occultist has control over nature forces which are no more supernatural than the intangible radio waves which were then unsuspected, and are even now as mysterious to the scientist as to the schoolboy who makes his amateur receiver.

Later, responsible and highly intelligent persons, such as Sir Wallis Budge and A. Weigall, eminent Egyptologists,

Mme. David-Neel, Buddhist scholar and Tibetan explorer, Lord Curzon, former Viceroy of India, Dr. Carl Jung, leading psychologist, Dr. J. B. Rhine, Dr. Alexis Carrel, Major F. Yeats-Brown, and many others, testified to their knowledge of the occult or psychic powers in man. Representative members of the Psychical Research Society now recognize that the nature of man is complex, and that strange powers, such as prevision, telepathy, and even worse "superstitions and old wives' tales" are latent in the "subliminal or supraliminal consciousness" and can emerge under certain conditions.

10

WORK IN INDIA AND CEYLON

ABOUT a year after the work was begun in India, an important Council meeting was held at Benares on December 17, 1879, at the palace of the Maharaja of Vizianagram, to reconsider the Rules. A new and revised Constitution was drawn up there and ratified by the Society on February 26–8, 1880, at Bombay. "Universal Brotherhood" was accentuated, and as the three degrees of Fellowship had been allowed to fall into abeyance they were reestablished on esoteric lines. The First Section consisted of the "Initiates in Esoteric Science and Philosophy," the Masters and high chelas, "whom none but such as they voluntarily communicate with have the right to know." The Second Section embraced those Fellows whose courage, fidelity, and devotion to the work had been demonstrated, and who had learned to regard all men as their brothers. The Third Section was probationary, and newly admitted Fellows remained there until they had proved their sincerity and their ability to conquer certain weaknesses, prejudices, etc. Private instructions received by any Fellow from the First Section were not to be put to selfish use nor were they permitted to be revealed without permission. The first object of the Society was defined as "To keep alive in man his spiritual intuitions." The name was modified to "The Theosophical Society or Universal Brotherhood," and advancement in its degrees depended entirely upon merit.

Olcott seems, however, to have had no great enthusiasm for the esoteric aspect of the new constitution, though always fascinated by the mysterious and phenomenal. He gives several pages of his semi-autobiographical *Old Diary Leaves* to activities at Benares between December 15 and 22, many quite trivial, yet he does not mention this Council meeting on the seventeenth at all. Nor does he discuss the formal ratification later. The only available record of the Council meeting occurs in *The Theosophist*, April 1880, in a brief formal Report. No discussion is mentioned and the names of Olcott and Sinnett do not appear. Although this constitution revived the public announcement made to inquirers in the circular issued by the parent society in New York in 1878, and gave it official recognition, the spirit of this forward move was soon disregarded.

More than eight years passed before H. P. Blavatsky was able, with the help of W. Q. Judge, to make within the Society an enduring and vital occult nucleus, such as the Masters wished, to serve as the beginning of the revival of the Mystery schools in the West. Olcott's predilection for the more mundane or, as he considered, more practical aspects of the movement, quite natural in a successful man of business, frequently proved embarrassing to H.P.B. She was not always able or even permitted to explain her reasons for certain acts, and there can be little doubt that the urge for the Benares reconstruction came to her from the Masters. The cool reception it received hindered progress, for it is a rule in occultism that the teacher can go no farther than the receptivity of the chela permits.

In the spring of 1880, shortly after the Bombay Congress, H. P. Blavatsky, Colonel Olcott, Dāmodar K. Māvalankar, and some Parsi, Hindu, and English members made a triumphant tour in Ceylon where they were received with the greatest enthusiasm by audiences of many thousands everywhere they went. H.P.B. and the president publicly identified themselves with the highest ideals of the Buddhas by "taking pansil," as the ceremonial of reciting the Five Precepts of the Good Law is called. One of the highest Masters, the Mahā-chohan, has written, "Buddhism, stripped of its superstitions, is eternal truth" (*L.M.W.*, I, 3).

At that time Buddhism was undergoing a serious crisis in Ceylon. Conditions were entirely different from those in India where complete religious freedom was guaranteed. Brutal attacks were being made on Buddhist meetings, Buddhist religious processions were prohibited, and many oppressive restrictions placed on the proper exercise of the popular religion, while every possible liberty was given to the Christian sects. These conditions were transformed in a few years by the indefatigable efforts of Colonel Olcott, helped by native and other theosophists of various religious affiliations. Olcott took an intense personal interest in the revival of Buddhism and worked hard for it during the remainder of his life. In 1881, with the help of the learned monk, Sumangala, and after long research and much correspondence with the leaders of the Buddhist sects, Olcott brought out a standard *Buddhist Catechism*, the first of its kind. It has been translated into many languages and accepted all over the Buddhist world. In 1884 he went to London to explain the real conditions of religious oppression in Ceylon to Lord Derby, the Colonial Secretary, who quickly authorized the local government to make drastic reforms which gave great satisfaction to the Buddhists of Ceylon, who now enjoy religious liberty. An immediate result was the establishment of schools where Buddhist children could get a modern education without the risk of losing their ancestral faith. Through Olcott's efforts several colleges and hundreds of schools were soon established, and today the standard of education in Ceylon is excellent.*

For a short time this activity aroused misgivings among the Hindu and Parsi theosophists in regard to the neutrality of the Society; but it was soon made clear that theosophy was not identified with exoteric Buddhism, nor was the Theosophical Society's neutrality violated in the least. One of the avowed purposes of the movement is "to help the followers of each of the ancient faiths to find and live up to its noblest ideals" – these "noblest ideals" being, of course, identified with theosophy, and the "ancient faiths" naturally including Hinduism, Christianity, Buddhism, and the rest. The Master K.H. took pains to declare that the work of preserving Buddhism in Ceylon was truly theosophical.

While H.P.B. was in Ceylon she was approached by a youth who afterwards was known throughout Asia and even

---

*[In its issue of December 8, 1967, *The Times of Ceylon* (Colombo) published an article written by Gamini Navaratne under the heading, "Colonel Henry Steel Olcott: The Only Foreigner on Our Roll of National Heroes," from which we quote the following:

"Today Ceylon honors an American by issuing a postage stamp in his memory. It is by no means the first or the only honor bestowed on Col. H. S. Olcott. There already is at least one school, several cultural and religious organizations, a hall, even a public highway named after him. . . . Early this year, a lifesize statue of him was unveiled in Colombo, . . . And now a stamp. Apart from British Royalty no other foreigner has so far been honored in this fashion. . . . Olcott involved himself fully with the life of the people, made them aware of their rich cultural heritage, aroused their nationalism and literally set them on the road to a new life . . . Olcott has several other notable achievements to his credit. As a banner for Ceylon Buddhists, he devised a flag . . . [which] has become the emblem of international Buddhism." – Ed.]

in the West as the greatest modern apostle and resuscitator of Buddhism. Hewavitarna Dharmapāla became a devoted theosophist and a lifelong supporter of H.P.B. He would probably have devoted his life to theosophy, but she told him that his true line of work for humanity was the promotion of the pure teachings of the Lord Buddha, knowledge of which was threatened not only by Western materialism, but still more seriously by the incompetence, ignorance, and superstition of so many of the Buddhists themselves. Acting upon this advice, Dharmapāla took up the study of Pali and, renouncing the "householder" life, spent the remainder of his days in the revival of the *Dhamma* in both East and West. He is said to have claimed to be a disciple of the Mahatma K.H., and he certainly never lost touch with H.P.B.

After the magnificent reception in Ceylon, H.P. Blavatsky and her workers returned to Bombay, leaving theosophy well established in the island. In this brief sketch much has to be omitted that is of great interest in regard to the spread of theosophy in India, of the striking successes and, sometimes, of the disappointments and failures inevitable in a work of such an unusual character and comprising such a varied personnel in its membership. H.P.B. must be pictured as working incessantly at her desk, writing innumerable articles and letters, interviewing inquirers, and occasionally sharing Colonel Olcott's long journeys in tropical heat and discomfort, by train, canal, or various forms of native transport, in order to start new branches, Sanskrit and other schools, and to discuss philosophical problems with learned Hindu, Parsi, Jain, Moslem, or other pandits. Many illustrations of the outer association and inner communion between

H.P.B. and other chelas and with the Mahatmas can only be referred to in passing. To many persons in India, including Colonel Olcott and other foreigners, the Masters were anything but 'mythical.'

A vivid idea of the trying conditions under which the pioneers of theosophy had to conduct their activities in India is given by Olcott in a letter to W. T. Brown, a Scottish volunteer for theosophical service who ultimately withdrew after having been given special opportunities. Olcott says:

> I wrote him from Hyderabad a kind but most explicit letter, warning him of the self-sacrifice he must expect to make; the public ingratitude, individual treacheries, libellous attacks on character, unjust suspicion of motives, bad fare and fatiguing journeys by nights and days in all sorts of conveyances: warning him to return to Europe if he had expected anything else, and leave H.P.B. and myself to continue the work we had begun with our eyes open.
>
> – *O. D. L.*, III, 20

The unremitting labor in the trying Indian climate with its humidity in the monsoons, its terrible summer heat and dust, and the unrelieved strain of wearing anxieties told seriously upon H.P.B.'s health, and she gradually became chronically ill. At last her condition became so alarming that in the late summer of 1882 her physician told her plainly that she had only a short time to live, "perhaps a few days." In a farewell letter to Sinnett she makes a significant remark in the quaint, humorous way that no troubles could silence:

> I tell you I am very very sick. Yes, I wish I could see you once more and dear Mrs. Gordon and my old Colonel whose "Grandmother" I may meet in some of the lower hells whither I will go – unless I am picked up by *Them* and made to stick in Tibet.
>
> . . . I hope Mrs. Gordon will not dishonour [me] by *evoking* me

with some medium. Let her rest assured that it will never be my spirit nor anything of me – not even *my shell* since this is gone long ago. — *Blavatsky Letters*, 37–8

Both H. P. Blavatsky and Colonel Olcott announced more than once that they would never appear through ordinary mediums, and it is perfectly safe to ignore all reports to the contrary, however plausible they may sound.

But H. P. Blavatsky's work was hardly begun in 1882 and, however critical her state might be, she could not be spared to go "Home," and so the Masters took quick action. They sent Gārgya Deva, a chela from the Nilgiri Hills, near Madras, to Bombay to help their almost helpless messenger to reach one of their retreats in the Himalayan jungle in Sikkim. The journey must have been very trying for her, and in addition to difficulties arising from her illness she had to face the impossibility of obtaining official permission to cross the British frontier into Sikkim. She succeeded, however, in reaching the āśrama where she found the Masters M. and K.H. with several of their chelas. During "the blessed blessed two days" as she calls them, that she spent there, she was restored to health.

This occasion was one of the three or more critical times when she was saved from death by her Master. Writing to a correspondent in France, she said that he had given her a medicine extracted from a Himalayan plant which she had to take seven times a day, and that within three days she was perfectly well. Her impressions of this visit to Sikkim are briefly but poetically described by her in the *Blavatsky Letters*, page 38.* In the *Mahatma Letters*, page 314, K.H.

*Further details (concerning the journey) are given by S. Rāmaswāmier, a chela of the Master M., in *The Theosophist*, Dec. 1882.

refers to this visit and describes her joy at meeting him and the Mahatma M. in bodily presence after a long separation during which she had only seen them clairvoyantly or in the māyāvi-rūpa or thought-body. The two Masters were on horseback accompanied by some of their chelas.

The first septenary cycle, the seven years from the formation of the Society until 1882, was a critical time, and during that initial period of growth it was necessary for the Masters and their chelas to take a more open and active part than was possible in later years. Efforts were made by them to form an "Inner Group" at Simla, in order to study in preparation for deeper teachings, and it dragged along for several years. Unfortunately, the would-be occultists failed to realize the basis on which the chela-life must be founded. Sinnett and Hume asked for instruction in occult science under conditions *arranged by themselves*, and impossible to accept. Subba Row agreed to give them "theoretical instruction" in *philosophy*, but not too willingly, as he foresaw the difficulties in store; and very little came from that effort. An extract from a letter from Subba Row, dated 26th June, 1882, is useful in showing the utter misconceptions that dominated the minds of even such intelligent men as Sinnett and Hume. He writes to them:

> The *qualified* assent which you were pleased to give to the conditions laid down by me necessitated a reference to the Brothers for their opinion and orders. And now I am sorry to inform you that anything like practical instruction in the ritual of Occult Science is impossible under the conditions you propose. So far as my knowledge goes, no student of Occult Philosophy has ever succeeded in developing his psychic powers without leading the life prescribed for such students; and it is not within the power of the teacher to make an exception in the case of any student. . . . for the present you must

be satisfied with such theoretical instruction as it may be possible to give you.

. . . You will be taking a very low view of Occult Science if you were to suppose that the mere acquirement of psychic powers is the highest and the only desirable result of occult training. The mere acquisition of wonder-working powers can never secure immortality for the student of Occult Science unless he has learned the means of shifting gradually his sense of individuality from his corruptible material body to the incorruptible and eternal *Non-Being* represented by his seventh principle. Please consider this as the real aim of Occult Science and see whether the rules you are called upon to obey are necessary or not to bring about this mighty change.

– *Mahatma Letters*, 458–9

Those would-be occultists found it difficult to realize that "Devotion to the interests of others is the first test of apprenticeship." A wish to investigate psychic phenomena in order to satisfy ordinary scientific curiosity does not carry the student one step toward true occultism. A real occult teacher does not need to use arguments or even words, but when his chela is in perfect accord with him his thoughts penetrate by occult telepathy. Subba Row did the best he could on intellectual lines for his Western pupils, as he knew the importance of encouraging men of their energetic type who were capable of rousing his own countrymen from their lethargy.

Unfortunately, the attempt to create even a semblance of an Inner Group had to be abandoned in 1885 because of the inharmony among the candidates and their craving for personal advancement. They failed to realize that their quarrels and egotistic desires were hindering a world movement described as one of the three most important movements of the nineteenth century, and which the Master K.H. said:

is a question of perdition or salvation to thousands; a question of the progress of the human race or its retrogression, of its glory or dishonour, . . . —Ibid., 365

Mr. Sinnett's efforts to force the phenomenal and purely psycho-intellectual aspect of theosophy at the expense of the truly spiritual or occult, caused increasing friction and ultimately resulted in the withdrawal of the Master's attention from him, and in a complete break in his relation with H. P. Blavatsky. In her letters to him, her bitter disappointment at his uncomprehending attitude is strongly expressed. It would be a hard heart indeed who can study these poignant letters without the deepest sympathy and reverence for the "real H.P.B."

Sinnett not only failed to appreciate the more spiritual aspect of the Masters' work, but he very early in his theosophical career lost his sense of proportion in regard to H.P.B.'s standing as the direct agent of the Masters. For instance, in consequence of his misunderstanding of a slightly obscure passage in one of the Master's letters to him he insisted that Mars and Mercury were part of the earth's chain of globes; and, although the Master, on H.P.B.'s personal request, explained this fallacy, Sinnett stuck to his original misapprehension. The matter was fully treated and the mistake corrected when *The Secret Doctrine* was published (I, 160–70), but, unfortunately, a certain school of theosophy accepted Sinnett's view and built an erroneous superstructure upon it.

The true position and importance of H. P. Blavatsky as a leader and teacher was not adequately recognized by even a majority of the members during the first septennate of the

Society, and, as she said, some of her most troublesome antagonists were not the open ones – she was prepared for them – but in too many cases members of her "own household." Even Colonel Olcott, with all his devotion and goodwill, had to be pulled up sharply at times by his Master as well as by H.P.B., and reminded that although he, as president, was the highest officer in the Society, she was the life and soul of the movement in the nineteenth century. As a pledged disciple of a Master, a beginner, he was undergoing the intensive training which invariably brings the weaknesses of the *personality* to the front, so that they can be recognized and conquered. It is the unavoidable rule and a most beneficent one. At the same time, Olcott had to keep up his official dignity as best he could in spite of various mistakes in judgment caused by outer pressure and inner conflict. Few could have sustained the strain of his position. Although not naturally mystical, his unselfish devotion to the service of humanity showed that the real *inner man* understood the issues even though the brain-mind at times was bewildered.

Even Olcott did not sufficiently allow for one difficulty that caused some misunderstanding in H.P.B.'s relation with him and others, and which again arouses sympathy for her. A chela of an Oriental guru who works in the outside world has to face trying problems to which those who live in retirement are not exposed. There are many things regarding his association with his teacher about which the rules of his Order forbid him to speak. While this may seem strange to Westerners, it is not artificial or formal but a necessary arrangement, and in the Orient it is well understood. H. P. Blavatsky suffered severely from unavoidable misconceptions arising from this source; her silence was misconstrued and it was impossible for her to explain. At times the strain was terrible and she was obliged to appear what she was not. Writing to Miss Francesca Arundale in 1884, she touches on this subject:

> . . . Now if these words are once more understood by you as implying that MASTERS *either* countenanced or *encouraged* deception then all I can say is you have not acquired yet the true perception of a theosophist—and I had hoped you had. There are things in the *Occult* circle which *no one outside of it* can rightly judge. That's all.
>
> —*Theos.*, LIII, 361, July 1932

In another letter written to Mrs. Gebhard of Elberfeld, H.P.B. tells of her distress when she saw suspicion generated in the minds of sincere people by the impossibility of explaining certain refusals to give reasons for her actions. She writes:

> Do you suppose for one moment that what you write to me now I did not know for years? . . . It is just that which killed me, which tortured and broke my heart inch by inch for years, for I had to bear it *in silence* and had no right to explain things unless permitted by Masters, and *They commanded me to remain silent.*
>
> —*The Path,* VII, 382, March 1893

Her complete devotion and undaunted courage carried her through without breaking under trials that were almost unendurable. It is said to be a royal thing to be misunderstood when doing service, but it was a terrible thing to lose friends and co-workers, and to be proclaimed a charlatan by those who, had they known the truth, would have stood by her to the bitter end, at any cost. That was the tragedy revealed to the world when her letters to Sinnett were published.

The following striking passage is quoted from the admirable *Defence of Madame Blavatsky* by Beatrice Hastings, writing from the standpoint of an outsider who has made a close study of the subject and who loathes to see injustice done. With pungent irony the author explains the conditions under which H. P. Blavatsky was said to have forged the Mahatma letters, and shows how impossible this was under such conditions. The letters reveal a quiet mind, an unruffled temper, an undisturbed attention in their writers, as well as being as different in style from H.P.B.'s sledgehammer style as those of the letters of the two different Masters are from each other – which is very marked. During the period when these letters appeared H.P.B. lived in a tumult of conflicting emotions, was frequently ill, immersed in a constant round of exhausting activities, and had no money to spare. Mrs. Hastings writes, with some legitimate sarcasm indeed, on page 23, volume I:

> It must not be supposed that Madame Blavatsky, at this period, had nothing to do but invent the style and forge the script of the "Mahatma Letters"; be the lioness of all the social gatherings, attend lectures, talk to all and everyone about Theosophy and the Society; sleep, bath, dress and eat; correspond with a hundred people all over India, write for the "Theosophist," read, and frequently comment on, articles sent in; keep in touch with her Russian editors and run an eye over the world's news and reviews; be ill; organise fraudulent phenomena, such as having diplomas buried under bushes miles outside Simla; hypnotise everybody everywhere to think, say and do just what she needed for the perpetration of her frauds; handle the network of confederates she had, the person who wrote the Jhelum telegram and the Amritsar postal employees who must have tampered with the post-mark, the god-like Hindu who bamboozled the Colonel with a rose in the Golden Temple and the "man in white" who must have stuck notes in trees; unpick a heavy old velvet and worsted cushion (and ensure that it should not be missed and asked for at

any moment), unpick the inner lining, stick in a note and a brooch and sew the cushion up again, with new thread exactly the same as the old, without leaving a trace (velvet!); have endless discussions with Hume and other sceptics; travel, attend new Branch inaugurations, talk to new members; pass hours and whole days in despair and rage under a hurricane of slander, explain to friends and reply to enemies all around the country; fall desperately ill and, barely convalescent, gather up unerringly all the threads of her huge conspiracy . . .

The references to the notes, the cushion, the telegram and the diplomas relate to phenomena at Simla described in Sinnett's *Occult World*, and are mentioned in various letters by H. P. Blavatsky and the Mahatmas. The Golden Temple of the Sikhs is at Amritsar, and Colonel Olcott writes in *Old Diary Leaves* that when he and H.P.B. visited it in October 1880, one of the Masters came forward and greeted them, giving each a fresh rose. This was K.H., who refers to his visit to the Golden Temple in the *Mahatma Letters*, page 12.

Letter V in the *Blavatsky Letters*, upon which K.H. precipitated a long comment, bears out the point Mrs. Hastings makes in the above quotation. In that letter, H.P.B. reveals to Sinnett her terrible physical suffering and her mental distress at that crisis and, under the almost unendurable pressure, she even reproaches the Master in words she would never use under ordinary conditions. Yet K.H.'s script, accompanying the letter and only intended for Sinnett's perusal, explains her outburst in calm and dignified terms, using it to give him a profound lesson on the duality of man's nature. Racked with pain, tortured by a series of insults, and almost overwhelmed by other difficulties, it would have been impossible for her to have written that philosophical communication under such circumstances.

II

THE SECOND SEPTENARY CYCLE OF THE THEOSOPHICAL SOCIETY

THE critical first seven-year cycle of the Society closed without disaster on November 17, 1882, but the lack of the proper understanding of the deeper meaning of the movement, of the need to act as well as to talk brotherhood, compelled the Masters to limit their personal contact with all but H.P.B., and a very few others, mostly their own chelas. Far too much publicity had been given regarding the Masters. As H.P.B. writes in a letter to Mrs. Gebhard, a barrier had been erected between even the reliable theosophists and the Masters ever since certain members –

> throwing Their names right and left, *poured in torrents* on the public, so to say, Their personalities, powers, and so on, until the world (the outsiders, not only Theosophists) *desecrated* Their names indeed from the North to the South Pole. . . . They were desecrated in every possible way by believer and unbeliever, by the former when he would *critically* and from *his* worldly standpoint examine Them (the Beings beyond and outside every worldly if not human law!), and when the latter positively slandered, dirted, dragged Their names in the mud! O powers of heaven! what *I* have suffered – there are no words to express it. This is my chief, my greatest crime, for having brought Their personalities to public notice unwillingly, reluctantly, and forced into it by –– and ––.
>
> – *The Path,* VII, 381–2, March 1893

This ill-advised exploitation of their personalities, *instead of their teachings,* exposed the Masters to a constant bombardment of appeals, prayers and even demands for attention

Ninth Anniversary of The Theosophical Society
Adyar, Madras, December 27–29, 1884

From left to right:

Standing: M. Krishnamachari (called also Babaji, Bowaji, Dharbagiri Nath) and Henry S. Olcott

Seated, back row: Major-General H. R. Morgan, W. T. Brown, T. Subba Row, H. P. Blavatsky, Franz Hartmann and Rudolf Gebhard

Middle row: Norendro Nath Sen, Dāmodar K. Māvalankar, S. Rāmaswāmier and P. Sreenivasa Row

Front row: Bhavani Shankar, T. Vijayaghavacharin, Tookaram Tatya and V. Coopooswami Iyer

in regard to personal matters – marriages, financial affairs, and the like – from all directions, and they were compelled to erect an isolating barrier in pure self-defense. H.P.B. ultimately became very reserved in regard to communications with the Masters, a wise policy continued by William Q. Judge when his turn came to take the direction of affairs.

More than six months before the close of the septenary cycle the Master M. sent Mr. Sinnett a severe warning, which is of considerable interest:

> For the 6½ years they [H.P.B. and Olcott] have been struggling against such odds as would have driven off any one who was not working with the desperation of one who stakes life and all he prizes on some desperate supreme effort. Their success has not equalled the hopes of their original backers, phenomenal as it has been in certain directions. In a few more months the term of probation will end. If by that time the status of the Society as regards ourselves – the question of the "Brothers" be not definitely settled (either dropped out of the Society's programme or accepted on our own terms) that will be the last of the "Brothers" of all shapes and colours, sizes or degrees. We will subside out of public view like a vapour into the ocean. Only those who have proved faithful to themselves and to Truth through everything, will be allowed further intercourse with us. And not even they, unless, from the President downward they bind themselves by the most solemn pledges of honour to keep an inviolable silence thenceforth about us, the Lodge, Tibetan affairs. Not even answering questions of their nearest friends, though silence might seem likely to throw the appearance of "humbug" upon all that has transpired. In such a case effort would be suspended until the beginning of another septenary cycle when, if circumstances should be more auspicious, another attempt might be made, under the same or another direction.
>
> – *Mahatma Letters*, 263–4

Fortunately the attempt was made in 1888, and under the same direction, and it did not fail.

Notwithstanding the various hindrances already mentioned, the opening of the second septenary of probation — which turned out to be far more trying than the first — was marked by a great increase in the general activities, the establishment of numerous new branches and the extension of the work to countries hitherto untouched. The first important event was the removal of the temporary headquarters from Bombay to Adyar, a suburb of Madras, where a suitable mansion with large grounds was obtained on very advantageous terms.

H. P. Blavatsky's unique mission in arousing wide interest in the treasures of Eastern religions, and especially in demonstrating that they had deeper meanings than were known to the laity, had aroused great enthusiasm throughout India and Ceylon. This was strongly manifested at the farewell ceremony held in connection with the departure of the theosophists from Bombay on December 17, 1882, which marked the opening of the second septenary cycle of the T. S.

The efforts made by the theosophists to revive the high ideals of antiquity, the spiritual wisdom, scientific knowledge, and high culture of ancient India, were warmly recognized. Colonel Olcott's indefatigable attempts to arouse the self-respect and the ambition of the people of India to help themselves culturally and economically, as well as morally and spiritually, by lectures given from one end of the country to the other, had attracted wide attention. An Address was read in connection with the presentation of a handsome testimonial (a silver cup and salver) by Fellows of the Society and friends, including a large number of the most prominent native residents of Bombay.

On the eve of your departure for Madras, we, the members of the

Bombay Branch, beg most respectfully to convey to you our heartfelt and sincere acknowledgement for the benefit which the people of this Presidency in general and we in particular have derived from your exposition of the Eastern philosophies and religions during the past four years. . . . By your editorial efforts and public lectures you have done much to awaken in the hearts of the educated sons of India a fervent desire for the study of their ancient literature which has so long been neglected; . . . you have often justly impressed upon the minds of young men the necessity of making investigations into the boundless treasures of Eastern learning as the only means of checking that materialistic and atheistic tendency engendered by an educational system unaccompanied by any moral or religious instruction. . . .

Your endeavors have been purely unselfish and disinterested, and they, therefore, entitle you to our warmest sympathy and best respects.

– *Theos.*, IV, Jan. 1883, Suppl. 8

On the arrival of the theosophical household at Madras, they received a hearty welcome. Reporting the enthusiastic reception, the newspaper, *Native Opinion*, wrote:

The intelligent thinking section of the Native Community, wherever a branch of the Society has been established has fairly been roused to take a greater interest in Sanskrit literature and science.

When H.P.B. reached Adyar she probably hoped that she could settle down in that peaceful retreat to write and teach without interruption or anxiety, but karma decreed otherwise. For a while, all went well, and when Mr. and Mrs. Sinnett visited her in March 1883, she and her heterogeneous household were comfortably installed, and many of the Anglo-Indians had become friends. Mr. Sinnett writes:

The upper rooms of the house were her own private domain. . . . The new room just built had been hurried forward that we might see it complete, and was destined by Madame to be her "occult room," her own specially private sanctum, where she would be visited by none but her most intimate friends. It came to be sadly desecrated by her worst enemies a year or two later. In her ardour of affection for all that concerned "the Masters," she had especially devoted herself to decorating a certain hanging cupboard to be kept exclusively sacred to the communications passing between these Masters and herself, and already bestowed upon it the designation under which it became so sadly celebrated subsequently—the shrine. Here she had established some simple occult treasures—relics of her stay in Tibet—two small portraits she possessed of the Mahatmas, and some other trifles associated with them in her imagination. The purpose of this special receptacle was of course perfectly intelligible to everyone familiar with the theory of occult phenomena—held by Theosophists to be as rigidly subject to natural laws as the behaviour of steam or electricity. A place kept pure of all "magnetism" but that connected with the work of integrating and disintegrating letters, would facilitate the process, and the "shrine" was used a dozen times for the transaction of business between the Masters and the chelas connected with the Society for every once it was made to subserve the purpose of any show phenomenon. —*Incidents,* 257–8

By "show" phenomena Sinnett did not mean sensational displays to attract the curious, which would not be permitted, but an occasional exhibition of occult power which the Master, or H.P.B. and a few other chelas, employed to show serious students the possibilities of a trained will. While this course was no doubt necessary under the prevailing conditions, it was the origin of much subsequent tribulation, and has long been entirely abandoned.

After a trying summer of hard work in the intense heat of the lowlands, H.P.B. and Colonel Olcott sought relief in a short vacation in the bracing climate of the Nilgiri Hills, staying with their staunch friends, Major-General and Mrs. Morgan at Ootacamund, where she made many new friends, although, as happened earlier at Simla, her passionate revolt against the conventions and insincerities of social intercourse, aroused resentment among some. As Olcott writes in regard to this visit:

> She railed at society, not like your parvenues, whose bitterness springs from their being kept beyond the threshold of the salons of the fashionable caste, but as one who, born in the purple and accustomed to equal association with peers and peeresses, had differentiated from her species and stepped up to higher ground.
>
> – *O. D. L.*, III, 3

While at Ootacamund she produced the exact counterpart of a valuable sapphire for a society woman, by the same occult means that she had duplicated a fine topaz for Mrs. Sinnett at Simla. The sapphire was appraised by a jeweler at quite 200 rupees. Even if H.P.B. had wished to impose the belief in her occult powers upon the new acquaintance, how could she have purchased such a costly jewel for the purpose – poor H.P.B. who was never free from financial difficulties! The highly-placed lady afterwards parted company with the donor – but she kept the sapphire.

During her visit, H. P. Blavatsky took the opportunity of studying the mysterious "white" aborigines (the Todas) and other peculiar tribes of the romantic Nilgiri district. Her observations were published in Russian, then in book form in French under the title, *Au Pays des Montagnes Bleues*, and ultimately in English. The Todas have many strange religious customs connected with cattle and dairy work, and there is much that is obscure about them which is discussed in the little book just mentioned and in *Isis Unveiled*, where the author says, "They are a people who fulfill a certain high purpose, and whose secrets are inviolable" (II, 615).

Before returning to Adyar, Colonel Olcott and H.P.B. paid a short visit to Pondichéry, the French settlement, where they were most hospitably received by the governor and other officials. A theosophical lodge was soon formed as the result of a large public meeting where Olcott spoke in French after the official interpreter broke down. On his return from this meeting he found H.P.B. entertaining a number of visitors, among whom was the Master Narāyan, who left after speaking a few words to her apart and greeting Olcott with a smile.

After the Pondichéry trip, H.P.B. returned to Adyar to the slavery of her desk, and a little later the president started on a long lecture tour in northern India. These fatiguing journeys were always diversified by varied experiences, ranging from lavish hospitality on the part of appreciative rajas and other prominent persons, down to the most uninviting conditions with Spartan fare and embarrassing inconveniences. H.P.B. accompanied him for a short distance on this northern journey, and then Dāmodar and W. T. Brown joined him, while she returned to Madras.

Colonel Olcott not only preached brotherhood but practiced it at the cost of his own health and comfort. For a long time he was permitted by the Master to employ his abundant natural magnetism for the amelioration and often for the permanent cure of disease. Enormous crowds mobbed him on his lecture tours, and his cures were so remarkable that he could easily have posed as a holy man, and formed a theosophical healing cult which would have attracted thousands of self-seekers. His tremendous exertions in magnetic healing, combined with the strain of incessant traveling, constant lecturing and interviewing, and the lack of proper sleep, food or rest, began to drain even his superabundant vitality. While on this journey in 1883, Olcott had treated some eight thousand patients within a twelvemonth, and the Master, noting his condition, ordered him to suspend further magnetic healing. H.P.B. writes a vivid description of a typical scene of healing. She is giving Sinnett, whose circumstances in life had been easy and congenial, a hint of what could be done by a sincere theosophist who was devoted to the welfare of humanity:

> Well, my dear Sir, allow me to tell you, that I, who have been just travelling with him for three weeks, I saw, and am a witness to it whether he has one moment of freedom from morning to night. At 5 o'clock in the morning the whole courtyard and veranda of the houses we stopped in were crowded with the lame and the cripple. At every station, the railway platforms were crowded with the sick lying in wait for him. . . . I saw him begin curing the sick at 6 in the morning, and never sit down till 4 p.m.; and when stopping to eat a plate of vegetable soup have to leave it to cure a possessed woman and his plate of soup remaining unfinished at 7 p.m. and then he would sit down and dictate to his Secretary till 2 in the morning; having only three or four hours sleep. —*Blavatsky Letters*, 61

In regard to another shining example of selfless devotion, that given for so many years by Dāmodar, she adds:

> I would be happy to find *one* member in your L.L. [London Lodge] doing unremunerated one fourth of the work done by Damodar . . . —Ibid., 61

During this year, 1883, an effort was made by the Master K.H. to enlist the journalistic ability of Sinnett in establishing a newspaper to be called *The Phoenix*, to help in raising the social and economic condition of the Indian masses, and thereby to arouse their sense of self-respect and their standing in the eyes of the world. This effort had, of course, nothing to do with party politics, nor had it any connection with the subject of Indian self-government, but one of its main objects was the protection of the depressed classes against the greed and oppression of their own countrymen. At that time some alarm was felt by the Indian government as to the intentions of Tsarist Russia, and H. P. Blavatsky, although a Russian, was outspoken in support of British rule. She warned the Hindus that an exchange of control from England to Russia would be a terrible misfortune for India.

Considerable efforts were made by Sinnett, Olcott and others to raise the funds needed to start this paper, but they failed to get enough money, owing to lack of patriotism in both poor and wealthy Indians, and the enterprise had to be abandoned.

Another interesting point in regard to the *Phoenix* incident is the indirect proof it gives of the authenticity of the Mahatma letters. While H. P. Blavatsky was second to none in devotion to the Masters, she did not always agree with their course of action, and occasionally her protests were unreservedly frank, though she always obeyed when positive orders were received. In the negotiations for the establishment of *The Phoenix* she was not fully informed of the plans of K.H., and she protested vigorously against the course Sinnett was pursuing, not knowing that he was doing his best to follow instructions. In the *Mahatma Letters* the reasons for the Master's action are disclosed, and the reader can see how her misunderstanding arose. One strikingly characteristic letter of protest in the *Blavatsky Letters* (Letter XXVI) exhibits her disturbed condition at this time.

The whole correspondence, which reveals such a conspicuous difference in opinion, is further evidence that H.P.B. did not "fake" those letters from the Master K.H. which led Sinnett to adopt a policy entirely at variance with her wishes. Another similar case occurred a little later, which is mentioned below.

Although to all outward appearance the Society was sailing on calm waters, trying times were not far off when it would require the support of determined men and women who could not be shaken by events which would seem to threaten complete disaster. About this time a few members were given the rare opportunity of meeting one or more of the Mahatmas and their advanced chelas, and of receiving direct personal instruction and advice. One of these was S. Rāmaswāmier, of Tinevelly.

Soon after H.P.B. had been restored to health in 1882 by the Masters K.H. and M. at their āśrama in Sikkim, as previously mentioned, Rāmaswāmier, a probationary chela and a devoted worker in the Theosophical Society, an official in government service, crossed the Indian frontier into Sikkim in a desperate attempt to find his Master. After walking through dangerous forests and having some narrow escapes, he saw the Master approaching him on horseback in the forenoon of a bright sunny day. Although Rāmaswāmier had never met his guru in the physical body till then, he recognized him at once, having seen his portrait at Bombay, where he had also seen him in the māyāvi-rūpa or mind-body. He had received instructions at times from his guru both by letter and by telepathic hearing. The Master talked with him for a long time and told him that he must wait patiently in order to become a fully "accepted chela," for only a few were found worthy, though none was rejected without trial. He was told to go no farther toward Tibet or he would come to grief. Two chelas then came up on horseback and the Master bade him farewell.

Rāmaswāmier described this interview in detail in *The Theosophist* for December 1882, and no reason has been given to doubt its literal accuracy. It is an independent corroboration of H. P. Blavatsky's letter to Sinnett where she describes her visit to Sikkhim.

In November 1883, shortly after the Pondichéry reception, which was attended by the Master Narāyan, as said, Colonel Olcott, Dāmodar K. Māvalankar, and W. T. Brown, while on their northern tour, were individually granted personal interviews with the Master K.H. at Lahore. Dāmodar and Olcott saw and conversed with him at least twice, and they declare that they had not the slightest doubt that they were speaking to a living man, and one possessing that majestic appearance observed by all who have seen him on other occasions. Olcott describes this incident in detail in his *Old Diary Leaves* (III, 36), and mentions that the Master K.H. gave him information about certain important future events which duly happened as foretold. A letter of advice was formed in Olcott's hand as the Master stood near him, and W. T. Brown received one in the same way.

Rather later, on November 25, while the theosophists were being entertained by the maharaja of Kashmir at Jammu, Dāmodar, who had already made great spiritual progress, was called to the Masters' āśrama for a few days' special training. He returned greatly changed in appearance. From a rather diffident, physically fragile youth, he had become, according to Colonel Olcott, "seemingly robust, tough and wiry, bold and energetic in manner." It was not long before Dāmodar had to take heavy responsibilities and to stand firmly in defense of the work during the absence of H.P.B. and Colonel Olcott in Europe. He describes his experience with the Masters in *The Theosophist* (V, 61, Dec. 1883) in an interesting article called "A Great Riddle Solved" and confirms Olcott's and Brown's accounts. Comparing his previous visions of the Master with this meeting in the flesh, Dāmodar writes:

> In the former cases, when making *Pranám* (salutation) my hands passed through his form, while on the latter occasions they met solid garments and flesh. Here I saw *a living man* before me, the same in features, though far more imposing . . .

On the way back to Adyar, the president broke his journey at Jaipur, the modern capital near the romantic and deserted city of Amber, which was abandoned in 1728 for reasons which have never been divulged, though semi-legendary explanations are preserved. There is apparently some mystic attraction in connection with Amber, for both H. P. Blavatsky and later Katherine Tingley made a point of visiting it. When Olcott was in Jaipur he received some curious information confirming similar statements previously obtained elsewhere. He writes:

> Our local colleagues took me the next morning to call on Atmaram Swami, a well-known and respected ascetic, who had been telling them long before my arrival that he was personally acquainted with our Masters, and that, eight years before, in Tibet, one of them known as Jivan Singh, Chohan, had told him that he need not be discouraged about the religious state of India, for they had arranged that two Europeans, a man and a woman, should soon come and revive the Eastern religions. This date corresponds with that of the

formation of our Society at New York, . . . I found the Yogi a man of dignified presence, with a calm, thoughtful countenance, quite a different sort of person from the ordinary ascetic now so common in and profitless to India. — *O. D. L.*, III, 59

12

TOUR IN EUROPE IN 1884

THE critical year 1884 opened auspiciously to all appearances, but strange destinies were impending, both tragical and fortunate. Early in the year Colonel Olcott, in fulfillment of his promise to the Buddhists of Ceylon, went to London to present their case to the Home Government. As mentioned above, he was completely successful in obtaining justice for the Buddhists, and his good work brought honor to the Theosophical Society and happiness to a nation. In addition to this, the president was needed in England to adjust some complications which threatened to disrupt the important London Lodge. He was accompanied by H. P. Blavatsky, whose health was beginning to break down again, and to whom a sea voyage had been recommended. Two Hindus and a Parsi, well educated in the English system, went with them. One of the Hindus was Mohini M. Chatterji, a brilliant thinker and a most promising young man, then striving for chelaship. After doing excellent work for some years, he "dropped out," spoiled, as H.P.B. said, "by male and female adulation, by incessant flattery and his own weakness." The party left India on February 20 and arrived at Marseilles on March 12, 1884. H.P.B. stayed for a while at Nice and then settled in Paris for some months.

In regard to this journey, an unexpected light is thrown upon it by certain letters which contain a valuable hint to those who have the intuition to penetrate in imagination a little behind the seeming, especially in regard to H. P. Blavatsky, the "Sphinx of the nineteenth century." In a letter to N. D. Khandalāvala, a highly respected Indian theosophist, she wrote, in reference to the illness which she thought was the reason for her being sent to Europe:

> ". . . Well, if the Masters want me to go, then I go – though I cannot make out why They should send me abroad to get relief, when They could as well cure me here, as They did twice before. Colonel is going to London, and I too. I do not know myself where and why I am going."
>
> – *Golden Book*, 75

It was not surprising that she was puzzled, for there was a far more important reason *which was not told to her* by the Master K.H., but was told to Mohini M. Chatterji, who was at that time filled with enthusiasm and devotion. Mohini received the following in March 1884, in Paris, where he was awaiting H.P.B.'s arrival from Nice:

> When Upasika arrives, you will meet and receive her as *though you were in India, and she your own mother*. You must not mind the crowd of Frenchmen and others. You have *to stun them;* and if Colonel asks you why, you will answer him that it is the interior man, the *indweller* you salute, not H.P.B., for you were notified to that effect by us. And know for your own edification that One far greater than myself has kindly consented to survey the whole situation under her guise, and then to visit, through the same channel, occasionally, Paris and other places where foreign members may reside. You will thus salute her on seeing and taking leave of her the whole time you are at Paris – regardless of comments and *her own surprise*.
>
> – *L.M.W.*, II, 124–5

The greater "One" is most probably the Mahā-chohan or Chief of the Himalayan Brotherhood of Adepts, the Occult Hierarchy. The Hindu salutation mentioned is, of course, very reverential.

Not only H. P. Blavatsky, but also Mohini himself, who was at that time free from reproach, was employed by the Master as the vehicle of a higher personality, in his case that of an advanced chela. She mentions this in a letter to Sinnett, who was then in London, written a month or two before she started for Europe, when she seems not to have known that she herself was to take the voyage. Observe the reference to the chela. She wrote:

> On February 17th [1884] Olcott will probably sail for England on various business, and Mahatma K.H. sends his chela, under the guise of Mohini Mohun Chatterjee, to explain to the London Theosophists of the Secret Section – every or *nearly* every mooted point . . . Do not make the mistake, my dear boss, of taking *the Mohini you knew* for the Mohini who will come. There is more than one Maya in this world of which neither you nor your friends and critic Maitland is cognisant. The ambassador will be invested with an *inner* as well as with an *outer* clothing. *Dixit.*
>
> As for me let me die in peace among my household gods. I have become too old, too sick and broken down to be of any use. I am dying by inches in my harness. – *Blavatsky Letters*, 65

But she was mistaken; her best work remained to be done. In another letter to Sinnett, dated April 25, 1884 and written in Paris, she refers to the great importance of Mohini's visit to London, where he had a far more urgent mission than merely to establish the London Lodge on a firm basis. This mission is indicated in the letter just quoted, in which 'Mohini' is mentioned as being overshadowed by a higher intelligence who had a special work to do.

To prevent any misunderstanding it should be realized that the overshadowing of a living person by a more spiritually developed individual is not mediumship in the ordinary sense. It is not the occupation of a living body by the supposed spirit of a deceased person, a "control." The temporary overshadowing or inspiration of a chela or even of an ordinary person by an adept is well known in the East, and is often mentioned in Indian literature. It is recorded that the great teacher Śankarāchārya exercised this occult power in his sacred work. It is called *āveśa*.

At this time the Society in Europe already consisted of the London Lodge, two lodges in Paris, one in Corfu, a group at Odessa, and many unattached members; but soon after the arrival of H.P.B. and her party, a considerable increase in lodges and membership took place.

Notwithstanding the minor difficulties that quite naturally arose, theosophy was making good progress in Europe in the early summer of 1884. England and France were the most energetic centers, but other European countries were awaking to the dawning light from the East. The great development in America had hardly begun. In March, H.P.B. arrived in France, where she stayed about three months. She attracted many persons of high social standing as well as serious students of occult philosophy such as Baron J. Spedalieri, the kabbalist and former disciple of the well-known Éliphas Lévi. Many were, as usual in those pioneering days, drawn by the tales of wonder associated with phenomena and Oriental mysteries; and the presence of the brilliant young Hindus – possibly, as some imagined, chelas or at least near-chelas – rather added to than diminished the glamor that was connected with the word theosophy. But there were exceptions to the wonder-seekers, such as the Countess of Caithness (Duchesse de Pomar), who became a lifelong friend and active helper of H.P.B.

By means of innumerable interviews and the large amount

of newspaper publicity, theosophy became well known in Paris. Victor Hugo's journal, *Le Rappel*, discussed theosophy under the title "The Buddhist Mission to Europe." Lady Caithness, who had written a book on theosophy, had started a study-group in 1883, and this became a lodge of the Parent Society in June 1884, while H.P.B. was in Paris. Within a few years many distinguished persons joined it, including the scientists C. Richet, Camille Flammarion, R. Thurman, and writers such as Édouard Schuré. Other lodges were formed in Paris, but for several years the French Society was the principal arena of controversy, and of serious anxiety to H.P.B. and Olcott.

Mme. Jelihovsky, H.P.B.'s sister, visited her in Paris. She writes:

> . . . we found her surrounded by a regular staff of members of their Society who had gathered at Paris, coming from Germany, Russia, and even America, to see her after her five years' absence in India; and by a crowd of the curious . . . Truth compels me to say that H. P. Blavatsky was very reluctant to satisfy idle curiosity. She has her own way of looking very contemptuously at any physical phenomena, hates to waste her powers in a profitless manner, and was, moreover, at the time quite ill. Every phenomenon produced *at her will* invariably cost her several days of sickness. —*Incidents*, 264

It was not only in France that people were craving for thaumaturgy. One evening when she unexpectedly arrived in London for a few days and dropped in to the London Lodge, she offered to give explanations of some of the difficulties in *Isis Unveiled*, but the members preferred to hear about certain astral apparitions! Real work, however, was being done, and new centers were forming in Europe and America.

H.P.B. spent most of her European visit in France and Germany, with a few short trips to London. She was the center of interest wherever she went, and her fame reached its highest pitch in public estimation in 1884. Prominent leaders in progressive thought and scientific achievement either joined the Society or became serious students of theosophy. Besides those mentioned in the Paris Lodge, Baron Karl du Prel, Professor Gabriel Max, Dr. Hübbe-Schleiden, in Germany; Dr. Gustav Zander in Sweden; Dr. Elliott Coues in America; F. W. Myers, and Professor William Crookes in England; and other noted scholars, scientists, etc., became active Fellows of the Society. Professor Crookes, the chemist to whom science owes the great discovery of "radiant matter," as he called it (now known as ionized matter), which led directly in his and other hands to the modern atomic theories and the "New Physics," became a councillor of the London Lodge and, it is said, received communications from Master M., who took great interest in his work. The Master's attention was attracted to him by the moral courage he showed in daring to investigate psychic phenomena, and in publicly declaring that they were facts, scientifically demonstrable, whatever their interpretation might be. Crookes suffered bitter persecution from many of his scientific colleagues, but even under the strongest pressure he never modified his statements or withdrew his records. He never accepted the regular spiritualistic belief in the return of the departed, but kept an open mind.

H. P. Blavatsky devotes many pages of *The Secret Doctrine* to Crookes' researches in chemistry which approached closely to the teachings of the ancient wisdom. She also used his famous demonstration of the existence of the astral or ethereal double in man, with its capacity for a temporary existence independently of the physical body, as an apt illustration of the ethereal condition of the human race in its earlier pre-physical evolution. Crookes' experiments with the so-called spirit of Katie King, apparently an astral projection from a medium, are of the greatest importance in support of the theosophical teachings in regard to human evolution and the early ethereal races of man. Students will find references to this problem in *The Secret Doctrine*, Volume II, pages 652–3, 737.

The great public interest in theosophy shown in London was aroused not only by the presence of H.P.B. and Colonel Olcott, but also by that of the Hindus, particularly Mohini. Sinnett's *Occult World* and *Esoteric Buddhism* had not long been published, and he was then living in London where his activities had attracted much attention. Olcott gives a glowing account of his own reception by many distinguished persons in April 1884, and adds:

> Everywhere the theme of talk was Theosophy: the tide was rising. The ebb was to follow, but as yet no one foresaw it in Europe, for it was to begin at Madras: the Scottish Missionaries its engineers, the high-minded [?] Coulombs their tools. —*O.D.L.*, III, 98

On July 21, a most important public meeting was held in Prince's Hall, London, in honor of H. P. Blavatsky and H. S. Olcott. A very large number of the most cultured persons in the city were present, including statesmen, scientists, writers, artists, as well as many distinguished Asiatics and other foreigners. The profound impression made on intellectual England bore good fruit, and H. P. Blavatsky's name became widely known. But she cared little for the bubble reputation and when the bubble burst she regretted it only because of the interference with her work for humanity.

On too many occasions, unfortunately, Colonel Olcott accentuated the phenomenal side of the theosophical philosophy, no doubt with the good intention of breaking down the prevailing skepticism in regard to anything but the physical plane. Too much was said about H.P.B.'s occult powers and too little about her philosophical teachings and her response to the cry of humanity for a solution of its pressing problems. Very serious trouble arose from this, and the error was committed in spite of her protest. In the simplicity of his heart, Olcott consented to be examined as to his private experiences with the Masters by those then inexperienced beginners in practical psychology who constituted the London Society for Psychical Research. He discussed occult matters which, as the Master K.H. said, "ought to have been limited to an *inner* and very SECRET circle" (*Mahatma Letters*, 323). In this and other ways, the false idea which has been difficult to eradicate was spread that theosophy is a form of psychic research. The psychical researchers were looking only for phenomena and had no interest in theosophy, or in studying the place that the occult powers in man occupy in its philosophy of nature. The same Master had warned Sinnett two years before:

> It is not *physical* phenomena that will ever bring conviction to the hearts of the unbelievers in the "Brotherhood" but rather phenomena of *intellectuality, philosophy* and logic, if I may so express it.
> —*Mahatma Letters*, 246

It turned out that Olcott's misdirected zeal to convert the psychists to a belief in the phenomena, and especially the extremely injudicious way in which he presented his case on one occasion prejudiced them very strongly, and the consequences were deplorable. H.P.B. was present on this occasion and she instantly saw the fatal effect of his ill-advised address, of which he was perfectly unconscious, and greatly surprised him when she castigated him later in no gentle terms.

Colonel Olcott's astonishment at the result of the inquiry is shown by his remarks in *Old Diary Leaves:*

> But to understand our feelings when, later on, the S.P.R. made its merciless attack upon H.P.B., our Masters, and ourselves, one should try to put oneself in our places. Here were we laying bare a series of personal experiences which had for us a most private and sacred character, for no possible benefit that could accrue to ourselves, but solely that our testimony might help the cause of spiritual science and give comfort to other students not yet so favored as ourselves; going before the Committee with no prepared case, but answering the questions sprung upon us, and hence putting ourselves at the mercy of those who had none of our enthusiasm, whose policy was to criticize, analyze, and pick flaws in our statements, and who in rendering their final judgment were unsparing of our feelings, sceptical as to our motives, and merciless to a degree. Worst of all, they were then incompetent through inexperience of psychical laws, misled by the conclusions of an agent – Dr. Hodgson – whom they sent out to India to verify our statements and collect evidence, and by an utterly incompetent handwriting expert's report, and so put themselves on permanent record as the self-righteous calumniators of a woman – H.P.B. – who had neither done an injury to a living person, nor asked or received any benefit or reward for her services to the world, yet whom they dared to brand as "one of the most accomplished, ingenious, and interesting impostors in history". . .
>
> – *O. D. L.,* III, 100–1

It is important to remember that when Colonel Olcott says "we were laying bare a series of personal experiences" and "we" were doing this and that, he means himself and Mohini M. Chatterji, and not H.P.B. Neither the Society for Psychical Research, nor their Committee of Investigation, nor Richard Hodgson, its representative in India, ever saw any of the phenomena they presumed to condemn.* This should always be borne in mind, as otherwise the reader might get the false idea that those people had tested her in the way Hodgson and other members of the S.P.R. tested ordinary mediums like the well-known Mrs. Piper, who converted some of them to spiritualism.

In view of the success attained during this European tour, the difficulties in the London Lodge which Olcott had to adjust are seemingly of little significance, but being the most important center in Europe it demanded the president's most earnest attention.

This lodge had been a center of discontent and trouble almost from its foundation. H.P.B. frequently complained that it had done nothing for the general welfare of the Society until Sinnett and a devoted American, Samuel Ward, joined it. She called it the "head and brain of the T. S.," but not the soul. It had many members who were prominent in intellectual and social circles, and an effort had been made to establish an Inner Group to which more advanced teachings could be given; but, here again, the lack of harmony and true cooperation were a severe handicap and, as H.P.B. ultimately said, it had to be "left to its fate." About three years afterwards, when she had settled in London for good,

*[Cf. *Journal of the American Society for Psychical Research*, LVI, 133–4, July 1962, for Walter A. Carrithers, Jr.'s statement that on July 5 and 26, 1884, F. W. Myers and Edmund Gurney, joint secretaries of the S.P.R., did hear the "astral bell" in H.P.B.'s presence. —Ed.]

she was obliged to start a new lodge, the Blavatsky Lodge, for those London members who would be willing to follow her advice, and who were worthy of her help. In 1884, however, there was hope that if the differences of opinion and in policies which had reached an explosive point could be adjusted, the lodge would become a very strong center.

The two most active members of the London Lodge were A. P. Sinnett and Dr. Anna Bonus Kingsford. Sinnett had recently returned home from India, and carried the authority and reputation of his Oriental experiences. Dr. Kingsford was the well-known Christo-theosophical and Hermetic mystic and seer, author of *The Perfect Way*, and president of the lodge for a while. She was a remarkable woman, self-confident and masterful. She had a great hatred of cruelty, especially to animals, and the unspeakable horrors of unrestrained and utterly heartless vivisection in the Paris hospital in which she had studied medicine had almost upset her mental equanimity at that time. Her noble work in defense of the tortured animals aroused the admiration of the Masters but, carried away by furious indignation at the callous materialism of the physiologists, she sometimes went to unjustifiable extremes which called forth H.P.B.'s condemnation. According to K.H. in the *Mahatma Letters*, she was a "fifth rounder," a technical theosophical term for those persons who have run ahead of the average in evolutionary development, a fact of which she herself had more than a suspicion.

At the time H. P. Blavatsky was writing *Isis Unveiled* in America, but quite independently, Dr. Kingsford wrote down mystical interpretations of biblical and classical myths and symbols which agree in the main with the theosophical teachings and show the existence of the "secret doctrine" of antiquity, the basic unity behind all the outward forms of religion. She writes, in the preface to *The Perfect Way*, ". . . the dogmas and symbols of Christianity are substantially identical with those of other and earlier religious systems," and that "the true plane of religious belief lies, not where hitherto the Church has placed it, – in the sepulcher of historical tradition, but in man's own mind and heart." In the *Mahatma Letters* on pages 345–7, K.H. pays Anna Kingsford a high tribute for her intuitive seership. Here is one sentence:

> Well may you admire and more should you wonder at the marvellous lucidity of that remarkable seeress, who ignorant of Sanskrit or Pali, and thus shut out from their metaphysical treasures, has yet seen a great light shining from behind the dark hills of exoteric religions.

Not long before Olcott reached London in 1884, a complication had arisen in the London Lodge in regard to the presidency. Mrs. Kingsford had held the office for some time in response to the expressed wish of the Masters as indicated to Mr. Sinnett, though H.P.B. had disapproved of her occupation of the post notwithstanding that she was the Masters' choice for the time. A study of the correspondence on this involved situation in the *Mahatma Letters* and the *Blavatsky Letters* reveals a positive difference of opinion between the Masters and H.P.B., which shows how utterly absurd it would be to think that she forged the Master's letters which urged Sinnett to adopt a policy entirely opposed to her outspoken protests.

Olcott arrived at the time of the new election, and many of the lodge members wished for a change, as they felt that their president did not represent the point of view of the majority. She and her small but active group of followers, including Edward Maitland, a well-known writer on mystical subjects, insisted that their Christo-theosophical interpretation was more suitable for the West – Christendom – than the Oriental presentation. Subsequent events have not confirmed this, for H. P. Blavatsky's method has made a far more profound impression on the world. Dr. Kingsford herself did not work for the masses, but, as she says in *The Perfect Way*, her teaching was intended only for "the educated and developed; its terms and ideas being beyond the conception of the generality." This was not in harmony with the spirit of theosophy, which is for all.

Assuredly, the mystical and devotional note that Dr. Kingsford struck was opportune, but it is not missing in the Oriental presentation of H. P. Blavatsky's *Voice of the Silence*, derived from Eastern sources, and which expresses it with deeper significance and greater poetic beauty than Dr. Kingsford's mystical odes. In any case, the fact that the English seeress' Hermetic or Christo-theosophical independent revelations so closely parallel H. P. Blavatsky's teachings, including as they do karma, reincarnation, the divinity of man, etc., is good evidence that theosophy is no "concoction," invented by the latter. Dr. Kingsford was surprised when she discovered that H.P.B. was teaching similar doctrines to those she herself had been promulgating and she had no difficulty in recognizing the existence of the Adepts, though she never fully accepted them as her teachers.

The majority of the London Lodge supported Mr. Sinnett in standing by the theosophical presentation of H.P.B. and her teachers, and as it did not seem possible for Dr. Kingsford and her followers to agree to this policy, the adjustment of the difficulty was left to Colonel Olcott. On his arrival in London he tried to make an acceptable compromise between the contestants, but after various complications the Kingsford party formed a Hermetic Society quite independent of the Theosophical Society, though without breaking off friendly association. Dr. Kingsford remained a Fellow of the T. S. for the few years still to run of her short life, and H.P.B.'s notice of her death contains the following:

> She was a Theosophist and a true one at heart; a leader of spiritual and philosophical thought, gifted with most exceptional psychic attributes. . . . The first and most important [of her books] was "The Perfect Way, or the Finding of Christ," which gives the esoteric meaning of Christianity. It sweeps away many of the difficulties that thoughtful readers of the Bible must contend with in their endeavours to either understand or accept literally the story of Jesus Christ as it is presented in the Gospels. . . .
>
> . . . the circle of her mystically-inclined friends will miss her greatly, for such women as she are not numerous in the same century. The world in general has lost in Mrs. Kingsford one who can be very ill-spared in this era of materialism. —*Lucifer*, II, 78–9, March 1888

Owing to the publicity that has been given by enemies of the movement to the slanders of a Russian writer, V. Solovyoff, whom H.P.B. met during the 1884 tour, a few words must be given to his case which, although deplorable, is an instructive example of misplaced desires. Solovyoff was greatly interested in her phenomena and professed great friendship and even devotion to her at first. He was one of the six witnesses who signed a document attesting their absolute assurance of the reality of one of her most remarkable phenomena. On request of one of the party she read the contents of a sealed letter which had just been received from the mail carrier and performed some other occult feats in connection with the same letter. Solovyoff wrote to the *Rebus*, a Russian periodical of psychological science:

> "The circumstances under which the phenomenon occurred in its smallest details, carefully checked by myself, do not leave in me the smallest doubt as to its *genuineness* and reality. Deception or fraud in this particular case *are entirely out of question.* Vs. SOLOVIEFF"
>
> —*Incidents*, 273

The demonstration contained other features showing her ability to "precipitate" words inside the closed envelope, and the particulars, signed by the six witnesses, are given in Sinnett's *Incidents*, page 269. Solovyoff saw many other even more noteworthy phenomena in connection with H. P. Blavatsky. His emphatic testimony to their authenticity was entirely voluntary.

Yet, one year after her death, he wrote a scandalous and melodramatic attack upon her, repudiating his signed testimonies, and containing such obvious falsities that his own translator, Walter Leaf, had to admit that Solovyoff was not trustworthy in his writing about H. P. Blavatsky. William Kingsland, in his *The Real H. P. Blavatsky*, G. Baseden Butt, and others, have thoroughly exposed the slanders and falsehoods of the unfortunate man, and in private letters of H. P. Blavatsky (never intended by her to be seen by anyone but the Sinnetts) the world has now learned of her knowledge of Solovyoff's highly questionable character which she never used against him, even after she learned that he was trying to ruin her reputation.

How did this transformation in Solovyoff's attitude arise?

Among the causes which brought trouble and anxiety to H.P.B. — independent of the furious attacks from the enemies of theosophy, which were natural and expected reactions to her onslaughts on materialism and dogmatism – were several which are not familiar to the average thinker in the West, but which explain much that would otherwise be obscure in her conduct. One of the most important was her consistent discouragement of unfitted persons, such as Solovyoff and many others, when they revealed themselves as being ambitious to possess the psychic powers of developed chelas without first having the right moral and spiritual foundation. Demands for occult teaching were made with assurance, even with effrontery and threats and, when kindly but firmly refused by H.P.B., the unqualified claimants too often retaliated with abuse and slander. Solovyoff's unhappy story is a notorious example, but there are even worse, such as that of one who spread the rumor that she had "murdered her two illegitimate children"! In a private letter to her sister written in 1885, H.P.B. says:

> "I am travelling with him [Solovyoff] in Switzerland. I really cannot understand what makes him so attached to me. As a matter of fact I cannot help him in the least. I can hardly help him to realize any of his hopes. Poor man, I am so sorry for him . . ."
>
> – *The Path*, X, 108, July 1895

She soon found out why he professed such attachment, and the utter worthlessness of it when his selfish ambitions were frustrated.

To close this chapter on a happier note: during H.P.B.'s visit to Paris in 1884, she was cheered by the presence of her trusted friend and disciple, William Q. Judge, who was on his way to India. He arrived at Adyar at an opportune moment when he was able to render valuable help in regard to the Coulomb conspiracy which was just being revealed. He had been appointed treasurer of the Society, and expected to remain in India, but domestic affairs compelled his return to New York, where he soon began the work of spreading theosophy throughout the United States after several years of enforced inactivity. While in Paris, Judge was able to give H.P.B. valuable assistance in her preparations for *The Secret Doctrine*. She even asked him to write for it.

An invitation from an American friend and devoted theosophical worker, the Countess d'Adhémar, to take a short rest at her château at Enghien, enabled H.P.B. to do some writing in peaceful surroundings and free from worries, an opportunity which rarely presented itself to her. Judge was also a guest at Enghien, and he writes with great feeling of the delightful hours when his friend and teacher was free to present "the phase of her many-sided nature which stimulated the spiritual yearnings of the heart." Under those harmonious conditions, among sensible people who were not craving for miracles, she would occasionally volunteer a demonstration of her control of hidden forces. A very beautiful and impressive example is quoted by W. Q. Judge from a memorandum written by the Countess d'Adhémar:

> "H. P. B. seemed wrapped in thought, when suddenly she rose from her chair, advanced to the open window, and raising her arm with a commanding gesture, faint music was heard in the distance, which advancing nearer and nearer broke into lovely strains and filled the drawing room where we were all sitting. Mohini threw himself at H.P.B.'s feet and kissed the hem of her robe, which action seemed the appropriate outcoming of the profound admiration and respect we all felt toward the wonderful being whose loss we will never cease to mourn." —*Lucifer*, VIII, 360–1, July 1891

13

THE COULOMB CONSPIRACY AGAINST THEOSOPHY

WHEN the 1884 visit to Europe was arranged, the Adyar headquarters was left in charge of a Council which included several disturbing elements, but only one, a Frenchman named Coulomb, was contemplating treachery, and of course he was not suspected by the other members. But he and his English wife – a "weird, witch-like creature" as Dr. Hartmann calls her – soon found an opportunity of preparing a cunning scheme to ruin H.P.B.'s reputation and destroy the Society. Fortunately, as will be shown, the Fates worked against them before it was consummated.

Though H.P.B. and Olcott suspected no special danger to the Society in India when they left, the Masters were perfectly aware of the coming crisis, for when Olcott and Mohini were alone in France in a compartment of a train on their way from Paris to London on April 5, 1884, a letter from K.H. dropped from the roof warning Olcott of the plot that was hatching at Adyar, and telling him not to be discouraged, however threatening it might appear. One sentence reads:

> You have harboured a traitor and an enemy under your roof for years, and the missionary party are more than ready to avail of any help she may be induced to give. A regular conspiracy is on foot. She is maddened by the appearance of Mr. Lane Fox and the powers you have given to the Board of Control. – *L.M.W.*, I, 51

"She" was Madame Coulomb, the real traitor, who had been omitted from the Council, her husband being little more than her tool. Mr. Lane-Fox was a new arrival from England.

On September 10, when the situation was becoming critical in India, a letter from Dāmodar was received at Elberfeld in Germany, where H.P.B., Olcott, and others were staying with her good friends the Gebhard family, stating that a plot was hatching, evidently with the help of Mme. Coulomb. On October 10, Sinnett received a letter by mail from K.H. warning him of the serious implications in the affair. Sinnett was in a disturbed condition, and the Master reminded him that this crisis was a probationary test for him as well as for others: "It is not the moment for reproaches or vindictive recriminations, but for united struggle." Sinnett had frequently opposed the principle of probation, and laughed at the suggestion that it could be applied to him, but the Master assured him that "he who approaches our precincts even in thought, is drawn into the vortex of probation" and that he was in danger of seeing his "temple" fall in ruins. K.H. writes:

> However caused . . . a crisis is here, and it is a time for the utmost practicable expansion of your moral power. . . . Whomsoever has sown the seeds of the present tempest, the whirlwind is strong, the whole Society is reaping it and it is rather fanned than weakened from Tchigadze. —*Mahatma Letters,* 367

The entire Letter LXVI in which the above words occur is worth study as it makes clear the difficulties the Masters had with Sinnett and the reason that they were obliged to sever their connection with him within a few years. Tchigadze (Shigatse), mentioned by the Master, is the seat of the Tashi Lama of Tibet, and it is one of the centers where the Masters work, so the remark that the whirlwind was rather fanned than weakened from there is significant, and may not be inappropriate to other critical and trying periods through which it was the destiny of the movement to pass.

Sinnett never understood that the farseeing vision and the knowledge of human nature and past karma possessed by a real occultist justify methods of dealing with issues which no ordinary person can understand in all its ramifications. Hence, a true chela must tread the path, not with blind faith, but open-eyed and with a splendid trust in his teacher and his great ideal. K.H. wrote to Sinnett in regard to the trouble about to break out in India that such things were sometimes necessary results of the karma of the persons concerned, but for all that they provided useful experience and valuable opportunities of studying certain laws of the occult world in regard to karma, painful though they might be.

> I grant you, those laws *do* seem very often unjust, even, at times cruel. But this is due to the fact that they were never meant either for the immediate redress of wrongs, or the direct help of those who offer at random their allegiance to the legislators. Still, the seemingly real, the evanescent and quick passing evils they bring about are as necessary to the growth, progress and final establishment of your small Th. Society as those certain cataclysms in nature, which often decimate whole populations, are necessary to mankind. An earthquake may, for all the world knows, be a bliss and a tidal wave prove salvation to the many at the expense of the few. The "fittest" were seen to survive in the destruction of every old race and made to merge into, and assimilate with, the new, for nature is older than Darwin.
>
> —Ibid., 358–9

The limited space at disposal forbids a lengthy treatment of the "Coulomb Conspiracy." Larger works are available for those few who wish to study the details. Thorough analysis and complete refutation of the Coulomb charges are contained in standard books such as William Kingsland's *The Real H. P. Blavatsky*, G. Baseden Butt's *Madame Blavatsky*, and Olcott's *Old Diary Leaves*, etc. Dr. Franz Hartmann's *Report of Observations* is a useful exposure of the plot by one who was present during the most critical time. Other writers, unconnected with the Theosophical Society, such as Geoffrey West, Victor Neuberg, and Dr. E. R. Corson, aroused by the injustice from which H.P.B. suffered, have also defended her honor with conclusive logic. Beatrice Hastings' admirable *Defence of Madame Blavatsky* contains a brilliant analysis of the Coulomb case as well as a devastating criticism of the other charges against the maligned messenger of the Masters.

The basis of the Coulomb-Missionary attack is not difficult to find. Theosophists, under H.P.B.'s leadership, were not only fighting materialism in science, and the dead letter interpretation of Oriental philosophies by scholars, but bigotry and literalism in theologies. Nor were they dealing only with the limited interpretations of the Bible by the missionaries. While they were revealing the deeper, the theosophical, meaning in those scriptures, they were also urging the Orientals to find the same obscured truths of the ancient wisdom-religion in their own sacred writings. But the restoration of Buddhism to its rightful place in Ceylon, and the increasing success of theosophy in India were sore subjects with the uncomprehending and ill-advised missionaries who felt that strong measures must be taken to suppress this growing movement before it was too late. Surely it could not survive if H.P.B.'s reputation were ruined; the Coulomb charges were perhaps a heaven-sent opportunity.

But they miscalculated the power behind the movement,

and the undaunted courage and strength of endurance of H.P.B. Though, as she said, she suffered "till she could suffer no more," the theosophical ship weathered the storm successfully, only losing the fair-weather friends who could not stand adversity.

As the whole case against H.P.B. rests upon the statements of Mme. Coulomb, her character and record are of primary importance. What is known of her?

When H.P.B. had reached Cairo in 1870 after the shipwreck in which she lost everything but her life, and while waiting for remittances from Russia, she received some immediate help from Mme. Coulomb, who was connected in some way with a small hotel in Cairo. H.P.B. has never been charged with forgetting a kindness, and when about nine years later Mme. Coulomb and her husband, who were in great destitution, begged for assistance, she tried to find them work. Failing in this, she gave them shelter and occupation at the Bombay headquarters and then at Adyar. All went fairly well for some years, but both H.P.B. and Olcott had occasional causes of complaint against her, and the former had to reprimand her severely for misdemeanors. No one but H.P.B. suspected her of treachery and, as she made herself useful and had nowhere to go, she was tolerated.

She began building her plan of treachery in 1880, from the first day she landed at Bombay with her husband, both shoeless, penniless and starving. She offered to sell *my secrets* to the Rev. Bowen of the *Bombay Guardian*, in July 1880, and she sold them actually to the Rev. Patterson in May 1885. But those secrets were "open letters" for years. Why should I complain? Has not Master left it to my choice, to either follow the dictates of Lord Buddha, who enjoins us not to fail to feed *even a starving serpent*, scorning all fear lest it should turn round and bite the hand that feeds it — or to face *Karma* which is sure to punish him, who turns away from the sight of sin and misery, or fails to relieve the sinner and the sufferer. I knew her and tried my best not to hate her, . . . —*Blavatsky Letters,* 110

Mme. Coulomb was constantly trying strange money-making schemes, even to the extent of pretending to locate treasure by alleged clairvoyance. Her efforts to extort money from members of the Society caused much trouble, and her last effort in that direction precipitated the final break. Many other causes for serious friction arose before H.P.B. went to Europe in February 1884, which cannot be enumerated here, but a second attempt to 'borrow' 2,000 rupees from Prince Harisinghi, a devoted member, was too serious to be passed over lightly. He complained to H.P.B., who immediately put a stop to what seems to have been an attempt at blackmail. The prince says in an affidavit published in Hartmann's *Report of Observations:*

"This seems to have greatly disappointed her, and as we came to know, that she wilfully misrepresented to H.P.B. the facts, and told her that the offer was made by me without her asking for it, I related to H.P.B. what had actually happened, and satisfied her that the whole was a downright misrepresentation on Mad. C.'s part. I cannot help remarking that I have found her very unsympathetic and from what she told me of Madame Blavatsky, I know that she is no good friend of hers, as I falsely imagined her to be at first." —p. 31

Dr. Hartmann says in the same report:

. . . her fury knew no bounds, and her passionate outbursts of anger and jealousy were in no way soothed down by Madame Blavatsky, reproaching her for her unjust attempt of [at] extortion. —p. 31

Shortly after being foiled in this attempt, as H.P.B. was

leaving for Europe, Mme. Coulomb bade her farewell and, says Dr. Hartmann:

> Stepping into her boat she waved a last adieu to Babula, the servant of Madame Blavatsky, and said to him: "*I shall be revenged on your mistress for preventing me from getting my 2,000 Rupees.*" —p. 32

When the theosophical party left India in February 1884, the Coulombs were left in charge of H.P.B.'s apartments on the then unoccupied upper floor of the headquarters, and they took the opportunity to plan cunning schemes of revenge which might prove useful for blackmail if the chance offered. One of these consisted in devising forged interpolations in H.P.B.'s handwriting to be inserted in letters written by her to Mme. Coulomb, which would imply that she was conspiring with the latter to produce fraudulent phenomena. The second, which was immediately inaugurated, was the fabrication by Coulomb, who was a very efficient carpenter, of holes and sliding panels in H.P.B.'s rooms which could be exhibited as evidence of trickery on her part.

Although no one at Adyar had any suspicion of these underhand doings, the friction between the Coulombs and the Council gradually became intolerable to the latter after H.P.B.'s departure. Finally, thoroughly exasperated by Mme. Coulomb's past and present provocations, including slander, lying, purloining of letters, eavesdropping, and attempted extortion, etc., the Council on May 13 laid twelve charges of serious misdemeanors against the Coulombs, supported by a large number of affidavits. Mme. Coulomb neither acknowledged nor denied the charges, and after considerable resistance she and her husband were finally expelled from headquarters.

In September, four months later – plenty of time to complete the forgeries – the Madras *Christian College Magazine* published the first letter of a series which the woman claimed was written by H. P. Blavatsky. These letters contained incriminating expressions. They had been paid for by the missionaries, and so Mme. Coulomb realized her desire for revenge and for money at one stroke! In *Old Diary Leaves*, Colonel Olcott mentions that the Coulombs threatened the Council that they would do this unless they were paid 3,000 rupees. Of course the Council indignantly refused, and the publication of the forgeries took place (III, 179–80).

When the news of the attack on the Theosophical Society was published, the widespread sensation it created at once showed what a strong impression the movement had made upon thinkers throughout the world, as well as upon the general public. However, without waiting to hear the defense, the British press hastily declared that H. P. Blavatsky was completely discredited and theosophy destroyed. Similar unwarranted conclusions were expressed by other ill-advised critics during subsequent crises in the T. S., and every time its cynical enemies have been put to shame by having their premature verdicts proved false.

H.P.B. instantly decided to return to India to confute the slanderers in the law courts, but before leaving Europe she wrote an indignant denial to the *Times* (London) in which these sentences occur:

> . . . I have to say that the letters purporting to have been written by me are certainly not mine. Sentences here and there I recognize, taken from old notes of mine on different matters, but they are mingled with interpolations that entirely pervert their meaning. With these exceptions the whole of the letters are a fabrication.

> The fabricators must have been grossly ignorant of Indian affairs, since they make me speak of a "Maharajah of Lahore," when every Indian schoolboy knows that no such person exists. —*Incidents*, 289

In the above she is referring to the *printed copies* of her alleged letters published by the missionaries in their magazine. She was never given an opportunity of seeing the *originals* which the Coulombs claimed to hold. She stopped at Cairo on her return to India, to obtain information regarding Mme. Coulomb's reputation when the latter lived there, and which might supply valuable evidence for use in the proposed lawsuit. Here she received timely help from Nubar Pasha, the premier, and she obtained both police and consular evidence which showed that Mme. Coulomb's Cairo record was of such a discreditable nature that its production in court would have been devastating to her competence as a witness.

During H.P.B.'s short visit to Egypt, she was received with great cordiality by Russian friends of her family and other Russians as well as by the wife of the khedive of Egypt and the court ladies. Mrs. Cooper-Oakley, then a prominent theosophist, who was in H.P.B.'s party, writes:

> Very deeply impressed on my memory is every incident connected with that memorable voyage. H.P.B. was a most interesting fellow-traveller, her varied information about every part of Egypt was both extensive and extraordinary. . . . Especially interesting was one long afternoon spent at the Boulak Museum on the borders of the Nile, where H.P.B. astonished Maspero, the well-known Egyptologist, with her knowledge, and as we went through the museum she pointed out to him the grades of the Initiate kings, and how they were to be known from the esoteric side. —*Lucifer*, VIII, 278, June 1891

On reaching Madras, H.P.B. was received by a large committee and, garlanded according to the graceful Indian custom, she was escorted to an immense and enthusiastic public assemblage. An address of confidence, gratitude, and sympathy was read, signed by five hundred college students, including three hundred students of the very college whose professors were trying to destroy her reputation! She made a short speech, one of the very few she ever delivered, denying the charges, and saying that "of all the letters published, not a single one, as it stood, had been written by her." Any that were genuine had been tampered with by interpolations, etc., so as to present a compromising appearance. It is significant that when the missionaries presented many letters alleged to have been written by H. P. Blavatsky, not one *telegram* was offered. Yet, according to Mme. Coulomb, H.P.B. sent her many telegrams containing instructions for the production of fraudulent phenomena. Why were these telegrams not produced? It is very simple. While letters, or sentences in letters, could easily be forged, it was impossible to forge official postal telegrams. Hence no telegrams!

With few exceptions, the Indian press and public opinion agreed with the majority of the students of the Missionary College. *The Indian Mirror* of December 20, 1884, said:

> "The Hindu community, in general, is the more attracted to Mme. Blavatsky, because they believe that the Missionaries have, in reality, attacked the ancient Hindu religion and philosophy under the guise and pretence of exposing the lady's 'trickery.' On that account the feeling of the Native community against the Missionaries and for Mme. Blavatsky is very strong."

The *Indian Chronicle* said:

> "We are not Theosophists ourselves . . . but we have a great respect for the founders of the Theosophical Society. . . . The Chris-

tian scoffers . . . are perhaps not aware that the existence of Mahatmas . . . is universally believed throughout India, and it is preposterous to suppose that the Padris of Madras will do any serious harm to that belief. . . . Theosophy, though it may have to bear much temporary annoyance . . . will come out of the fiery ordeal purer for having gone through it."
— *O. D. L.*, III, 184–5

Allan O. Hume, whose open criticism of H.P.B. in certain matters was never concealed, and who was at the time of writing, as he says, "only a nominal member" of the Society, pointed out in the Calcutta *Statesman* that:

Madame Blavatsky is no fool; on the contrary, as all who know her, be they friends or foes, will admit, she is an exceptionally clever and far-sighted woman, with a remarkably keen perception of character. Would such a woman ever give a person like Madame Coulomb the entire power over her future, that the *writing* of such letters involves? Or again, say she *had,* in some mad mood, written such letters, would she have come to an open rupture with the holder of them? Parts of the letters may be genuine enough; one passage cited has a meaning quite different from that in which I see that the *Times of India* accepts it, but believe me, Madame Blavatsky is far too shrewd a woman to have ever *written* to any one, anything that could *convict* her of *fraud.*
— *Madame H. P. Blavatsky,* K. F. Vania, 224

Detailed refutation of the Coulomb forgeries of H.P.B.'s writing would be out of place here. It has been pointed out that their style (in French) is illiterate, while H.P.B. wrote a highly cultured French. In this connection it is worth quoting a significant passage from a French letter by M. L. Dramard hitherto unpublished in English, so far as ascertained. Dramard was a leading and scholarly member of the French T. S., and after a careful study of the whole case he wrote (Nov. 12, 1885) the following criticism of the literary aspect of the letters which include the forged passages:

> The compromising passages are of an entirely different style throughout. Madame Blavatsky's prose is vivacious, impulsive, not squeamish by any means — hardly enough so — the ideas are large, elevated, and, although the utmost fervor is revealed, delicate as amber, notwithstanding her frequent irrelevancies in whatever aim she is following. Now the compromising passages are sickening platitudes, such as a cook would write to his master's valet to arrange some smart business deal. These passages, which are after all very few, are obviously the work of a forger. — *Contributions to the History of The Theosophical Society in France,* by C. Blech, 166

Again, however incredible it may seem, neither H.P.B. nor her friends were allowed to examine or even to see the so-called original letters upon which the charges were based, charges which were supported only by the testimony of a woman of the indifferent character of Mme. Coulomb. How would such a violation of propriety be treated in any court of justice? Had Mme. Coulomb been a witness on H. P. Blavatsky's side of the case, Hodgson would have contemptuously refused to pay any attention to the testimony of a witness whose self-contradictions and bad character were proclaimed by her own acts and by her own letters and words.

Major-General H. R. Morgan, the distinguished Anglo-Indian, who was active in the defense, wrote:

> When we consider the characteristics of this woman, her eavesdropping, purloining of letters, her hatred of the members composing the Society, her swearing she would be revenged, her incessant espionage of Madame Blavatsky, and those she might be talking with, the motive and manner of her concocting these letters, is not difficult to understand.
>
> — *Reply to a Report of an Examination by J. D. B. Gribble,* 4

The second main charge made by the Coulombs was also

supported by false evidence. They asserted that the so-called shrine, already mentioned, had been used to deceive recipients of letters which appeared to come by occult means, but which they charge were really inserted through smooth-sliding secret panels and holes in the wall and which, according to the Coulombs, had been in constant use for many months. But evidence is available, signed by thoroughly responsible witnesses, that the wall and the 'shrine' were absolutely intact until the Coulombs were left in sole charge of the 'occult rooms.' Complete exposure of the Coulomb lies in regard to these points has been widely published and can be consulted in larger works than this. The following quotation from *The Arena*, March 1892, by W. Q. Judge, who carefully examined and measured the 'shrine,' etc., covers the ground sufficiently for our purpose. Having exposed gross misstatements by the Rev. M. Conway, the man whose false charge in a condemnatory article in *The Arena* against H. P. Blavatsky of having invented the name Koot Hoomi (or Kuthumi) has already been treated on a previous page, Mr. Judge continues:

> Having now directly answered Mr. Conway's article I will take advantage of the opportunity to append some facts directly known to myself, about the "shrine" and the rooms at Adyar.
>
> I went to Adyar in the early part of the year 1884, with full power from the president of the society to do whatever seemed best for our protection against an attack we had information was about to be made in conjunction with the missionaries who conducted the Christian College at Madras. I found that Mr. Coulomb had partly finished a hole in the wall behind the shrine. It was so new that its edges were ragged with the ends of laths and the plaster was still on the floor. Against it he had placed an unfinished teak-wood cupboard, made for the occasion, and having a false panel in the back that hid

> the hole in the wall. But the panel was too new to work and had to be violently kicked in to show that it was there. It was all unplaned, unoiled, and not rubbed down. He had been dismissed before he had time to finish. In the hall that opened on the stairs he had made a cunning panel, opening the back of a cupboard belonging to the "occult room." This was not finished and force had to be used to make it open, and then only by using a mallet. Another movable panel he also made in the front room, but even the agent of the psychical society admitted that it was very new. It was of teak, and I had to use a mallet and file to open it. All these things were discovered and examined in the presence of many people, who then and there wrote their opinions in a book I provided for the purpose, and which is now at headquarters. The whole arrangement was evidently made up after the facts to fit them on the theory of fraud. That it was done for money was admitted, . . .
>
> . . . He [the principal of the Christian College] was then asked in my presence by Dr. Hartmann what he had paid to Coulomb for his work, and replied, somewhat off his guard, that he had paid him somewhere about one hundred rupees. — pp. 479–80

It is of course not charged that the principal employed Coulomb to fake the panels and holes.

After the Coulombs were sent away from Adyar, they were hospitably received by the missionaries, who saw a rare opportunity to discredit H. P. Blavatsky and theosophy by utilizing the revengeful feelings and the straitened circumstances of the discharged couple.

For a while no reason appeared why the Society's work should not proceed without further interruption. Resolutions and letters of confidence and support were received from lodges and members everywhere in the Society, as well as from numerous friends and sympathizers in India and abroad.

But now Richard Hodgson comes into the picture. This young man was sent to India by the Society for Psychical

Research, recently organized in London, "to investigate phenomena connected with the Theosophical Society," of which the Researchers had heard from Olcott and Mohini, as already mentioned.

Mr. Hodgson never saw a single phenomenon produced by H. P. Blavatsky. He never even heard a "fairy bell" or one of the raps she could easily make in different parts of the room, or, as in one famous case, *inside* the mouth and against the artificial teeth of a skeptic! Nor did he ever see the so-called shrine. In later years, when the S.P.R. investigated Eusapia Paladino, Mrs. Piper, and other noted psychics, they very properly spent months or years in close and detailed observation of their phenomena before venturing to render a verdict. The Psychical Society delegated H. P. Blavatsky's case to a committee which entrusted this responsible task to a single young and self-confident agent, who may have been well-intentioned at first, as she believed, but who was entirely ignorant of occultism, and who only had reports of events that had taken place several years before on which to form a judgment.

The Psychical Researchers overlooked the fact that, if her phenomena were fraudulent, she must have been often assisted by accomplices, and that such confederates must have been, by the nature of the case, the very persons whom she wished to convince of the genuineness of her occult powers. Some of the most important pieces of evidence on this line, which should have been submitted to the S.P.R., were omitted from Hodgson's *Report*. Why? In many places, *his* lack of straightforwardness is apparent when he wants to force a point, as Kingsland in his analysis of the *Report*, and other writers, have demonstrated. For instance, he deliberately suppressed the positive conclusion of his own handwriting expert which stated that "Madame Blavatsky was not the writer of the letters attributed to the Master."

Hodgson even went so far as to charge Dāmodar with being an accomplice, naively disregarding the fact that his chief witness, Mme. Coulomb, made only one attempt – a very feeble one – to inculpate him, seemingly in order to bolster up her reputation with Hodgson. In all her dealings with Dāmodar she treated him as a dupe, not a confederate. One of her charges against H.P.B. was that she was asked to convey a pretended Mahatma letter to Dāmodar "in a miraculous way," in order to deceive him, "the accomplice," according to Hodgson. In one of her letters to H.P.B. she shows that she well knew that the latter's phenomena were not all fraudulent, for she gives details of a phenomenon that took place in the 'shrine' in H.P.B.'s absence. She speaks of her astonishment, and of her belief that it was done by occult means – she calls it "Old Nick"! This letter was written in 1883, months before she got her husband to make trick panels and holes in the walls. General Morgan was present on this occasion and described the phenomenon in great detail in a letter to the press.

Among the witnesses of many other striking phenomena, are found the names of General and Mrs. H. R. Morgan, Mr. A. O. Hume, Colonel and Mrs. Gordon, Mr. and Mrs. A. P. Sinnett, and other Anglo-Indians, as well as of numerous native Indian gentlemen of high standing. Though some if not all of these persons must have conspired with H.P.B. in producing the phenomena if they had been fraudulent, yet neither Hodgson in his *Report* nor Mme. Coulomb ever hinted at such an absurdity. Colonel Olcott, who testified to having seen a large number of the phenomena of H.P.B. and of the Masters, both in America and in India, was categorically exonerated by the Psychical Research Committee from any possible collusion or deception.

In later years, many persons of equal responsibility and irreproachable character such as Countess Wachtmeister, Dr. Hübbe-Schleiden, Countess d'Adhémar, Dr. A. Keightley, Mrs. Besant, and others in Europe, testified to phenomena similar to those that took place in India. Were these confederates? According to this absurd accomplice theory, inevitable unless H. P. Blavatsky was genuine in her claims, the Theosophical Society would be a mutual-deception organization, playing fantastic tricks upon itself!

The conspiracy against H.P.B. had some astonishing features, more than one of which would have thrown the case for her traducers out of court if it had been legally examined. The only witnesses against her, the Coulombs, were admittedly paid cash for their evidence and, according to their own statements, they were accomplices in fraud. More than one hundred other witnesses testified positively to H.P.B.'s ability to produce phenomena. The verdict of guilty was given without the defense having an opportunity of rebuttal or cross-examination. There was no impartial judge or arbitrator to see that justice was done. The adverse decision of the 'inquiry' – really a criminal prosecution – was widely published and discussed six months before the official report was issued, and thus public opinion was in the meantime powerfully influenced against H.P.B. before the defense knew the details of the charges. Richard Hodgson, who enjoyed the privilege of being prosecuting attorney, witness, and, in essentials, judge and jury, was himself not so reliable as his

Committee supposed. William Kingsland and others have shown this in their analyses. For example Charles Johnston, the well-known Orientalist, in his study of the case given at a conference in 1907, mentions a letter produced by Hodgson in which a remark occurs entirely destroying his argument but, as he points out, Hodgson *suppressed that sentence in his Report* (Cf. *Theosophical Quarterly*, V, 1, July 1907).

As already said, this is not the place to discuss the case in detail, but readers who, in the name of common justice, wish to defend the honor of the great theosophist on broad and incontrovertible lines should remember that a wise Teacher of old asked:

> Do men gather grapes of thorns, or figs of thistles? . . . A good tree cannot bring forth evil fruit, neither can a corrupt tree bring forth good fruit. . . . Wherefore by their fruits ye shall know them.
> — *Matt.*, vii, 16–20

Is her life history reconcilable with the character of a self-seeking, disreputable, and ambitious charlatan, as her enemies alleged?

Hardly. Even the worst calumniators admit that she spent long years of self-sacrificing and incessant labor under most trying conditions, including ill health and tropical climates; and that she was beset with endless worries, anxieties, insults, and mortifications from which she could have instantly escaped into peace and comfort by dropping her theosophical leadership. She lived simply and economically, all her spare earnings being devoted to the cause so near her heart. She had given up a comfortable home (always open to her), high social standing, the so-called pleasures of life, and assured fame as a writer — all this for a noble ideal, to help ignorant and suffering humanity.

In the Conclusion of his *Report* (313) even the unimaginative Hodgson wonders "what has induced Madame Blavatsky to live so many laborious days in such a fantastic work of imposture?"

It was impossible, he says, to see her as an egotist seeking notoriety, a religious maniac, or a mercenary adventuress. She never even claimed the rightful credit due for her books, but always said that nearly everything original in them was directly owed to her Masters for whom she was little more than amanuensis. The embarrassed and puzzled young man had to find some explanation, however farfetched, for this strange problem and, like the proverbial drowning man, he grasped at a straw, the discredited charge that H. P. Blavatsky was a Russian spy, and that her theosophical activities were nothing but a plausible make-believe to conceal political intrigue. Hodgson jumped at this easy solution for he had nothing else to present to his employers, although he privately admitted to Colonel Olcott and Mr. Cooper-Oakley that it was absurd. Still he published in his *Report* that "her real object has been the furtherance of Russian interests . . . a supposition which appears best to cover the known incidents in her career." As even Hodgson could find nothing more credible to offer than the preposterous Russian spy yarn, it is no wonder that impartial critics have condemned his entire procedure. For some time the spy slander was widely circulated, and it is even now occasionally resorted to by some ignorant journalist who does not know that today the more intelligent of the carping critics of H. P. Blavatsky have abandoned it as absurd and indefensible.

The Committee of the Psychical Research Society made no proper effort to understand the background of the problem of H.P.B. They ignored the available firsthand evidence regarding her astonishing childhood and youth, so inextricably associated with psychic and occult phenomena and with her claim that she was helped by the Masters who were invisible to others and yet were not "spirits." They ignored her serious studies in Oriental philosophies and her strenuous efforts to revive Sanskrit learning, which were publicly and gratefully recognized by competent scholars. They paid no attention to the fact that the Brahmans, jealous of their secret knowledge, recognized that she possessed many of their guarded teachings which include the laws governing the employment of occult powers. Nor did they consider certain striking teachings on scientific matters by her and her Masters and their chelas, which in all reason should have appealed to serious investigators who really wished to understand the problem before them. By disdainfully ignoring this line of inquiry the S.P.R. missed a great opportunity; for although certain scientific teachings of theosophy were unsuspected in 1885 many of them have since been discovered by scientific research, and others have become promising subjects of intensive investigation.

When Mme. Coulomb's charges that H. P. Blavatsky had fabricated certain letters from the Masters were made, very few such letters were available for consideration, but a large number have been published in late years, making it clear by internal evidence alone that she could not have written them. The difference of style as well as of handwriting between the letters of H.P.B. and her Masters is marked, although there is at times evidence that her mentality colored the phrasing, at least in cases where she was their direct instrument of transmission. Many of the Masters' letters and notes were never seen by her. They contained criticisms of her actions, or even instructions to various people about matters of which they, the Masters, wished her to remain ignorant. They passed through other channels, and in some cases the instructions were quite opposed to her own desires.

In regard to more recent charges in connection with the Masters' letters, C. Jinarājadāsa has done good service in publishing his *Did Madame Blavatsky Forge the Mahatma Letters?* in which he gives photographic copies of letters from various Mahatmas, a study which shows the striking differences between them, and demonstrates the marked individuality of their characters. In presenting these facts, he gives unanswerable evidence that H.P.B. was in some cases thousands of miles away from the places where the letters were written, or received, or both, and that it was physically impossible for her to have written them.

Dr. Eugene R. Corson, the independent writer of *Some Unpublished Letters of Helena Petrovna Blavatsky*, and not a theosophist, says on page 63 of his book:

> When we view to-day, after so many years and after all the actors in the affair are dead, the methods of the English Society for Psychical Research in their attack on H.P.B., we are filled with a moral nausea.

In "A Plea for a Just Understanding," in *The Aryan Path* for May 1931, Theodore Besterman, editor, librarian, and research officer for the Society for Psychical Research, appeals to its members and to theosophists alike to drop the disputed question of H. P. Blavatsky's phenomena, and to concentrate on her writings which, he says, "merit the most serious consideration." He fully recognizes "the unquestionable services she rendered in making the Oriental Scriptures known in the West." Besterman almost repeats the encomium of the lama Kazi Dawa-Samdup (see p. 94).

This is a good sign, for it is a complete reversal of Hodgson's childish sneer that scholars would pay no attention to her Oriental studies. Their intrinsic value has attracted the attention of many serious scholars who are now studying theosophical literature in various centers of learning. She herself predicted that her works would not be recognized by the learned world generally until well on in the twentieth century.

Besterman also says that Hodgson's conclusion was only that of "a plain and uninspired individual" and carries no "final authority." He suggests that the results of recent psychical research would have greatly modified Hodgson's outlook if he had known them in 1884. The Society for Psychical Research, warned by past experiences, now disclaims responsibility for facts, reports, or reasonings published in its *Proceedings*, leaving that with the authors. While Mr. Besterman's position is not too generous in view of the established facts, it must stand until a larger *amende honorable* is made to the world.*

It was hardly possible for such a body as the Committee of the Society for Psychical Research to have understood such a complex being as H. P. Blavatsky. They knew nothing about occultism, occult laws, or the methods of occult teachers, and felt it necessary to be meticulously careful lest their garments should be splashed by any suspicions of being anything but rigidly scientific, according to the conventions

*[Cf. OBITUARY: *The "Hodgson Report" on Madame Blavatsky — 1885–1960* by Adlai E. Waterman, published in 1963, for a detailed refutation of the charges made against H. P. Blavatsky. — ED.]

of the day. Diplomacy, outward coolness, and self-control under petty worries, were not the qualifications for which she was selected as the messenger for the nineteenth century. She had no time to waste upon the unresponsive characters after they had thrown away their opportunities. As W. Q. Judge says, she was so regardless of worldly prudence, that she would brusquely turn away from her friends when they showed signs of coolness toward the movement, or causeless distrust of herself. In this way she made many bitter enemies, who almost necessarily misunderstood her actions when they affected their personal feelings. K.H. said she brought many of her troubles on herself by well-meant indiscretions.

In spite of these handicaps – serious enough, indeed – she had the absolute devotion to the theosophical work and to her Masters, the utter disregard for trials and dangers both open and hidden, and other magnificent qualities of mind and heart which carried her mission to success and which will be more and more recognized as time passes. From an outsider's standpoint, Geoffrey West sums up her character in these few words:

> Her character was compounded of contradiction. In some directions profoundly perceptive, in others she seemed almost wilfully blind. . . . She totally lacked ordinary discretion! Faced by either superior scepticism or open-mouthed gullibility she would 'pull the legs' of her audience mercilessly, quite careless of the charges of fraud she might sometimes thereby invite. She defied convention, and laughed at if she did not ignore the gossip she provoked. Thus she laid herself open at times to the gravest suspicions, and yet, with them all, *one turns from a study of her life with the final impression of a fundamentally honest, a deeply serious and sincere personality, possessed of, at once, courage, will, and purpose.*
>
> – *The Aryan Path*, V, 268, May 1934

14

AFTEREFFECTS OF THE CONSPIRACY

TO H.P.B. it was obvious that positive and immediate defense should be made against *The Christian College Magazine* attack, or the progress of theosophy would be seriously hindered, and so she strongly urged the necessity of taking an action for libel. Colonel Olcott, however, felt that the matter should be submitted to the annual Convention of the Society, shortly to assemble at Adyar (December 1884). A special committee, mostly composed of Hindu lawyers, was appointed to consider the position, and the Convention adopted its decision that there was no chance of justice being obtained in a court of law, because the case would be prejudged on account of the (legally) a priori impossibility of occult phenomena, and because of other technical reasons. H.P.B. was forced to yield to what she called a cowardly and foolish retreat. She would have fought to the last rather than see the forces of darkness gain even a temporary advantage. She felt, and rightly, that, as Dr. E. R. Corson says in his book (p. 66):

> Had this case been tried in court every witness on which Hodgson based his reports [practically the Coulombs alone] could have been discredited by opposing counsel, either on the ground of bad character or incompetency.

But there was another reason against taking legal action which H.P.B. did not perhaps appreciate at first. The experienced Indian lawyers and judges were no doubt right in realizing that evidence in regard to the so-called supernatural would be ruled out of court and so the strongest defense would be unavailable, but they were also aware of another and more serious obstacle. Being Asiatics themselves they knew the intense reluctance the Indian chelas would have in giving evidence which even remotely brought in the sacred names of their Masters. To them anything would be better than the certainty that the Masters would be ridiculed and their names desecrated by the smart attorneys in defense of the Coulomb-Missionary clique. H.P.B. imagined at first that the charge could be confined by her lawyers to the Coulomb forgeries of the incriminating parts of her letters, but the lawyers knew that this was impossible, and she afterwards saw that from their standpoint they were justified. The missionaries were eagerly looking forward to the case because they hoped to place her in an embarrassing position in the witness box.

Writing somewhat later to Mrs. Sinnett, H.P.B. told her that any lawsuit in which occult matters were bandied about, whether the chelas gave evidence or not, would have caused them all unendurable agony. She wrote:

> The Masters being involved in this also, and I, determined to RATHER DIE A THOUSAND DEATHS than pronounce Their names, or answer questions about Them in a Court of law – what can I do? Ah, Mrs. Sinnett, the plotters proved too cunning, too crafty for the T. S. and especially for myself. *She* [Mme. Coulomb] . . . knew well, I *would and could not* defend myself in a Court because of the accusations, of myself and friends, and the whole of my life being so intimately connected with the Mahatmas. . . . I have learned the whole extent and magnitude of the conspiracy *against the belief in the Mahatmas;* it was a question of life or death to the Missions in India, and they

thought that by killing *me* they would kill Theosophy. They very nearly succeeded. —*Blavatsky Letters*, 99–100

No appeal to the law being made by the Society, this failure to act was regarded as a sign of weakness, just as H.P.B. foresaw and struggled to avoid. While the decision may have been justified on grounds of ordinary prudence, who knows what a far-reaching effect might have been made for the future by the tremendous protest against injustice which she could, and surely would, have made before the world, even if the heavens fell! The wisdom of this world is not always the wisest. But even though the decision may have been reasonable, many of those who made it were anything but staunch defenders of her honor. H.P.B. soon found that there was weakness and more than weakness on the part of many of her fair-weather friends. Treachery was soon apparent, and also the cowardly desire on the part of some to repudiate one against whom the world had turned and was trying to destroy. As she wrote to Mr. Sinnett:

> Oh! the poor miserable cowards!! . . . I tell you I suffer more from theosophical *traitors* than from the Coulomb, Patterson [missionary], or even the S.P.R. Had all the Societies held together as one man; had there been unity instead of personal ambitions and passions awakened, the whole world, . . . could not have prevailed against us. Sacrifice *me* I am willing, but do not ruin the Society—love it and the Cause. —Ibid., 114

It was, however, not merely the attack on herself or on the T. S. that caused her so much anguish. It was the failure of such a large part of the Society to live up to its ideals. K.H. writes to Sinnett in regard to the position in 1881:

> You must have understood by this time, my friend, that the centennial attempt made by us to open the eyes of the blind world—has

nearly failed: in India – partially, in Europe – with a few exceptions – absolutely.

— *Mahatma Letters*, 362

In spite of innumerable warnings, too many would-be theosophists directed their attention the wrong way, selfishly looking for psychic powers and purely intellectual information, ignoring and even belittling the true aim of the Masters in starting the "centennial attempt" for the present cycle. To quote a passage in a letter from the Master M., which is most touching in its appeal for understanding:

> How many times had we to repeat, that he who joins the Society with the sole object of coming in contact with us and if not of acquiring at least of assuring himself of the reality of such powers and of our objective existence – was pursuing a mirage? I say again then. It is he alone who has the love of humanity at heart, who is capable of grasping thoroughly the idea of a regenerating practical Brotherhood who is entitled to the possession of our secrets. He alone, such a man – will never misuse his powers, as there will be no fear that he should turn them to selfish ends. A man who places not the good of mankind above his own good is not worthy of becoming our *chela* – he is not worthy of becoming higher in knowledge than his neighbour. If he craves for phenomena let him be satisfied with the pranks of spiritualism.
>
> — Ibid., 252

This growing failure on the part of so many to respond to the call of brotherhood had been preying on H.P.B.'s mind for some years, and the revelation of the weakness and vacillation of some of the prominent members in regard to the Coulomb defense almost broke her heart. The pressure of the whole situation brought on another long and severe illness. Her life was despaired of, and she was saved only by the direct interposition of the Master on a night which was indeed critical for the movement, for if she had chosen to abandon her work and "go Home" we should never have had *The Secret Doctrine*, or her other most important writings. The magnitude of her personal sacrifice for others is hinted at in a letter to Mrs. Sinnett dated July 23, 1885:

> My heart is broken not for what my *true, open* enemies have done – them, I despise; but for the selfishness, the weak-heartedness in my defence, . . . I shall never – nor could I if I would, forget that forever-memorable night during the crisis of my illness, when Master, before exacting from me a certain promise, revealed to me things that He thought I ought to know, before pledging my word to Him for the work He *asked me* (not *ordered* as He had a right to) to do. On that night when Mrs. Oakley and Hartman and everyone *except Bowajee* (D.N.), expected me every minute to breathe my last – I learned all. I was shown *who was* right and who wrong (unwittingly) and who was entirely treacherous; and a general sketch of what I had to expect outlined before me. Ah, I tell you, I *have* learned things on that night – things that stamped themselves for-ever on my Soul; black treachery, assumed friendship for selfish ends, *belief in my guilt*, and yet a *determination to lie in my defence*, since I was a convenient step to rise upon, and what not! Human nature I saw in all its hideousness in that short hour, when I felt one of Master's hands upon *my heart, forbidding it cease beating*, and saw the other calling out *sweet future* before me. With all that, when He had shown me *all, all*, and asked "Are you willing?" – I said "Yes," and thus signed my wretched doom, for *the sake of the few* who *were entitled to His thanks*. . . . Death was so welcome at that hour, rest so needed, so desired; life like the one that stared me in the face, and that is realised now – so miserable; yet how could I say *No* to Him who wanted me to live! But all this is perhaps incomprehensible to you, though I do hope it is not quite so. – *Blavatsky Letters*, 104–5

In the morning following this crisis, H.P.B. awoke from her apparently fatal coma and seemed comparatively well, saying to her doctor, whose amazement at this unexpected recovery was undisguised: "Ah, doctor, you do not believe in our great Masters!"

Disruptive forces were working at headquarters, and the cause of H.P.B.'s greatest suffering, the failure of many influential members to take a courageous stand, was not removed. Her poor-spirited and over-cautious advisers – as they appeared to be, though she must have known that their judgment was largely swayed by some influence more subtle than mere prudence – having overruled her passionate urge to protect the movement by challenging her persecutors in the law courts, insisted that she withdraw from public activities, at least for a while. Let her confine herself to writing until the public was better informed of the unwarrantable nature of the Coulomb charges. She strenuously resisted this retreat in the face of the enemy, knowing the risks if she left her work exposed to the secret as well as to the open forces against which she, as the direct agent of the Masters, had been the "guardian wall." But it was useless; tortured with sickness, worn out by anxieties and pressed by her impatient councillors, she finally submitted to an arrangement which Olcott considered the best. She resigned her official connection with the Society as Corresponding Secretary, entrusted *The Theosophist* to Olcott, and agreed to retire to some quiet place in Europe where she could write and try to regain a measure of health. On March 31, 1885, she bade farewell to India, which she never saw again. She was accompanied by a companion, Miss Flynn, Dr. F. Hartmann, and Babaji, a young Hindu who was striving for chelaship. Although the Master had rescued her from the jaws of death, she was still a very sick woman, and her convalescence was likely to be very slow. Her weakness was so great that she had to be hoisted in a hospital chair to the deck of the vessel on which they sailed, and her physician, who had insisted on a change of climate for her, said it was doubtful if she could live a year.

Shortly before she left, the missionaries, who were eager to force her into the witness box, planned a suit against Major-General Morgan, ostensibly in defense of the Coulombs whom he had openly charged with fraud. He was ready and indeed anxious to defend himself in court, but when the missionaries found that H.P.B. had left India they abandoned the idea and let the Coulombs save their shreds of reputation as best they could.

After she left, Colonel Olcott did his best to arouse the Society in India to renewed efforts. His devotion to the work never failed, though his judgment was sometimes at fault. He continued his laborious tours as before, lecturing and establishing new lodges, and heartening the members by placing the real facts of the Coulomb conspiracy before them. Among his other more or less theosophical activities was the promotion of fraternization among the various Buddhist authorities in Japan, Ceylon, Burma, Siam and Cambodia, on the basis of the fundamental principles of pure Buddhism. His efforts were so highly appreciated that if he had wished – and he was greatly tempted – he could have taken a high position in the Buddhist world, instead of confining his splendid energy chiefly to the theosophical movement.

His theosophical work was conducted under the greatest difficulties, being handicapped by serious dissensions within the managing group, conspiracies to get the control out of his hands, great financial embarrassment, and other anxieties. He learned much about ingratitude and treachery. For a while Olcott was so hard pressed that he says he was "nearly crazy and capable of writing and saying almost anything."

Although H.P.B. was far away in Germany, she did not fail to point out his mistakes in no complimentary manner when writing to him. But he held on and faced his trying problems.

> But when I put the question to myself what I was working for, whether for the praise of men or the gratitude of H.P.B., or that of any other living person, all this despondency drifted away and my mind has never gone back to it. The sense of the paramount obligation of doing my duty, of serving the Masters in the carrying on of their lofty plans – unthanked, unappreciated, misunderstood, calumniated . . . came in to me like the flash of a great light, . . .
>
> – *O.D.L.*, III, 221

He also frankly admits, in regard to the severe discipline he received from H.P.B. at certain times, that –

> No doubt all this heckling was just the discipline I needed, and undoubtedly still need as much as ever, to bring me down to my bearings, but I can't say it was nice. . . . I could have spared three-fourths of the discipline to any other needy neophyte without regret, although, doubtless, it was best for me to have it.
>
> – Ibid., III, 313–14

Writing on November 21, 1889 H.P.B. gave this tribute to Olcott:

> One thing I do know – and my Master and his know it too – he has done his best which is all that any of us can do. I have too many faults of my own (whatever may be his accusers) to sit over him in judgment. To me he has been ever a true friend and defender, and I will not throw him overboard because of his faults.
>
> – *Theos.*, LIII, 622–3, Aug. 1932

The above recognition of the true state of the case should be remembered when false charges are made that H.P.B. treated Olcott with injustice or unnecessary harshness. He was a very strong, determined character, and she was often compelled to handle him without gloves, as the saying goes. He admits that some of the Masters themselves found him quite unmanageable and impossible to work with, saying:

> From time to time one or another Brother [Master] who had been on friendly terms with me . . . has become disgusted with me and left me to others, who kindly took their places. Most of all, I regret, a certain Magyar philosopher, who had begun to give me a course of instruction in occult dynamics, but was repelled by an outbreak of my old earthly nature. —*Hints on Esoteric Theosophy*, I, 78–9

15

T. SUBBA ROW AND BRAHMANISM

A Defense Committee had been established to counteract the bad effect of the Coulomb charges, but a careful *Analysis and Report* drawn up in defense of H. P. Blavatsky, which had been prepared as a substitute for the abandoned lawsuit, was apparently suppressed, and no resolute public protest was made in India. Dāmodar had been called to the Himalayas, and Subba Row had become profoundly disturbed by the dissensions and cabals, as he called them, within the managing council in India after H.P.B.'s departure into exile in Germany.

Further, he had disagreed with H.P.B. about her method of presenting the "principles of man," and the controversy that arose between them was published in *The Theosophist.* Finally, in 1888 Subba Row resigned from the Society. But of course he remained faithful to the principles of theosophy and to his Master till his death in 1890, and he never had the least doubt that H. P. Blavatsky was an occultist and a high chela of Master M. Colonel Olcott writes:

> A dispute – due in a measure to third parties – which widened into a breach, arose between H.P.B. and himself about certain philosophical questions, but to the last he spoke of her, to us and his family, in the old friendly way. – *O. D. L.*, IV, 235

Olcott was a close friend of Subba Row and, with his usual kindly feeling, he used his experience in magnetic healing to relieve Subba Row's suffering during the painful illness which ended his life at the age of thirty-four. The cause of his affliction was unknown. His early death, and the distressing symptoms falling on a young man of blameless life, belong to the class of events which are explained only by the fact that unexpended karma has often to be met before further progress is possible.

In his obituary notice of Subba Row, Colonel Olcott writes:

> . . . T. Subba Row gave no early signs of possessing mystical knowledge: . . . I particularly questioned his mother on this point, and she told me that her son first talked metaphysics after forming a connection with the Founders of the Theosophical Society: . . . It was as though a storehouse of occult experience, long forgotten, had been suddenly opened to him; recollections of his last preceding birth came in upon him: he recognized his Guru, and thenceforward held intercourse with him and other Mahatmas; with some, personally at our Head-quarters, with others elsewhere and by correspondence. He told his mother that H.P.B. was a great Yogi, and that he had seen many strange phenomena in her presence. His stored up knowledge of Sanskrit literature came back to him, and his brother-in-law told me that if you would recite any verse of Gita, Brahma-Sutras or Upanishads, he could at once tell you whence it was taken and in what connection employed. —*Theos.*, XI, 577–8, July 1890

When Hume and Sinnett tried to get information from him about practical methods of producing psychic effects instead of the theoretical knowledge of what he calls "the ancient Brahminical Religion and Esoteric Buddhism" (note the combination!) he became dissatisfied with their attitude. Further complications ensued which can be followed in the Masters' and H. P. Blavatsky's correspondence; and finally, when Hume included him with H.P.B. in Hodgson's ridiculous Russian spy charge, his indignation knew no bounds.

Subba Row was a most conservative and rigid Brahman.

an initiate into the deeper side of the Brahmanical teachings, and he was not only horrified by the vulgar profanation of the Masters' names and all that they stand for in the Orient, but, *as a Brahman*, he strongly disapproved of H.P.B.'s revelation of some of the inner meanings of the Hindu scriptures, hitherto concealed in the secrecy of the temples and utterly unsuspected by outside scholars. In his excitement he must have overlooked the fact that in giving these theosophical teachings to the world she was obeying her (and his) superior officers, when he wrote her:

> "You have been guilty of the most terrible of crimes. You have given out secrets of Occultism – the most sacred and the most hidden. Rather *that you should be sacrificed* than that which was never meant for European minds." – *Blavatsky Letters*, 95–6

She was sacrificed by the persecution and slander which was heaped on her and which had the effect with so many of discrediting her teachings, and therefore of obscuring them in the view of Western scholars. H.P.B. frankly admitted that Subba Row's protest was not unreasonable; she was, however, carrying out her instructions as best she could and she had to take the responsibility of any mistakes she might make. Her position was extremely delicate and of course utterly incomprehensible to the Western mentality, at least at that time. K.H., writing to Sinnett, says that although "most if not all of the Secrets are incommunicable," because the true "illumination *must come from within*," and that it is with the greatest reluctance that the Masters have opened the doors to their secret knowledge a very little way, their action has been called forth by the great development of psychism in the West with all its potential dangers. They felt that by giving certain teachings to the few receptive minds who might be ready they risked a great deal, but it was necessary in order to attract such persons from the psychic lure by showing them glimpses of true occultism. (See page 284 of the *Mahatma Letters.*)

The significant point in regard to H.P.B.'s knowledge and rank in the eyes of those *who were competent to judge* is brought up by this matter, for Subba Row had not the least doubt that she possessed occult power and knowledge and that she was in close touch with the Mahatmas. His complaint was that she was lacking in caution in presenting the teachings – a heinous fault to an initiated Brahman – not that she had invented them, as her enemies said.

At the T. S. Convention in 1885, the Society recognized Subba Row's great learning and ability by establishing a Subba Row Medal in his honor, to be given annually for the best work on Eastern or Western philosophy.

When H. P. Blavatsky's teachings appeared, many learned Brahmans were horrified at the possibility of a Western woman possessing their cherished secrets, and yet Subba Row, Dāmodar, and other high caste Brahmans had to yield to evidence that they knew could not be simulated. Among these was Rai B. Laheri, F.T.S., who passed away in 1936, and who wrote most emphatically about this shortly after her death:

> There is not the least doubt that H.P.B. is a woman of mysterious and wonderful occult powers, . . . now-a-days it is very rare to find out, *i.e.*, to recognise, a powerful Yogi in India, . . . the more so by a woman born of Mlecha tribe [outcaste or foreigner]. That, however, . . . she has succeeded in getting the key of the true Hindu and therefore of the subsequent Buddhistic Secret Philosophy, there can

be no question, . . . Those who really understand anything about the sublime and mysterious philosophy of the Hindus . . . can at once find out what she knows and what she is; it does not require the demonstration of her occult powers to convince such a person. A few words on the real point, nay, only one word and the sign of a particular place, and he knows at once what she is.

. . . Is it not sufficient for the Westerns to know that a proud Brahmin, who knows not how to bend his body before any mortal being in this world, except his superiors in relation or religion, joins his hands like a submissive child before the white *Yogini* of the West? Why so? because she is no longer a Mlecha woman; she has passed that stage; and every Hindu – the purest of the pure amongst the Brahmins – would be proud and delighted to call her Hindu and a mother. . . . I myself certainly do not like the idea of publishing the Secret Philosophy of the East for the information of the people of the West, who have nothing but contempt and hatred for everything called Eastern, and especially Indian; there may be very, very few exceptions to these; but there is one consolation in this; that those books are dead letters for the *Saheb loks* unless fully explained, and H.P.B. is the only person who can explain them in the West. . . . As a Brahmin, I would always object, and I consider it my duty to do so, to the publishing of the secret sublime Truths of my religion and ancestors, especially amongst the people whose food is beef, who drink spirituous liquors, . . . – *Lucifer*, VIII, 309–11, June 1891

It was not unnatural that the proud Brahmans would cherish more passionately than life itself their ancestral knowledge and should have looked with little friendliness upon the theosophical revelations. But in the wider view of the Mahatmas, Brahmanism had degenerated into another of the "religions of pomp and gold" and was reeking with idolatry and other superstitions believed in by the masses, and tacitly if not deliberately encouraged by the exclusive coterie who exploited them. In the famous "Prayag Letter" republished in the *Mahatma Letters*, page 461, the Master M., addressing the Brahmanical Fellows of the Prayag (Allahabad) Lodge, declares in his characteristically trenchant language that if a man wished to come in touch with the Great Lodge he must become a "thorough" theosophist and "do as D. Mavalankar did, – give up entirely caste, his old superstitions and show himself a true reformer." Otherwise "he will remain simply a member of the Society with no hope whatever of ever hearing from us." M. shows that he has no sympathy with exoteric "Orthodox Brahmanism," and that even though the Europeans may have distasteful physical customs in eating and drinking, such things are far more easily corrected than are ingrained and bigoted habits of thought.

The Masters recognized not only the dangers of psychism in the Occident but also the increasing call for true occultism in the West. In line with their policy which, as Tsong-kha-pa stated, was largely intended for the benefit of the Western "barbarians," they had chosen their messenger from the West, one who, in addition to special training, had the understanding and world perspective gained by years of travel and study of human nature.

It cannot be too strongly emphasized that the recognition of that messenger as a genuine occult teacher, *possessing real knowledge*, by a goodly number of high-caste and well-informed Brahmans, deep students of their own philosophy, is one of the strongest proofs of her sincerity and of the significance of her mission. It is also important to remember that her teaching was *far from being welcome* to all the Brahmans, and that there would have been no great regret among many if it could have been quietly suppressed and confined to their exclusive caste. Is it mere coincidence that the Committee of the Adyar Convention which recommended that no legal action be taken against *The Christian College Magazine*, such as she so earnestly desired, was composed of ten Brahmans and only four Europeans? The name of G. N. Chakravarti, at one time professor of mathematics at Muir College, Allahabad (Prayag) occurs in the list, and the same learned professor and lawyer became a notable figure in the circumstances which caused the split in the Society ten years later. According to Mr. Judge, some Brahmans were greatly annoyed at the Master M.'s Prayag Letter, and he says that Chakravarti tried to make him believe it was "a pious fraud by H.P.B."! Colonel Olcott, living in India and surrounded by Brahmans, professed to be shocked at the plain speaking in the letter regarding the Brahman superstitions and bigotry, and suggested that it was a "mediumistic" production by H.P.B. and not genuine. This astonishing and utterly unfounded statement, which Olcott published in *The Theosophist*, XVI, 475–6, April 1895, after H. P. Blavatsky's death, brought forth a magnificent arraignment of Olcott's inglorious fling at his teacher, written by Judge in *The Path*, in which he defends with conclusive logic the authenticity and great importance of the letter. He says:

> Olcott does not like the one in question because he lives in India, and it is too gallingly true. . . . For my part, the message in question testifies to its genuineness by its text, except for those who are hit by it, or those who have the Indian craze and think themselves Brahmans, or those whose self-interest and comfort are against it.
>
> —*The Path*, X, 82, June 1895

16

H. P. BLAVATSKY IN EUROPE

IT IS now necessary to follow H. P. Blavatsky's fortunes in Europe where, by her indomitable will and devotion to duty, and after enduring many more trials, she succeeded in reviving the interest in theosophy. She attracted the attention of a class of intelligent and enthusiastic students who had a far better understanding of the real importance of theosophy to the world than many of the earlier members whose loyalty depended too much upon the gratification of personal, selfish desires for the occult information which they knew H.P.B. alone could give. It was not long before it was possible to give higher teachings, not only intellectual but spiritual and moral, to an audience better qualified to profit by them.

She reached Europe in April 1885, and settled for a while at Torre del Greco, near Naples, where she remained for some months under very depressing conditions, suffering in health and enduring many hardships from lack of money which, during the crisis caused by the Coulomb-Missionary conspiracy, was very scarce. This was one of the most trying periods of her life. Exiled from India, the brilliant theosophical successes of her last visit to Europe little more than a vanished dream, in poverty and isolation, what could the future hold for her? Yet this poor broken-down invalid with the heart of a lion, never lost courage, and never doubted for an instant the wisdom and protection of her Masters, and in no long time she had regained far more than she had lost, except in health and strength. But she still had many trials to undergo, and the young Hindu, Babaji, who accompanied her and Miss Flynn to Italy and did not remain with her long, provided some of the hardest. He was a would-be chela under probation, and in many ways seemed very devoted, but he was an extremist and lacked judgment. The strange story of his conduct in the unfamiliar European conditions can be traced in the *Blavatsky Letters* and in other published correspondence, and it is another outstanding illustration of the extraordinary anxieties from which she was never free.

After the dreary months in Italy she moved to Würzburg in Germany, to be nearer her friends, and for other reasons. She says:

> . . . I must have a warm and dry room, however cold outside, since I never leave my rooms, and here [Italy] healthy people catch cold and rheumatics unless they have palaces. I like Würzburg. It is near Heidleberg and Nürenberg, and all the centres one of the Masters [K.H.] lived in, and it is He who advised my Master to send me there.
>
> —*Blavatsky Letters*, 105

When she reached Würzburg and found accommodation at Ludwig Strasse, No. 6, she was still very poor, and as she was not free to write popular paying articles for the Russian journals she had to endure much privation at first. She writes to Sinnett on August 19, 1885:

> For myself — I am resolved to remain *sub rosa*. I can do far more by remaining in the shadow than by becoming prominent once more in the movement. Let me hide in unknown places and write, write, write, and teach whoever wants to learn. Since Master forced me to live, let me live and die now in relative peace. It is evident He wants me still to work for the T. S. since He does not allow me to make a

contract with Katkoff — one that would put yearly 40,000 francs at least in my pocket — to write exclusively for his journal and paper. . . . for — He says — my time "shall have to be occupied otherwise."
— Ibid., 112

A few words in regard to H. P. Blavatsky's literary distinction is in place here. Her brilliant essays and stories were so greatly in demand in Russia that publishers had been paying her at the same rates as those asked by the famous novelist Turgenev. When *The Secret Doctrine* no longer demanded her entire attention, she was again able to send occasional articles to Russia, and she was then placed on the list of regular contributors to *The Russian Review (Russkoye Obozreniye)*, "a Literary-Political and Scientific Journal." A copy of this magazine for August 1890 was sent by her to America in support of the legal defense made by Judge in rebuttal of the attack made upon her by Dr. Elliott Coues and *The Sun* (New York), which is mentioned in a later chapter. A note written by her and attached to the cover of the magazine contains these words in English:

My well known pseudonym "Radda Bai" (H. P. Blavatsky) published monthly since Feb. 1890 among the names of the best known writers in Russia, and the names of the eminent foreign contributors, prove plainly enough that I am not quite the person having no name in literature, as the *Sun* and Dr. Elliott Coues would represent me in their joint libel. — H. P. BLAVATSKY ("Radda Bai")

The foreign names include among many other notabilities such famous ones as William James, Bret Harte, Eduard von Hartmann, Jules Simon, and Paul Bourget. The same copy of the magazine contains a long and appreciative review article of H. P. Blavatsky's *The Key to Theosophy* by the great Russian philosopher, Professor Vladimir Solovyoff, who was a kind of Russian Herbert Spencer in reputation, though more spiritual in outlook. (He must not be confused with H.P.B.'s false friend, Vsevolod Solovyoff, who slandered her after her death when she could no longer expose his vindictive misunderstandings and misrepresentations.) The eminent reviewer shows great acumen and a profound knowledge of Eastern philosophies, and he immediately recognized the serious importance of his author's presentation of theosophy. He was deeply interested in the revival of the wisdom-teaching of Bodhi or Budhi which H.P.B. makes clear and which he distinguishes from exoteric Buddhism, observing that theosophy, or what he calls "Neo-Budhism," is not "an embroidery upon the doctrine of Gautama." He strongly approves of H.P.B.'s emphasis upon the concept that the *individuality* in man is a pure ray from the universal Principle, refracted through the personal human consciousness. In regard to her revelation of the inner meaning, he points out that it is not found in the best-known systems of Hindu philosophy, although they offer no small number of diverse opinions not suggested by H. P. Blavatsky, who gave the pure wisdom-teaching, Bodhi. An interesting passage, translated from Professor Solovyoff's article on *The Key to Theosophy*, reads:

> It has been said that Theosophy is a paying proposition and that a good deal of money can be made through it. The same opponent also claims that the Tibetan Guides of the Society, Mahātmans and Chelas, have never existed but were invented by H. P. Blavatsky. To the first accusation the author answers by convincing data and figures; as to the second, we ourselves, a disinterested party in the matter, can vouch that it is false. How could H. P. Blavatsky have invented the

Tibetan Brotherhood or the Order of the Chelas, when it is easy to find definite and authentic data regarding the existence and character of this Brotherhood[*] in the book of the French missionary Huc [*Travels in Tartary, Thibet and China*], who visited Tibet in the early forties, i.e., some thirty years before the founding of the Theosophical Society.

However it may be, and having taken due account of all the theoretical and ethical shortcomings of the Theosophical Society, it is evident that this society, whether in its present form or otherwise, and the Neo-Budhist movement reawakened by its efforts, have an important historical role to play in the near future . . . This latest work of H. P. Blavatsky is particularly interesting to us because it presents Buddhism from a new angle, unsuspected heretofore, i.e., as a religious movement without dogmas or creeds and yet with a very definite and unique trend (toward the raising of man to Divine Self-Evolution, and against the belief in any superhuman principle). . . .

The careful use of the words Budhism and Buddhism in Solovyoff's article show his clear understanding of the distinction H. P. Blavatsky made between the ancient wisdom (Budhism) and the exoteric religion called after the Buddha, the enlightened Teacher.

In her darkest hours H.P.B. knew that she had only to return to Russia and devote herself to literature to be assured

---

*H.P.B. writes to Sinnett in January 1887, when the Russian papers were warmly discussing her "powers" etc.:

"A Tibetan who came back with the Prjivolsky expedition (or after it) – 'a plant doctor' they call him as he produces mysterious cures with simples, told Solovioff [not the philosopher quoted in the text, but the would-be chela who turned traitor] and others it appears, that they were all fools and the S.P.R. asses and imbeciles, since all *educated* Tibet and China know of the existence of the 'Brotherhood in the Snowy Range,' I am accused of having invented; and that he, himself, knows several 'Masters' personally."

– *Blavatsky Letters*, 228

of ending her days in ease and comfort, as well as honor. Her sister, Mme. Jelihovsky, earnestly implored her to come home to the family. But that would have meant the desertion of her duty to humanity and the Masters' work, and that was an impossible line of action for H. P. Blavatsky, the chela. Her strength was failing, and she realized that the time was soon coming when she could no longer hold a pen, and *The Secret Doctrine*, the most important work of her life, was hardly begun. So she declined every outside offer and gave her entire time and energy to its completion.

Fortunately, a devoted member came to her rescue in the autumn of 1885 when she was quite alone in Würzburg. This was Countess Constance Wachtmeister, an Englishwoman, widow of a former Swedish ambassador to London. As H.P.B. and the countess lived in close association for a long time, the latter is an excellent and independent witness to the character and daily life of her friend, and to the genuineness of her phenomena, as is shown in a letter to *The Occult Word* (July 1886, Rochester, N. Y.), where the countess says:

> . . . I offered to spend some time with her and do what I could to render her position more comfortable, and to cheer her in her solitude. . . . I had been told a great deal against her, and I can honestly say that I was prejudiced in her disfavor. . . . Having heard the absurd rumors circulating against her, and by which she was accused of practising Black Magic, fraud and deception, I was on my guard, and went to her in a calm and tranquil frame of mind, determined to accept nothing of an occult character and coming from her without sufficient proof; to make myself positive, to keep my eyes open, and to be just and true in my conclusions . . . therefore my frame of mind was bent on investigation, and I was anxious to find out *the truth*.

In her *Reminiscences of H. P. Blavatsky*, the countess gives an intimate picture of the severe routine of her friend's life at this time. She had already begun to write *The Secret Doctrine*, and this work was continued with hardly an interruption from morning till night. It required all the will-power she possessed to do this in her weak state of health. Countess Wachtmeister gives an example of her unconquerable determination. She once found the floor strewn with sheets of paper, and was told:

> "Yes, I have tried twelve times to write this one page correctly, and each time Master says it is wrong. . . . but leave me alone; I will not pause until I have conquered it, even if I have to go on all night."
>
> — *Reminiscences*, 32

The thousand adverse thoughts directed against her from the outside world were a serious handicap and, thoroughly exhausted by the day's labor, she would rest her mind in the evening by arranging the cards in a game of patience or solitaire, and by reading the news from her homeland in the Russian journals.

But it was not long before this comparatively peaceful existence was violently interrupted by the publication of the Hodgson *Report*. This cruel blow, and the resulting confusion among some of the weaker members of the Society, wounded her sensitive nature very deeply, and she was unable to resume her writing for several weeks. It was with difficulty that she was persuaded not to rush off to London and take some rash action which would not have improved matters. The countess finally convinced her that the right course for her was to treat the slander with contempt and to let the theosophists make a dignified and united protest. Countess

Wachtmeister wrote to Sinnett, "If we all *keep true and firm* nothing can really hurt us." H.P.B.'s indignation and agony were not for herself but, as she passionately exclaimed:

> ". . . who will listen to me or read *The Secret Doctrine?* How can I carry on Master's work? O cursed phenomena, which I only produced to please private friends and instruct those around me. What an awful Karma to bear! How shall I live through it? If I die Master's work will be wasted, and the Society will be ruined!"
>
> —Ibid., 26

Indeed, she had a right to be distressed at such a prospect for, as the world knows now, the last few years of her life were by far the most valuable. They were to see the production of her most important work, not only *The Secret Doctrine*, *The Voice of the Silence*, and *The Key to Theosophy*, but the private instructions she prepared for her more qualified pupils.

The clouds gradually lifted, and she returned to her writing with renewed courage and zeal. While the shadow of the Hodgson *Report* was still lying heavily upon her, Sinnett felt that by far the best method of refuting the slanders would be to publish a complete memoir of her life, giving facts which were quite unknown to the world at large. It would thus be seen that she was no charlatan striving for notoriety, but a philanthropist who had given up everything to redeem the world from its own ignorance. After much hesitation, chiefly caused by reluctance to drag her Russian relatives and friends into the glare of publicity, she gave Sinnett permission to publish some information about her early life and adventures, including the extraordinary story of her psychic experiences in childhood, which could be supported by the evidence of thoroughly reliable witnesses.

Sinnett brought out his *Incidents in the Life of Madame Blavatsky* in 1886. This book contains not only the general sketch of the highlights of her life, but a careful analysis of the Coulomb conspiracy, giving the documentary evidence then available in her defense. The book proved an immediate success; the obvious sincerity and common sense displayed by the author in the treatment of much that was startling and unfamiliar at that time attracted a large number of independent and intelligent thinkers to H. P. Blavatsky and her work. The movement spread more widely than ever before in Europe and America, as the end of the second septenary cycle mentioned by the Master approached.

During the months Countess Wachtmeister spent with her teacher in Würzburg she had numerous opportunities to study the strange occult happenings that took place, and she was always on guard against mistaken observation. She writes:

> I have shared her room and been with her morning, noon and night. I have had access to all her boxes and drawers, have read the letters which she received and those which she wrote, . . .
>
> — Ibid., 29

She describes many of the phenomena with care, including some which took place when H.P.B. was asleep. She noticed, just as Olcott and Judge observed in New York when *Isis Unveiled* was being written, that with H.P.B. such phenomena were part of the day's work, so to speak — intended to serve practical purposes and not for display. The countess possessed at times a certain clairvoyant power of her own, and was able to see the Masters or their chelas, more or less clearly, when they telepathically talked with H.P.B. in the māyāvi-rūpa.

Probably the most striking phenomena in connection with this period were the precipitated messages from the Masters, containing instructions for *The Secret Doctrine*, which were found on her desk morning after morning as she needed them as material for her writing. These communications, as well as the interior instruction she constantly received from her teachers, were as matter-of-fact transactions to her as the interchange of notes and questions between an ordinary author and his amanuensis. Others, besides Countess Wachtmeister, testify to the constant receipt of written instructions in a phenomenal way from the Masters by H.P.B., while she was writing her books.

The countess sums up her impressions in a few pages of her *Reminiscences*, from which the following passages are specially informative:

> All who have known and loved H.P.B. have felt what a charm there was about her, how truly kind and loveable she was; at times such a bright childish nature seemed to beam around her, and a spirit of joyous fun would sparkle in her whole countenance, and cause the most winning expression that I have ever seen on a human face. . . . The weak traits in everyone's character were known to her at once, and the extraordinary way in which she would probe them was surprising. . . . But to many of her pupils the process was unpalatable, for it is never pleasant to be brought face to face with one's own weaknesses; and so many turned from her, but those who could stand the test, and remain true to her, would recognise within themselves the inner development which alone leads to Occultism. A truer and more faithful friend one could never have than H.P.B., and I think it the greatest blessing of my life to have lived with her in such close intimacy, . . . —Ibid., 54–5

In the spring of 1886 H.P.B. left Würzburg for Belgium, in order to spend the summer with her sister and niece at

Ostend. She broke the journey at Elberfeld in Germany to see the Gebhard family but, owing to a fall, she had to remain there till August 1886, when she proceeded to Ostend where she stayed till May 1887.

The year 1886 had been one of severe anxieties and strange difficulties. Complications arose in regard to affairs in India, America, France and Germany. The young Hindu who had come from India had caused serious trouble by his erratic conduct, and finally he had to be shipped back to his native land. Fortunately, Countess Wachtmeister, who had gone to her home in Sweden for a while, again became free to resume her devoted care of the increasingly suffering patient – for that is what H.P.B. was until the end of her life, with occasional intervals of partial relief.

But, as the countess said, ill health could not break her spirit, and she fought on to complete her work, no matter how severe were her pains, so long as it was possible. However, it seemed as if even her indomitable will would have to yield at last, for her complication of diseases finally reached another dangerous crisis. In the spring of 1887, while at Ostend, the doctors gave her up, and she sank into unconsciousness. But her work was not completed, and again the Master intervened and she was enabled to use that worn-out body for another four years. Awaking out of what seemed her last sleep, she said:

"Countess, come here. . . . Master has been here; He gave me my choice, that I might die and be free if I would, or I might live and finish *The Secret Doctrine*. He told me how great would be my sufferings and what a terrible time I would have before me in England (for I am to go there); but when I thought of those students to whom I shall be permitted to teach a few things, and of the Theosophical Society in general, to which I have already given my heart's blood, I accepted the sacrifice, and now to make it complete, fetch me some coffee and something to eat, and give me my tobacco box.

— Ibid., 75

When viewed in retrospect, it is hardly too much to say that the situation at the time H.P.B. decided to make the sacrifice of going on to complete her work was a critical turning point for the welfare of humanity. The Adepts had chosen the one available messenger whose special endowments, such as her sympathetic and penetrating knowledge of her fellowmen, her indomitable determination and her occult training, enabled them to write a saving clause of brotherhood in world affairs. This was done in no sentimental way, but by the scientific demonstration that harmony, love and cooperation are fundamental in the structure of the universe, and that departure from such principles is opposed to the course of evolution. The general selfish grasping for material power and possessions if not counteracted would drag every mental, material, and psychic resource into a conflict that would shake modern Western civilization to its foundations — a threat that still looms large on the horizon. The Hindus had failed to make their land a vitalizing center for world enlightenment. Their learned men were traditionally out of touch with even the lower castes of their own people; and there was a complete lack of understanding, even distrust, between them and the Anglo-Indians and Westerners generally. Even the Brahman theosophists, who recognized H. P. Blavatsky as the accredited messenger of their Rishis, in some cases found the situation difficult.

But the Teachers themselves, unknown to the world at large, yet perfectly aware of its existing and its oncoming conditions, knew that the time had come to make a great effort to arouse the inquisitive and self-confident West to think on new lines now that it was beginning to throw off its leading-strings. Three important world cycles coincided at this time, and the most favorable opportunity known for centuries depended upon this impoverished, sick, and suffering European woman, sorely wounded in mind and heart by traitors and secret as well as open enemies. It indeed seemed a forlorn hope, yet, as Victor B. Neuberg says: "the Intelligences that despatched H.P.B. as Messenger to her Age did not err. Her mission has been accomplished. She changed the current of European thought, directing it toward the sun."

As soon as possible she prepared to leave Ostend, and when some of the staunch English members invited her to take up her residence with them in London she gratefully accepted the offer as it was in line with the Master's plan. Qualified helpers, well equipped in every way, were ready to give the assistance she needed to bring out *The Secret Doctrine* and other new literature. The strong revival of interest in theosophy in England provided the opportunity for a great expansion of her work in the West.

Her arrival in England was warmly welcomed by the loyal majority of the English members who recognized her true position as messenger of the Masters, and who did noble service in relieving her from the practical difficulties which heretofore had handicapped her. All that was possible was done to ameliorate her physical sufferings. After a few months' stay at Maycot, Upper Norwood, London, a pleasant though small house was taken at 17 Lansdowne Road, Notting Hill, and a large group of earnest men and women of literary ability and recognized public standing, such as Dr. Archibald

H.P.B. at "Maycot," Upper Norwood, London, 1887

Keightley, Bertram Keightley, E. D. Fawcett, G. R. S. Mead, and others, who had not been affected by the Coulomb slanders, gathered around her. Rather later she was able to write (April 1890):

> . . . it is not solely on account of bad health that I do not return to India. Those who have saved me from death at Adyar, and twice since then, could easily keep me alive there as They do me here. There is a far more serious reason. A line of conduct has been traced for me here, and I have found among the English and Americans what I have so far vainly sought for in India.
>
> In Europe and America, during the last three years, I have met with hundreds of men and women who have the courage to avow their conviction of the real existence of the Masters, and who are working for Theosophy on *Their* lines and under *Their* guidance, given through my humble self.
>
> In India, on the other hand, ever since my departure, the true spirit of devotion to the Masters and the courage to avow it has steadily dwindled away. At Adyar itself, increasing strife and conflict has raged between personalities; . . .
>
> . . . in 1884, Colonel Olcott and myself left for a visit to Europe, . . . It was during that time and Col. Olcott's absence in Burma, that the seeds of all future strifes, and – let me say at once – disintegration of the Theosophical Society, were planted by our enemies. What with the Patterson-Coulomb-Hodgson conspiracy, and the faint-heartedness of the chief Theosophists, that the Society did not then and there collapse should be a sufficient proof of how it was protected.
>
> . . . While in the West, no sooner had I accepted the invitation to come to London, than I found people – the S.P.R. Report and wild suspicions and hypotheses rampant in every direction notwithstanding – to believe in the truth of the great Cause I have struggled for, and in my own *bona fides*. – *Theos.,* XLIII, Jan. 1922

Unfortunately, Sinnett did not share the general enthusiasm, and H.P.B. soon was obliged to take positive steps in order to carry out the Master's plan and to prepare for the new cycle. His equivocal attitude toward her emphasis on the spiritual, and therefore the vital side of theosophy, became conspicuous soon after her arrival. With all his good intentions, he never recognized his error in mistaking a subtle intellectualized form of psychic research for spiritual development, and as he had been such a prominent and influential figure in the work, H.P.B. had to take a very firm position to protect it from his disintegrating influence. More than thirty years after her death, an utterly unreliable book, written in his old age, was published which reveals how little he had understood her real mission. At the outset of his connection with the movement, the Masters had told him in the plainest language – very bluntly at times – "Rather perish the T. S. with both its hapless founders, than that we should permit it to become no better than an academy of magic and a hall of occultism" (*L.M.W.*, I, 10). And "If you cannot be happy without phenomena you will never learn our philosophy" (*Mahatma Letters*, 262). It is to be feared that he never took this counsel to heart.

Sinnett also attempted to inaugurate a policy which was entirely opposed to the strongly expressed wish of the Masters. The Master M. had warned him in plain language that social standing had nothing to do with spiritual development or the real progress of the movement, yet Sinnett quite ignored this advice. In a letter to him written in 1882, long before he returned to England and tried to make the London Lodge an exclusive body which would attract only cultivated persons of "the upper levels of society," as he said, who could attend the meetings in formal dress, etc., the Master spoke very seriously about Sinnett's wrongheaded views on this subject. Illustrating his point, he referred to an excellent man named Bennett, a freethinker who had suffered terribly from religious persecution in America. Bennett came into touch with the movement in India, and was warmly welcomed by Olcott and H.P.B. He was, however, rather a diamond in the rough; his ways were not those of the best society, and Sinnett shrank from contact with him. The Master pointed out that few had a more kind and unselfish heart than Bennett, and that he was spiritually far superior to many of the fine gentlemen of Sinnett's acquaintance. M. said further that if superficial manners were Sinnett's criterion of moral excellence –

> how many adepts or wonder producing *lamas* would pass your muster? This is part of your blindness.
>
> . . . B——— is an honest man and of a sincere heart, besides being one of tremendous moral courage and a martyr to boot. Such our K.H. loves – whereas he would have only scorn for a Chesterfield and a Grandison. . . . See how well K.H. read your character when he would not send the Lahore youth [a rather unkempt Hindu ascetic] to talk with you without a change of dress.
>
> – *Mahatma Letters*, 261

After Sinnett left India he lost touch with the Masters (after many warnings) and weakened in the support of H. P. Blavatsky to such a degree that he was intensely disturbed by her coming to London to upset his plans and policies, as he complained. He declined to participate in her activities, and endeavored to communicate with the Masters through other "intermediaries," mediums as some called them, though the Masters had expressly stated that she was their "direct agent." The situation was somewhat disquieting, and H.P.B. felt that the members as a whole must have the serious responsibilities of their position made clear to them. In the first number of the English *Vahan* she wrote (Dec. 1, 1890):

> We are in the very midst of the Egyptian darkness of *Kali-yuga*, the "Black Age," the first 5,000 years of which, its dreary first cycle, is preparing to close on the world between 1897 and 1898. Unless we succeed in placing the T. S. before this date on the safe side of the spiritual current, it will be swept away irretrievably into the Deep called "Failures," and the cold waves of oblivion will close over its doomed head.

But the Theosophical Society was not destined to perish; it had an inner vitality and support that has kept it alive, similar to that which H.P.B. herself had been able to call upon when the waters of death seemed to be closing over her head. The warning just quoted was not without a saving clause and was apparently one of those rhetorical expressions which she sometimes used to emphasize her meaning, but which must be weighed against equally strong statements to the contrary, in order to discover the truth in the paradox. For example, in contrast to this rather pessimistic outlook, she even more positively declares that the Society has come to stay. For instance, she wrote in 1886:

> the T. S. *cannot be destroyed as a body*. It is not in the power of either Founders or their critics; and neither friend nor enemy can ruin that which is *doomed to exist,* all the blunders of its leaders notwithstanding. That which was generated through and founded by the "High Masters" and under their authority if not their instruction — MUST AND WILL LIVE. Each of us and all will receive his or her *Karma* in it, but the *vehicle* of Theosophy will stand indestructible and undestroyed by the hand of whether man or fiend.
>
> — "The Original Programme," *Theos.*, LII, 581, Aug. 1931

Again, although H. P. Blavatsky said in her letter to the

American Convention in 1891, just before her passing, that "The period which we have now reached in the cycle that will close between 1897–8 is, and will continue to be, one of great conflict and continued strain," etc., yet in the same letter she visioned a great future for the T. S. in the coming century after the crisis was over. After warmly congratulating the American theosophists for their well-considered plans and unremitting labors which were producing such excellent results, she said:

> The English character, difficult to reach, but solid and tenacious when once aroused, adds to our Society a valuable factor, and there are being laid in England strong and firm foundations for the T. S. of the twentieth century.

The following statement by Master M. is even more encouraging:

> You have still to learn that so long as there are three men worthy of our Lord's blessing in the Theosophical Society, it can never be destroyed. —*L.M.W.*, I, 111

W. Q. Judge repudiated the idea that the help of the Masters would be absolutely withdrawn after the end of the first five thousand years of the kali-yuga cycle. He wrote:

> At the end of the twenty-five years the Masters will not send out in such a wide and sweeping volume the force they send during the twenty-five years. But that does not mean they will withdraw. They will leave the ideas to germinate in the minds of the people at large, but never will they take away from those who deserve it the help that is due and given to all. However, many will have gone on further by that time than others, and to those who have thus gone on from altruism and unselfish devotion to the good of the race continual help and guiding will be given. —*The Path,* IX, 238, Nov. 1894

When reading the warning sounded by H.P.B. in *The Vahan*, there comes strongly to mind, in addition to the unremitting opposition of the dark forces to all such work as hers, a most serious crisis which the Society (especially the European and American sections) had to pass through a few years after her death. Not long before that event she wrote an earnest appeal to the members to stand by W. Q. Judge "when the time comes."

But in spite of Sinnett's prestige, his influence rapidly waned after her arrival in London, and was little felt outside of the small body remaining in his London Lodge. The majority of the London members established a new lodge in which H.P.B. could work without hindrance and called it by her name, the Blavatsky Lodge.

Under the new conditions, and supported by an enthusiastic body of workers, she was able to start many new activities, the Blavatsky Lodge being the vital center of inspiration. Some philanthropic work among the London poor was begun, and an anonymous contributor gave H.P.B. one thousand pounds for the establishment of the East London Club for Working Women, a refuge for homeless and friendless factory girls. Her compassionate heart always took pleasure in the relief of suffering, mental or physical. For instance, she writes this touching letter to Mrs. Besant, who was doing some work in the London slums:

I have just read your letter to ———, and my heart is sick for the poor little ones! Look here, I have but 30 s. of *my own* money, of which I can dispose (for, as you know, I am a pauper, and proud of it), but I want you to take them *and not say a word*. This may buy thirty dinners for thirty poor little starving wretches, and I may feel happier for thirty minutes at the thought. Now don't say a word and do it; take them to those unfortunate babes who loved your flowers and felt happy. Forgive your old uncouth friend, *useless* in this world!

Ever yours, . . . H.P.B.

—*Lucifer,* X, 446, Aug. 1892

But H. P. Blavatsky knew well enough that all such 'practical' expressions of brotherhood were only palliatives, and that the truly practical work of theosophy is to set new currents of thought throughout the world from which reforms will inevitably arise, to give men *ideas* which will change their minds and hearts. H.P.B. put the case in a few words in her letter to the American Convention, 1888:

We are the friends of all those who fight against drunkenness, against cruelty to animals, against injustice to women, against corruption in society or in government, although we do not meddle in politics. We are the friends of those who exercise practical charity, who seek to lift a little of the tremendous weight of misery that is crushing down the poor. But, in our quality of Theosophists, we cannot engage in any one of these great works in particular. As individuals we may do so, but as Theosophists we have a larger, more important, and much more difficult work to do. People say that Theosophists should show what is in them, that "the tree is known by its fruit." Let them build dwellings for the poor, it is said, let them open "soup-kitchens" etc. etc., and the world will believe that there is something in Theosophy. . . . The function of Theosophists is to open men's hearts and understandings to charity, justice, and generosity, attributes which belong specifically to the human kingdom and are natural to man when he has developed the qualities of a human being. Theosophy teaches the animal-man to be a human-man; and when people have learnt to think and feel as truly human beings should feel and think, they will act humanely, and works of charity, justice, and generosity will be done spontaneously by all.

To the Aryan Theosophical Society of New York –
with H P B's & H S O's good wishes
London, October 1888.

17

H. P. BLAVATSKY ORGANIZES NEW WORK, EXOTERIC AND ESOTERIC

WITH the rapid increase of the Society in the West, and the new energy pulsing through its channels, it was impossible in the prevailing conditions to avoid difficulties and frictions arising from the clash of undisciplined personalities. Petty ambitions, lack of discrimination between the permanent and the impermanent, and a want of impersonal, kindly consideration for others – the enemies within the household – inevitably brought trouble. When the aspirant strives consciously for self-conquest, the duality of his nature quickly shows itself, because the personal and selfish component, the intellectual-animal, feels that its sway is threatened, and it instantly challenges the spiritual side to mortal combat. The lower nature is so subtle that in order to dominate it will even steal the weapons of the higher and masquerade as an angel of light. Much that seems strange in theosophical history becomes clearer when the interplay of the dual forces in every man is understood.

Only the briefest mention can be made of the local troubles that sprang up in America and Europe to embarrass H.P.B. just as she was starting the most important enterprises in her career – *The Secret Doctrine*, and her esoteric school for more advanced students. In America they were chiefly confined to the disruptive activities of a few who were dissatisfied because they were not immediately brought into communication with the Masters. One of H.P.B.'s most trenchant and instructive articles was called forth by this affair. She explains to these disturbers that they had no grounds for complaint:

> Yet, to those Theosophists, who are displeased with the Society in general, no one has ever made to you any rash promises; least of all, has either the Society or its founders ever offered their "Masters" as a *chromo-premium* to the best behaved. For years every new member has been told that *he was promised nothing*, but had everything to expect only from his own personal merit. The theosophist is left free and untrammeled in his actions. . . . no harm in trying elsewhere; unless, indeed one has offered himself and is decided to win the Masters' favors. To such especially, I now address myself and ask: Have you fulfilled *your* obligations and pledges? Have you, . . . *led the life* requisite, and the conditions required from one who becomes a candidate? Let him who feels in his heart and conscience that he has, — . . . let him, I say, rise and *protest*. . . . I am afraid my invitation will remain unanswered. — *The Path*, I, 260–1, Dec. 1886

Further trouble was caused by a prominent member, a well-known scientist, Dr. Elliott Coues, who was dabbling in psychism and claimed to be an occultist. By devious ways he tried to oust W. Q. Judge from the leadership of the American work, in order to take his place. Eventually H.P.B. was forced to take a firm stand against his claims and he then began a campaign of slander against her, which was so outrageous that it became necessary to expel him from the Society. When relieved of these handicaps, the work in America advanced rapidly under Judge's guidance.

In Europe the difficulties were mainly centered in France, and the president left India in August 1888, for a European tour with, he feared, the prospect of considerable trouble awaiting him. Much of the trouble, however, was of his own making. He was particularly agitated by what he called

H. P. Blavatsky's "obstinacy," and her defiance of the presidential authority in regard to her action in the adjustment of a crisis in Paris. In order to prevent disruption and grave injury to the work she had, without consulting Olcott, dissolved the staff of the "Isis" Branch and its bylaws, and authorized new bylaws to be prepared. The matter was urgent, and she had very good reasons to act rapidly.

This French affair, however, seemed to Olcott only a symptom of the possibility of further "autocratic" action by H.P.B. which he was likely to disapprove, and he left India in no pleasant state of mind. He says he was ready for "a pitched battle" with her for her "unconstitutional" tendencies which seemed to him to threaten the sacrosanct rules and regulations to which he attached so much importance.

He understood that H.P.B. was about to start a private group of the more earnest students who were ready for deeper teachings, in fact that she was pressing the esoteric aspect of the work which the Master had said might be revived at the opening of another septenary cycle.

During Olcott's voyage to Europe on the S.S. *Shannon*, he was gloomily brooding over H.P.B.'s intentions; and really serious consequences might have followed if Master K.H. had not immediately interfered. Such a course was rarely adopted except in emergencies.

When the ship was crossing the Mediterranean, about a day's run from Brindisi, K.H., who had noticed Olcott's disturbed state of mind, precipitated a long letter of kindly reproof and advice in his cabin as an immediate corrective. This letter is very important for several reasons. It showed that, according to the Masters, the final authority in matters affecting the welfare of the movement lay in the hands of their "direct agent," H. P. Blavatsky. Olcott was quite alone on this voyage, and had no one to consult in his difficulties. The letter reads, in part:*

Misunderstandings have grown up between fellows both in London and Paris which imperil the interests of the movement. You will be told that the chief originator of most, if not all, of these disturbances is H.P.B. This is not so; though her presence in England has, of course, a share in them. But the largest share rests with others, whose serene unconsciousness of their own defects is very marked and much to be blamed. One of the most valuable effects of Upasika's [H. P. Blavatsky's] mission is that it drives men to self-study and destroys in them blind servility for persons. Observe your own case, for example. But your revolt, good friend, against her "infallibility" — as

*Colonel Olcott gives a brief extract from this letter in his *Old Diary Leaves*, III, 91, and by a singular oversight refers it to the year 1884, during the Sinnett-Kingsford disturbances in London, instead of to the proper date, August 1888, when he was on his way, aboard the *Shannon*, to attend to the French difficulty. (See *Theos.*, Suppl., Oct. 1888, xvii.) Discriminating readers of *O. D. L.*, IV, ch. iv, which deals with H. P. Blavatsky's handling of the French affair, who have regretted his ungoverned remarks about her, such as "language violent, passion raging," "to rule or ruin," a "mad person," etc., will observe that if he had published the full text of the Master's severe though kindly admonition, it would have destroyed the force of Olcott's emotional outburst against H.P.B. on which he wasted so much space.

Old Diary Leaves is far from reliable where the author's prejudices — and, perhaps, his self-importance as president, of which he was not entirely free — were aroused. This is still more evident when he discusses, from a purely ex parte standpoint, charges which were brought against W. Q. Judge at a later date. If he had known certain facts that have come to light since he wrote his book, he might have taken a different stand, and certainly would never have made many of his accusations against Judge, which can only be accounted for by ignorance of the truth.

Writing in 1896, in his *Historical Retrospect* pamphlet (page 15), he makes a casual reference to the "letter phenomenally given me on board my steamer," but this time he gives the correct date, 1888.

you once thought it — has gone too far, and you have been unjust to her, for which, I am sorry to say, you will have to suffer hereafter, along with others. Just now, on deck, your thoughts about her were dark and sinful, and so I find the moment a fitting one to put you on your guard.

. . . Her fidelity to our work being constant, and her sufferings having come upon her thro' it, neither I nor either of my Brother Associates will desert or supplant her. As I once before remarked, *ingratitude* is not among our vices. With yourself our relations are direct, . . . That they are so rare is your own fault as I told you in my last. To help you in your present perplexity: H.P.B. has next to no concern with administrative details, and should be kept clear of them, so far as her strong nature can be controlled. But this *you must tell to all: — with occult matters she has everything to do.* We have *not* abandoned her. She is *not* given over to chelas. She is *our direct agent.* I warn you against permitting your suspicions and resentment against "her many follies" to bias your intuitive loyalty to her. In the adjustment of this European business, you will have two things to consider — the external and administrative, and the internal and psychical. Keep the former under your control and that of your most prudent associates, jointly; *leave the latter to her.* You are left to devise the practical details with your usual ingenuity. Only be careful, I say, to discriminate when some emergent interference of hers in practical affairs is referred to you on appeal, between that which is merely exoteric in origin and effects, and that which beginning on the practical tends to beget consequences on the spiritual plane. As to the former you are the best judge, as to the latter, she.

— *L.M.W.*, I, 52–3

It is a pity that Richard Hodgson and the members of the S.P.R. whom he so sadly led astray had given that ill-advised *Report* to the world before this letter to Olcott came to light. The conditions under which it was received — when Olcott was alone on the high seas and far away from H. P. Blavatsky or any other chela or theosophist, and its immediate relation to Olcott's "dark and sinful thoughts," as well as the subject matter, unwelcome to him – would have given the deniers of the Mahatmas a problem they could not solve on the theory of trickery by H.P.B. or the Hindu chelas! Owing to the conditions of this phenomenon, which was accepted naturally by Olcott as nothing unusual, it is one of the most conclusive testimonies to the existence of the Masters and their close connection with the Society.

When Colonel Olcott reached London he found H.P.B. working hard at one of her "emergent interferences" spoken of by the Master K.H. In this case it was the organization of the esoteric work so distasteful to him. In regard to the French "interference," he fortunately found that she had kept within her rights as cofounder of the T. S. The formation of the new lodge in Paris had only been provisional, and he recognized that it was necessitated by the crisis then prevailing. He accepted the situation, and all was well for the time being (Cf. *Lucifer*, III, 145, Oct. 1888).

Her esoteric activity was, however, another matter, and but for the warning he had received on the *Shannon* a serious rift might have occurred. Even so, when Olcott found that W. Q. Judge was wholeheartedly supporting her plans, his friendly relations with the third cofounder were impaired, with unfortunate results after the death of H. P. Blavatsky. He loyally tried to suppress his irritation and he says that he even helped a little in her preparations, but his disapprobation was revealed in a letter he wrote to Judge in 1893, when trouble was brewing:

The E.S. and especially the I.G., Svastika and other rings within rings I consider a danger and a possible source of great wrong and evil. . . . So long as the E.S. does not work against the Constn. of the T. S. I shall not oppose it, but when it does then I fight.

. . . I should be sorry to have either of you [Mrs. Besant or W. Q. Judge] P.T. S. [President of the T. S.] if that devilish Cabinet Noir of yours is to be kept up . . . — *Theos.*, LIII, 608, Aug. 1932

It has been said that Colonel Olcott never became a member of the Esoteric School, though as president he was called upon to charter it as a section. Sinnett did not apply for membership, apparently being more interested in the psycho-intellectual researches he mistook for occultism.*

After the French troubles were disposed of, at least temporarily, Colonel Olcott made a successful lecturing tour in Europe and then returned to India where he found new difficulties. These were chiefly brought about by the policy of Richard Harte, the temporary editor of *The Theosophist*, who was pushing notions entirely opposed to H.P.B.'s intentions. He was minimizing her authority and bitterly criticizing her proposals for the esoteric work. He held the mistaken belief that the T. S. should make its principal appeal to ordinary mundane intelligence, and he showed animus toward W. Q. Judge, who was strongly supporting H.P.B.'s line of action. He talked loudly about "loyalty to Adyar,"

*[It should be added here that neither Olcott nor Judge ever signed the pledge of the E.S., they having already pledged themselves to Masters' work in the early New York period ("By Master's Direction," W. Q. J., Nov. 3, 1894). Although as "President in Council" Olcott had issued an order announcing the formation of the Esoteric Section (*Lucifer*, III, 176, Oct. 1888), and a year later, on December 25, H.P.B. had appointed him her "confidential agent and sole official representative of the Esoteric Section for Asiatic countries" (Ibid., V, 437, Jan. 1890), Olcott withdrew more and more from association with its activities, whereas Judge identified completely with the Esoteric effort. — Ed.]

meaning subservience to whatever was given out from the head office, regardless of H.P.B.'s wishes. He even asserted that she was conspiring, with the support of the Americans and most of the Europeans, against the authority of "Adyar"!

It was necessary for the true leader of the movement to deal firmly with this extraordinary situation, and one of her letters to Harte paints in vivid colors this example of the internal troubles which were everlastingly harassing her. No wonder she said that her worst enemies were those of her own household. In this letter of sharp reproof, dated London, September 12, 1889, a notable passage occurs which should be borne in mind in view of subsequent events, the more so as H.P.B. tells Harte that Olcott is beside her as she writes and will read the letter before it is sent:

> The Theosophist my dear sir, belongs to myself and Olcott only. . . . I will not permit Judge to be lowered or humiliated in it. Judge is one of the Founders and a man who has ever been true to the Masters. . . . And *Judge will be the president of the T. S. after our death* or the T. S. will die with us. —*Forum*, V, 133, Jan. 1934

In addition to the general attitude prevailing at Adyar against herself, there were indications that even Olcott was weakening under pressure and abandoning the "original programme" in favor of turning the T. S. into nothing more than a philosophic and philanthropic movement. To her clearer vision, and by her knowledge of the Masters' wishes, all this spelled a possible worldly success but a complete occult failure and abandonment of the unique work for which the Society had been established. The transgression went so far in India that she had to threaten the controlling party there with strong action, finally publishing an uncompromising manifesto under the title "A Puzzle from Adyar" which contained the following:

It is pure nonsense to say that "H.P.B. . . . is loyal to the Theosophical Society and *to Adyar*" (!?). H.P.B. *is loyal to death to the Theosophical* CAUSE, *and those great Teachers whose philosophy can alone bind the whole of Humanity into one Brotherhood*. . . . Let it break away from the original lines and show disloyalty in its policy to the CAUSE and the original programme of the Society, and H.P.B. calling the T. S. *disloyal*, will shake it off like dust from her feet.

. . . Let the new Exoteric Theosophical Society headed by Mr. Harte, play at red tape if the President lets them and let the General Council expel me for "disloyalty," if again, Colonel Olcott should be so blind as to fail to see where the "true friend" and his duty lie. Only unless they hasten to do so, at the first sign of *their* disloyalty to the CAUSE – it is I who will have resigned my office of Corresponding Secretary [which she had resumed by invitation] for life and left the Society. This will not prevent me from remaining at the head of those – who will follow me. – *Lucifer*, IV, 507–9, Aug. 1889

She had no fear that such action would destroy *theosophy*. But Olcott, far away in India, was becoming more and more out of touch with the fast-moving current of events in London as well as on the Continent. He did not understand why H.P.B. took certain measures. Finally, the active lodges in Britain and Europe appealed to H. P. Blavatsky to form a new section with herself as president (*Lucifer*, VI, 428, July 1890). At about this time she wrote to Olcott:

"If, recognizing the utmost necessity of the step, you submit to the inexorable evolution of things, nothing will be changed. Adyar and Europe will remain allies, and, *to all appearance*, the latter will seem to be subject to the former. If you do not ratify it – well, then there will be two Theosophical Societies, the old Indian and the new European, *entirely independent of each other*." – *O. D. L.*, IV, 55

He came to an understanding with her at last, for his heart was true, though it was not easy for him to yield. Master M. had told him in the early days in New York that "a mysterious tie . . . which could not be broken, however strained it might be at times," had drawn him and his colleague together (ibid., I, 380). As he himself says, he knew that:

> She was the Teacher, I the pupil; she the misunderstood and insulted messenger of the Great Ones, I the practical brain to plan, the right hand to work out the practical details. — Ibid., IV, 21

A society entirely under his control would not, however, have been at all what the Masters wanted, for his judgment was not always sound — unselfishly active and well-meaning though he was. The Society was intended as a channel through which the Light from the Lodge might reach mankind in spiritual currents which must be generated by the earnest efforts of each member to *live* the ideals of theosophy. Success in the eyes of the world, such as rapid increase in membership, new buildings, great libraries, a big literary output, are very well in their place, but the real success is not so sensational. H. P. Blavatsky's *Voice of the Silence*, which was written "for the Few," shows how the *individual* can prepare himself to spread the noble theosophical ideals of life and duty in the world by the living power of example. Members of an association united in such endeavor are not like a congregation listening to comfortable platitudes or praying for self-benefits. Shocks which might destroy the latter are not permanently harmful to a theosophical organization whose members know they must work out their own salvation. Such shocks also act as the "Great Sifter" when drastic action may be necessary. Several severe crises have occurred in theosophical history and, as we have seen in the Coulomb conspiracy, such prunings may not be looked upon with entire disfavor.

Around 1888, K.H. told H.P.B. with regret that—

> the Society has liberated itself from our grasp and influence and we have let it go—we make no unwilling slaves. He [Olcott] says he has saved it? He saved its body, but he allowed through fear its soul to escape; it is now a soulless corpse, a machine run so far well enough, but which will fall to pieces when he is gone. Out of the three objects the second alone is attended to [*], but it is no longer either a brotherhood, nor a body over the face of which broods the spirit from beyond the Great Range. His kindness and love of peace are great and truly Gautamic in their spirit; but he has misapplied that kindness. —*L.M.W.*, II, 68–9

Exaggerated claims have been made that Colonel Olcott was indispensable to the existence of the Society. This is unquestionably true in regard to the early years when the work was struggling for recognition, and it is a fact that the Masters chose him, although, as they say, "He was far from being the best, but (as Mr. Hume speaks in H.P.B.'s case)—he was the best one available" (*Mahatma Letters*, 263). Olcott himself did not feel he was indispensable, for in 1885 he offered to resign, saying with true impersonality: ". . . I have ever from the first been convinced that an abler and better man than myself ought to fill the post of chief executive in so vast an organization as ours," and that someone else should have the "chance to display his abilities" (*O. D. L.*, III, 329, 328).

In 1890 he repeated his offer, and in January 1892, he

*In 1888 the second object was: "To promote the study of Aryan and other Eastern literatures, religions, and sciences."

actually did resign in favor of W. Q. Judge, the vice-president, and his withdrawal would have been accepted by the majority of the Society but for the action of Judge himself, who learned that the Masters wished Colonel Olcott to retain his office.

It took all H.P.B.'s strength to restore the movement to its rightful path, and it was in that work that she had the unwavering help of W. Q. Judge who, as she said, had been a part of herself for aeons.

The Master's hint that the intellectual aspect of theosophy was being overstressed at the expense of the spiritual, as previously quoted, showed that something more had to be done to prepare the members for the esoteric work that was in prospect or the main purpose of the movement would fail. The output of literature dealing with spiritual development and the training for chelaship must be increased. Some inspiring articles had already appeared, such as H. P. Blavatsky's magnificent appeal, "Chelas and Lay Chelas" (*Theos.*, July 1883, Suppl., 10–11), her first great call to intuitive aspirants. But more were needed. This had been followed by a remarkable letter from 109 Hindu students, many of them theosophists, defining the sublime exploit of chelaship as understood in India, the tests and the experiences that face him who would "become victor and trample under foot every temptation, to show himself worthy of taking his rank among the gods of true science" (Ibid., Aug. 1883, Suppl., 2).

Within a few years, W. Q. Judge in America was able to establish his magazine *The Path*, whose title indicated its esoteric basis. H.P.B. soon was enabled to pay a high tribute to its spiritual authority. In 1887, she started *Lucifer*, "the combative Manas" (intellect) as she characterized it, in which she could speak directly to her students without hindrance from Adyar. Its early numbers contained her extremely valuable and timely studies on "Practical Occultism," and "Occultism versus the Occult Arts" (April and May 1888). Her letter to the American Convention in 1888 was another stirring appeal to learn and spread abroad the teachings of theosophy so much needed in this sorrowful world; for, as she said: "the essence of Theosophy is the perfect harmonizing of the divine with the human in man, the adjustment of his god-like qualities and aspirations, and their sway over the terrestrial or animal passions in him."

The first volume of *The Path* (1886–7) contained "A Hindu Chela's Diary," a record of great value and unusual interest to aspirants, as it shows how naturally and unassumingly the chela life can be lived while fulfilling all the normal duties of everyday life. The Chela's Diary is in part a paraphrase of the two letters by Dāmodar mentioned on p. 100. The real names of the persons mentioned under pseudonyms in the Diary are given in the letters. Other instructive articles on the meaning of chelaship as a spiritual discipline for workers for humanity by H. P. Blavatsky and W. Q. Judge followed in subsequent volumes of *The Path* as well as in *Lucifer*.

There remains, however, a widespread misunderstanding in the West in regard to the meaning of chelaship – the system of self-discipline and unselfish work for others which ultimately attracts the attention of a Master and leads in time to his direct guidance. Glittering promises of psychic and other rewards, which mislead the unwary, are worlds apart from the noble ideals of chelaship. Serious students will find in H.P.B.'s *Voice of the Silence*, in Judge's *Letters That Have*

Helped Me, and elsewhere, clear and unalloyed directions regarding the first steps on the Path.

When the first seven years of the T. S. were closing in 1882, the Masters told Sinnett that unless matters improved they would not be able to continue their open activities on behalf of the T. S. but would subside "out of public view like a vapour into the ocean" until the opening of another septenary cycle when, "if circumstances should be more auspicious, another attempt might be made, under the same or another direction" (*Mahatma Letters*, 264). The cause seems in part, if not entirely, to have consisted in the failure to arouse the true chela spirit which, in an esoteric section, could make possible the revival of the old Mystery schools that had been closed in the West for some sixteen centuries.

In the New York days an effort had been made to conduct the Society in a semi-esoteric way, with signs and passwords, and in 1878 grades or degrees to mark the stages of proficiency attained in self-control and enlightenment were instituted. This, however, did not last long. As mentioned, another attempt to place the Society on an esoteric basis was made at Benares, on December 17, 1879, under the plenary powers granted to the president by the Council in New York on August 27, 1878 (as quoted on p. 79).

The Council at Benares officially decided to divide the Society into three sections – the Masters; the more advanced Fellows; and the Probationers. Although the new regulations were adopted by a Convention of the Society in February 1880 at Bombay, little or nothing more was heard of the three degrees.

In India, at a somewhat later date, efforts were made to establish a special private body of students who might receive instructions from the Masters through Subba Row and Dāmodar, but the utter lack of harmony and understanding of the true purpose of the theosophical movement prevented anything satisfactory being done at that time. When Sinnett returned to London further efforts were made by the London Lodge to receive private teachings but the conditions were not encouraging. Rather later, Miss Francesca Arundale, a devoted member of the London Lodge who evidently understood the only basis upon which such a group can succeed, appealed to H.P.B. to organize one for a few of the more earnest members in England. She wrote, in part:

> we the undersigned members of the London Lodge, being convinced that no spiritual education is possible without absolute and sympathetic union between fellow students, desire to form an inner group.
>
> . . . to establish a bond of true brotherly union of such a nature as to realise those conditions, which we are convinced are unattainable in the London Lodge as it is constituted. —*L.M.W.*, I, 25–6

This Inner Group in its special work was to be entirely independent of the London Lodge. H.P.B. approved the application, and Masters M. and K.H. countersigned and annotated it with some warnings.* Judging by some casual references in H.P.B.'s letters, little or nothing came of the effort, but it probably encouraged her to proceed quickly with the establishment of esoteric work on a permanent basis. She regarded the T. S. not so much as just a "philanthropic organization" per se, however effectual, but as a recruiting camp for training individuals who would carry on the work for humanity into the future.

*[Cf. *H. P. Blavatsky: Collected Writings*, VI, 252–4, for facsimile of above document, written in the summer of 1884. —Ed.]

In 1887, W. Q. Judge voiced a strong demand on the part of a number of aspiring members in America for more advanced teaching and guidance, and H.P.B. responded quickly. The psychological moment came in April 1888, a little before the opening of the third septenary period of the Theosophical Society, when she took the first step to prepare the Society for the coming change by publicly and officially declaring the high estimate in which W. Q. Judge was held by the Masters and herself. Although she could not then announce it openly, he was destined to be her direct representative in the esoteric work in America and the only channel of communication between the American and Himalayan thought.

In a special message to W. Q. Judge read to the American Convention in 1888, she used the following strong expressions of confidence:

> It is to you chiefly, if not entirely, that the Theosophical Society owes its existence in 1888. Let me then thank you for it, . . . from the bottom of my heart, which beats only for the cause you represent so well and serve so faithfully. I ask you also to remember that, on this important occasion, my voice is but the feeble echo of other more sacred voices, and the transmitter of the approval of Those whose presence is alive in more than one true Theosophical heart, and lives, as I know, pre-eminently in yours.

It is not surprising, then, that she called him to London to help in drawing up the Rules, etc., of what was first called "The Esoteric Section of the Theosophical Society," and that she placed him, the "chela of thirteen years standing," the one who, "of all Chelas, suffers most and demands, or even expects, the least," as her fully trusted representative and head of the Esoteric Section in America.

Owing to the many misconceptions that have been cir-

William Q. Judge

culated about W. Q. Judge, and to the fact that his importance in the theosophical movement is so great and his writings so valuable, it is necessary that H. P. Blavatsky's high opinion of him and her absolute trust in his honor, ability, and impersonal devotion to the "Great Cause of Human Perfection," as he called the theosophical movement, should be given in her own words. This appreciation increased, if possible, until the last day of her life. She writes:

London Oct. 23, 1889

He or she, who believes that under any circumstances whatever, provocations, gossips, slander or anything devised by the enemy H.P.B. will ever dream even of going against W. Q. J. – does not know H P B – even if he or she *does* know H. P. Blavatsky, or *thinks* he knows her.

The idea is absurd and preposterous. . . . H.P.B. would give . . . the whole esoteric brood in the U.S.A. for one W.Q.J. *who is part of herself since several æons. . . .*

The Esoteric Section and its life in the U.S.A. depends on W. Q.J. remaining its agent & what he is now. The day W. Q. J. resigns, H.P.B. will be virtually dead for the Americans.

W. Q.J. is the *Antaskarana* [connecting link] between the two *Manas*(es) the American thought & the Indian – or rather the trans-Himalayan Esoteric Knowledge.

DIXI H.P.B.∴

PS. W. Q.J. had better show, & impress *this* on the mind *of all those whom it may concern.* H.P.B.

– *Forum,* III, 192–3, June 1932

In the above she makes a distinction between "H.P.B." the high occultist and "H. P. Blavatsky" the Russian woman, *the outer personality* with its marked idiosyncrasies, of which the Masters speak very plainly in their letters to Sinnett. She half-humorously indicated this distinction, of which no one was more aware than herself, in the words she wrote in her own copy of *The Voice of the Silence:* "H.P.B. to H. P. Blavatsky with *no* kind regards."

To quote further from her tributes to Judge:

> If, knowing that William Q. Judge is the only man in the Eastern and Esoteric School in whom I have confidence enough not to have extracted from him a pledge . . . He has to be defended whether he will or not. He has much to endure.
>
> . . . Take my place in America now [in the Esoteric School], and, after I am gone, at Adyar. If you have no more personal ambition than I have . . . and I know you have not – only combativeness – then this will be no more sacrifice for you than it was for me to have Colonel Olcott for my president. – *Forum,* I, 3–4, May 1930

Other evidences of her high estimation of W. Q. Judge are available, and of her desire that he should ultimately become president of the T. S. as well as head of the Esoteric School.

The Esoteric School was a strictly private group, although certain *Preliminary Memoranda* written by H.P.B. have been published. These give an outline of the lofty ideals and aims of the E.S., as well as her reasons for starting it. A few passages may be quoted:

> The Theosophical Society has just entered upon the fourteenth year of its existence [in 1888], and if it has accomplished great, one may almost say stupendous, results on the exoteric and utilitarian plane, it has proved a dead failure on all those points which rank foremost among the objects of its original establishment. Thus, as a "Universal Brotherhood," or even as a fraternity, one among many, it has descended to the level of all those Societies whose pretensions are great, but whose names are simply masks, – nay, even SHAMS. . . .
>
> The object of this Section, then, is to help the future growth of the Theosophical Society as a whole in the true direction, by pro-

moting brotherly union at least among the few. . . . and now it must be saved from future dangers by the united aim, brotherly feeling, and constant exertions of the members of this Esoteric Section. . . .

The Esoteric Section is thus "set apart" for the salvation of the whole Society, and its course from its first steps will be an arduous and uphill work for its members, though a great reward lies behind the many obstacles once they are overcome. . . . in this degree, the student – save in exceptional cases – will not be taught how to produce physical phenomena, nor will any magical powers be allowed to develop in him; . . .

Each person will receive in the way of enlightenment and assistance, just as much as he or she deserves and no more; . . . The apparent favour shown to some, and their consequent apparent advancement, will be due to the work they do, to the best of their power, in the cause of Universal Brotherhood and the elevation of the Race.

– *First Preliminary Memorandum*, 1888

The Esoteric Section was not concerned with the outer forms of the Theosophical Society, nor was it compelled to observe neutrality in matters of belief which, in the Theosophical Society, is a constitutional provision and an essential to its method of work in the world. The Esoteric Section was devoted to the study of and individual training in theosophy in the full sense of the word – divine wisdom. As such, the E.S. was not an official part of the T. S., though it drew its membership from the Society. Shortly before she died, H.P.B. changed its name to "The Eastern School of Theosophy."

A few passages from a letter by H. P. Blavatsky dated December 1, 1888, about the time she started the Esoteric School, throw a strong light upon its true significance:

The Esoteric Section is to be a School for earnest Theosophists who would learn more (than they can from published works) of the true Esoteric tenets. . . . There is no room for despotism or ruling in it; no money to pay or make; no glory for me, but a series of misconceptions, slanders, suspicions, and ingratitude in almost an immediate future: but if out of the . . . Theosophists who have already pledged themselves I can place on the right and true path half a dozen or so, I will die happy. Many are called, few are chosen. Unless they comply with the lines you speak of, traced originally by the Masters, they *cannot* succeed. I can only show the way to those whose eyes are open to the truth, whose souls are full of altruism, charity, and love for the whole creation, and who think of themselves *last*. — *The Path*, VII, 121, July 1892

In regard to the revival of the ancient wisdom in the West, in which H. P. Blavatsky took the first effective steps, she writes:

But if the voice of the MYSTERIES has become silent for many ages in the West, if Eleusis, Memphis, Antium, Delphi, and Crèsa have long ago been made the tombs of a Science once as colossal in the West as it is yet in the East, there are successors now being prepared for them. We are in 1887 and the nineteenth century is close to its death. The twentieth century has strange developments in store for humanity, and may even be the last of its name.
— "The Esoteric Character of the Gospels," *Lucifer*, I, 310, Dec. 1887

18

REVIVAL OF THE WORK IN AMERICA

BEFORE considering the last remaining years of H. P. Blavatsky's life, the progress of the Society in America must be reviewed.

While India and Europe were passing their stage of growing pains, little could be done in America owing to the lack of available leadership. William Q. Judge, with all his fiery energy and devotion to theosophy, not only had to struggle desperately to earn a living for his wife and child, but he was constantly being called away on legal business to distant places, including the Latin American countries. For several years his poverty prevented him from giving much time or energy to theosophical work, and he suffered severe hardships, sometimes hardly knowing where to find the price of a meal. He would walk miles to save carfare in order to pay the postage on letters to inquirers. Yet his trust and enthusiasm never failed, and although at times the shadows were heavy he never despaired.

After the arrival of the "Delegation" to India in 1879, Judge kept up a regular correspondence with Olcott, Dāmodar and a few others. For many months, however, H.P.B. ignored him. She did not answer his letters and left him to find his own way by his own efforts. At first he suffered deeply from being apparently neglected by his friend and teacher; but he soon realized that "this great loneliness" was a part of the training of a chela, and a real, though stern, tribute to his inner spiritual resources. H.P.B. knew exactly what she was doing; and several years later she confided her knowledge of his real inner status to him. Writing in 1886, she says:

> The trouble with you is *that you do not know the great change* that came to pass in you a few years ago. Others have occasionally their *astrals* changed & replaced by those of Adepts (as of Elementaries) & they influence the *outer*, and the *higher* man. With you, it is the NIRMANAKAYA[*] not the "astral" that blended with your astral.
>
> – *Forum*, III, 253, Aug. 1932

After H. P. Blavatsky and Colonel Olcott went to India, the small group at New York – probably never more than forty, mostly spiritualists – were not able to do much. General Doubleday, the acting president, although devoted and sincere, himself said he was conscious of his own ignorance and inexperience. C. C. Massey, then a very active member, had gone to England. Much delay and anxiety was caused by the difficulty in getting a proper form of initiatory ritual from India, without which new members could not be accepted. Judge wrote for it many times, and Olcott admits that he was largely to blame for the suspension of activities. He writes:

> It must be said, in justice to Mr. Judge, General Doubleday, and their associates in the original Theosophical Society, whom we left in charge on leaving for India, that the suspended animation was for two or three years mainly due to my own fault. There had been some

Nirmānakāya is the Sanskrit name for a highly advanced Adept who has evolved beyond the need of a physical body, and while living on the plane of being next superior to the physical one, yet remains closely in contact with mankind in order to help by continually instilling thoughts of spiritual and moral beauty into the hearts of men.

talk of converting the Society into a high Masonic degree, and the project had been favourably viewed by some influential Masons.

– *O. D. L.*, I, 142

He says he expected to draft an appropriate form of ritual on his arrival in India, but this was prevented by the pressure of theosophical work which soon became much greater than he expected and, after Judge and General Doubleday had made vain appeals for something to be done, the idea was abandoned. Olcott says: "But by this time Judge had gone abroad, and the others did nothing." The time finally came when conditions permitted a revival of theosophy in America, and a ritual of a kind was introduced in at least one lodge.

In 1882, the first American branch was started in Rochester, N. Y., and it began to work with such energy that, within two years, it was able to establish a well-written theosophical magazine, *The Occult Word*. *The Theosophist* (IV, Nov. 1882, Suppl. 2) published a note about the general conditions which is historically interesting:

Professor A. L. Rawson, LL.D., F.T.S., as delegated representative of Major General A. Doubleday, Acting President of the (New York) Theosophical Society, organized at Rochester, N. Y., on the 27th of July, the local branch for which a charter had been duly issued from the Bombay Head-quarters. A new form of ritual for initiations was used for the first time on this occasion.

From the above it is seen that the headquarters in India was regarded by the Society in New York as the rightful office for the issue of new charters.

The Rochester Lodge was quickly followed by another in St. Louis, and on December 4, 1883, the historic Aryan Theosophical Lodge was formed out of the original New York Society, William Q. Judge being made president. After a few years, the Aryan became the throbbing heart of the American work, and many of the activities initiated there were adopted by the lodges throughout the world. At its first meeting a Hindu of distinguished appearance, but whose name is not recorded, was introduced by General Doubleday and, after saying that the time had come for active work, read a passage from the *Mahābhārata*, and then retired after presenting a copy of the *Bhagavad-Gītā* to the General.

Olcott, in reviewing this revival of theosophy, said that America

> was almost a graveyard of Theosophy when Mr. Judge felt what you may call the "divine afflatus" to devote himself to the work and to pick up the loose threads we had left scattered there and carry it on. The result shows what one man can do who is altogether devoted to his cause.
>
> —*First Annual Convention of the T. S. in Europe*, London, July 1891, p. 49

When W. Q. Judge returned from his brief but important visit to Adyar, India, his financial position improved so greatly that he was able to give far more time and energy to the work. An energetic body of helpers was soon attracted to this strong, able, quiet man, and many new lodges were started.

In W. Q. Judge's report to the American Section in 1888, page 7, he said that, at his suggestion, in 1884 Colonel Olcott in London,

> under his powers as President, constituted the American Board of Control which was to supersede the Presidency of General Doubleday, . . .
>
> But in 1885, on my return from India, I found that the importance of the Society had so increased that a radical change was demanded . . .

In accordance with my request, Madame Blavatsky suggested to the Board of Control to form the American Section, and Col. Olcott presented the matter to the General Council in India, . . .

The American Section was formed in 1886 with Judge as general secretary, and when he gave the above report it contained twenty-two lodges, while more were in process of formation.

The American Section soon became so prosperous under the great organizing ability of W. Q. Judge that it was able not only to initiate various new activities, but to give much needed support in money and other ways to the Society in general and especially to the Indian Section.

In April 1886, before this satisfactory condition was reached, Mr. Judge boldly started his magazine, *The Path*. Though the funds were low and suitable writers were very scarce, he saw the necessity of an American magazine in which the new era of thought and aspiration could be represented. Fortunately for all later students, the paucity of qualified contributors compelled Judge to write a large proportion of its contents under various pseudonyms, such as American Mystic, Eusebio Urban, Rodriguez Undiano, Hadji Erinn, and especially William Brehon. (Brehon meant a *judge* in ancient Ireland.) His series *Letters That Have Helped Me* (1888–1889) has been reprinted in book form, and continues to be invaluable to students who are starting on the path in search of themselves. His clear exposition of matters of practical mysticism, free from psychism, and the high spiritual quality of *The Path*, quickly attracted attention.

With the increasing demand for more theosophical information on the problems of life, *The Theosophical Forum*, chiefly consisting of answers to questions, was started, and in 1891 conditions warranted the engagement of qualified Hindu scholars to translate Sanskrit and other manuscripts. A large number of valuable pamphlets were published by the Oriental Department. W. Q. Judge's clear and concise handbook *The Ocean of Theosophy*, which has been the means of introducing theosophy to innumerable inquirers, appeared in 1893, and has never been equaled in its own line.

Information, unavailable until recently, has thrown a vivid and hitherto unsuspected light upon Judge's psychological development, and it adds greatly to the estimation in which he should be held. After his first seven or eight years in the T. S. a definite change took place in him. He showed a marked and rapid increase in power and knowledge toward the end of that period, and began to stand out as a natural leader of men. He was quickly recognized by the members as the one who had the capacity to organize successfully the spreading of the theosophical movement in America. H. P. Blavatsky relied on him more and more as her "only friend" in a very deep sense. This development is seen in his writings. His contributions in the early volumes of *The Theosophist*, though few in number, are practical and interesting; but they are very different from those which flowed in abundance from his pen when he started his *Path* in 1886. When H. P. Blavatsky started her magazine *Lucifer* in 1887, in order to have a freer opportunity to speak to the members than she could get in *The Theosophist* after leaving India, it seems to have been suggested that *The Path* might cease publication. Blazing with indignation, she promptly wrote to Judge:

If I thought *for one moment* that *Lucifer* will "rub out" *Path* I would never consent to be the editor. But listen, then, my good old friend. Once that the Masters have proclaimed your *Path* the

> *best*, the most *theosophical* of all theosophical publications, surely it is not to allow it to be rubbed out. . . . One is the fighting, combative Manas; the other (*Path*) is pure Buddhi. . . . *Lucifer* will be Theosophy militant and *Path* the shining light, the Star of Peace. . . . No, sir, the *Path* is too well, too *theosophically* edited for me to interfere.
> — *Irish Theosophist*, III, 156, June 1895

The remarkable advance in power and spiritual illumination on the part of Judge was no ordinary development. H.P.B. explained the secret cause to Judge himself when she told him, as noted earlier, that the Nirmānakāya, a high spiritual Adept, had mystically blended with his astral, although he did not know it till then. The enlightening of a trained personality by a higher spiritual consciousness is fully recognized in Eastern occultism. Judge himself, a chela for many preceding lives, had consciously incarnated in childhood into a chosen body, which, *as W. Q. Judge*, required the training and self-discipline partially obtained through struggles for a livelihood and through certain domestic difficulties. When the time arrived for his own work as teacher, inspiration came from the inner realms from which the nirmānakāyas help humanity.

In the meantime an important work had been going on in Ireland, in which Judge was greatly interested. In April 1886, theosophical activity began by the establishment of the Dublin Lodge, and the work of this remarkable group of original thinkers soon began to produce far-reaching effects in the world at large. Judge kept up an active correspondence with the members, and attended the lodge whenever he visited his native country.

The facts of the important literary work initiated by this lodge should be known to all theosophists and kept in mind, both as a tribute to William Q. Judge, and as an example of the real standing of the theosophical movement as shown by its power to inspire new achievements in the thought-life of the world. It is regrettable that only the briefest reference can be made to the unique work of the Dublin Lodge in starting the new current of research into, and appreciation of, the greatness of the Heroic Age in ancient Ireland, with its theosophical mythology and other spiritual factors so long obscured by misrepresentation and suppression. It was through this lodge, indirectly from H. P. Blavatsky and more directly through W. Q. Judge, that this revolution in thought was initiated, and the broad-minded and liberal Irish Literary Revival became a cultural power which has enriched the modern world with the forgotten treasures of Celtic antiquity.

In 1892, the group of brilliant young writers and other enthusiastic workers (including Fred. J. Dick, his wife, and Robert E. Coates, who in later years helped to build up the center at Point Loma) forming the Dublin Lodge, started a small magazine under the greatest financial and other difficulties. The high standard and unusual character of the articles and poems in *The Irish Theosophist* soon attracted wide attention, and the little periodical very quickly took a distinguished place in contemporary literature. Two challenging articles by George W. Russell (Æ) on "Priest and Hero" and "The Hero in Man" struck the keynote of the new liberating movement. It was in this journal that his poems, unique for their mystical insight and spiritual beauty, first found an appropriate setting and obtained public recognition. Russell, afterwards so famous as poet and essayist, never failed to give credit to H. P. Blavatsky and W. Q.

To the "Dublin Lodge"
of the T. S.

HAPPY NEW YEAR 1891.
&
CEAD MILLE FAILTHE
[A Hundred Thousand Welcomes]

S novim godom, s novim schastyem.
[Wishing you a New Year with New Happiness.]

FROM YOUR SERVANT
H P B.

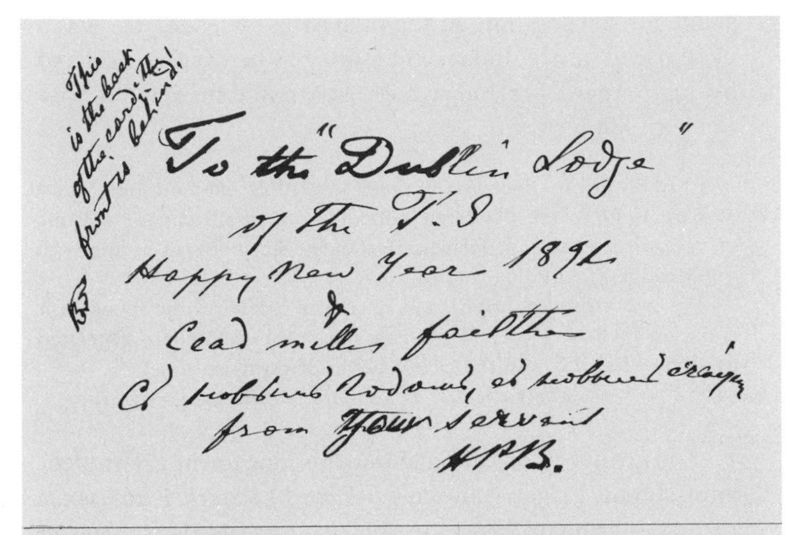

New Year Card drawn by H. P. Blavatsky
with greetings in English, Gaelic, and Russian

Judge for starting him on the path of knowledge. He was a close friend of Mr. Judge, and as long as he lived he declared his high regard for Judge both as a noble man and a wise teacher. He writes:

> I had no private doctrine: nothing but H.P.B. eked out, for beginners by W. Q. J.; the Bhagavad Gita; Upanishads; Patanjali; and one or two other classics. I did what I could to keep always in line with the Message of H.P.B., . . .
>
> My own writing is trivial, and whatever merit is to be found in it is due to its having been written in a spiritual atmosphere generated by study of H.P.B. and the sacred books of the East.
>
> — *The Canadian Theosophist*, XVI, 163-4, Aug. 1935

For further information about this movement the student must consult Ernest A. Boyd's *Ireland's Literary Renaissance* (1916), a standard work, in which he treats the subject at length. The following is quoted from that book:

> The study of mysticism was the common factor which brought together the younger writers, W. B. Yeats, Charles Johnston [the accomplished Sanskritist who married H. P. Blavatsky's niece], . . . Charles Weekes and George W. Russell (A.E.), to mention only some of the names which have since come into prominence in Irish literature. By an irony of history, the late Professor Dowden seems to have given the impulse to the Theosophical Movement in Dublin. . . . It was at Dowden's house that W. B. Yeats heard the discussion of A. P. Sinnett's *Esoteric Buddhism* and *The Occult World* which induced him to read these two books, and to recommend them to his school-friend, Charles Johnston. . . .
>
> Johnston's interest did not stop at reading and commentary. He went to London to meet Mr. Sinnett, through whom he became acquainted with various people of prominence in theosophical circles, and finally he returned to Dublin as a Fellow of the Theosophical Society. It was not long before he obtained recruits, who in time

became the Charter-members of the Dublin Lodge of the Theosophical Society. This Lodge . . . was as vital a factor in the evolution of Anglo-Irish literature as the publication of Standish O'Grady's *History of Ireland,* the two events being complementary to any complete understanding of the literature of the Revival. The Theosophical Movement provided a literary, artistic and intellectual centre from which radiated influences whose effect was felt even by those who did not belong to it. . . . It was an intellectual melting-pot from which the true and solid elements of nationality emerged strengthened, while the dross was lost. . . . Depth without narrowness was their reward for building upon a human, rather than upon a political, foundation. . . .

It would, of course, be rash to assert that the newcomers would not have written but for that Movement, but there can be no doubt of its having helped many to find themselves, and of its having given a definite mould and impulse to their work. George Russell (A.E.), . . . Charles Weekes, and Charles Johnston [and others] were the specific contribution of the Theosophical Movement to the Revival. As writers, editors and publishers they are directly and indirectly responsible for a considerable part of the best work in Anglo-Irish literature. . . . pp. 213–17

The Theosophical Movement in Dublin not only gave us a great poet in A.E., but also our only essayist, . . . — p. 239

The year 1886 also saw the first mention of a new activity, the work for children, which developed into Lotus-Circles or Theosophical Sunday-Schools and the Junior Theosophical Clubs. In a letter dated May 28, 1886,* W. Q. Judge writes advising the establishment of weekly meetings where the children of theosophists can be taught reincarnation and karma. The children of today, he said, will be the men and women of tomorrow, and by teaching them the elements of

*[Cf. *Practical Occultism: From the Private Letters of William Q. Judge,* 28. — ED.]

the laws of being in ways adapted to their growing intelligence, especially the divinity of their real nature, a new generation will arise fitted to take great responsibilities in the redemption of humanity.

The first effective work for the children, of which definite record is available, began in California at Orange in 1888 and rather later in San Francisco. This purely theosophical work must not be confused with the numerous Sanskrit schools for young people already established in India under H.P.B.'s direct inspiration and help.

A rapid development was taking place in California in 1886, and H.P.B. watched it with great interest. About that time she sent two pictures of the Masters to the Pacific Coast Committee in token of her prevision that California would take an important part in the spread of theosophy.

Mention was previously made of troubles that arose from Dr. Coues' ambition to become leader. Enraged by his expulsion and anxious for revenge, in 1890 he wrote one of the most scandalous attacks ever made on H.P.B., Colonel Olcott, and Judge, which was published in full in the New York *Sun*. This produced a most dignified reply from H.P.B. in which she said that as one of the slanders – an attack on her moral character – brought into disrepute the name of a dead man, an old family friend, the Prince Emil Wittgenstein, she could not remain silent. She had therefore taken an action against the New York *Sun* and Dr. Coues for libel for, as she said, if this rich and powerful newspaper could prove only one of the dastardly charges made in this article her character would be ruined and the Society disrupted. The onus was on the publishers to prove her guilty by the production of facts, not by claiming a verdict on false evidence, innuendo, or hearsay, as was attempted in the Hodgson-Coulomb travesty of justice.

In spite of every effort to press the case by her counsel, it was a long time before it came into court, and early in 1891 the attorneys for *The Sun* admitted that they could not prove the charge on which the suit depended – immorality – and asked Judge Beach of the Supreme Court of New York to be allowed to retain a mass of irrelevant matter. The Judge refused, as this was only meant to prejudice the jury. This decision was a substantial victory, and the only question seemed to be the amount of damages to be assessed. Before the judgment was given, however, H. P. Blavatsky passed away, and her death automatically terminated the suit.

But the matter was not closed. *The Sun* decided to make further inquiries on its own account, and finding that it had been entirely misled and victimized by Dr. Coues, made a most honorable retraction and apology and, as the best method of restitution, published a long article by W. Q. Judge, "The Esoteric She," outlining the truth about H. P. Blavatsky and exposing the slanders. Judge comments on this voluntary action in *The Path* (VII, 249, Nov. 1892):

> As many newspaper men since have said, it is as complete as anything of the kind that was ever published. And in view of the fact that no suit by H.P.B. was then pending, it reflects credit on the paper in this age when newspapers in general never retract except when forced by law or loss of money. Thus ends this libel.

19

THE CLOSING YEARS OF H. P. BLAVATSKY'S LIFE

PUTTING aside the evidence of the earlier years of H. P. Blavatsky's theosophical career, the last five years of her life, of which the most intimate knowledge is on record, is indeed a convincing refutation of the charges by which sensational writers, ex-F.T.S., and others, have tried, and still occasionally try, to belittle her character. Every moment of her days after leaving Würzburg was a physical misery, yet this heroic and extraordinary being toiled incessantly for the accomplishment of her greatest literary achievements, *The Secret Doctrine*, *The Voice of the Silence*, and *The Key to Theosophy*, which were written in the last few years of her life.

In addition to this labor, H.P.B. took an active part in the editorial work for *Lucifer*, and contributed long articles to that and other theosophical journals. The Blavatsky Lodge was given special instruction, and much time was required for her private teaching in the Esoteric School.

Rather less than two years before H.P.B. passed away, Mrs. Annie Besant, the well-known reformer and philanthropist, who afterwards became a prominent figure in theosophical history, joined the Society. This was largely the result of a thorough study of *The Secret Doctrine*, which she made when asked by the famous journalist, W. T. Stead, to review it for his *Review of Reviews*. But before H.P.B. would accept her as a Fellow of the Society she insisted upon her reading the *Report* of the Society for Psychical

Research prepared by Richard Hodgson. Her keen mind at once saw its unfairness and other outstanding faults, and she quickly became an ardent defender of H. P. Blavatsky and helped her in every way possible until the death of the great theosophist. All the tremendous energy Mrs. Besant had devoted to the help of humanity through her work for Free-thought and social reforms, her brilliant oratory and her forceful literary style, were directed toward theosophical activities. She was appointed president of the Blavatsky Lodge and co-editor of *Lucifer*.

In July 1890, H.P.B. and her household moved from Lansdowne Road to a much larger and more suitable house, 19 Avenue Road, Regent's Park, which then became the European headquarters. A large hall was built in the garden, effectively decorated with symbolic paintings by a devoted member, R. W. Machell. This artist afterwards resided at the Point Loma headquarters where his peculiar genius again found expression, especially in woodcarving and decorative work of unusual and original character. In addition to this large hall a small room with a blue glass dome was built near H.P.B.'s workroom, in which she gave instruction to her most advanced pupils. Later, when the house was pulled down, the glass and other parts were taken to Point Loma.

Ever since H.P.B. established the British Section in 1888 in order to obtain more freedom for her Esoteric and other plans, considerable opposition had smoldered not only at Adyar, but among a few in England. A. P. Sinnett went his own way, and persisted in his efforts to have independent communication with the Masters through clairvoyants. Yet they had definitely stated that H.P.B. was their only direct agent of communication.

European T. S. Headquarters
19 Avenue Road, London

At last, after two more years, she found it necessary to act vigorously in protest against the crippling, if not indeed the destruction, of her crucially important Esoteric work. She therefore took stronger measures than had hitherto been possible and, in response to constant appeals by members to be relieved from unnecessary interferences from Adyar, she united the European members more closely to her by establishing a European Section with herself as president. What was almost a declaration of independence from Adyar was announced in *Lucifer* (VI, 428, July 1890):

NOTICE

In obedience to the almost unanimous voice of the Fellows of the Theosophical Society in Europe, I, H. P. Blavatsky, the originator and Co-Founder of the Theosophical Society, accept the duty of exercising the Presidential authority for the whole of Europe; and in virtue of this authority I declare that the Headquarters of the Theosophical Society in London, where I reside, will in future be the Headquarters for the transaction of all official business of the Theosophical Society in Europe.

H. P. BLAVATSKY

Colonel Olcott, of course, remained president of the Society as a whole, but this new departure on the part of H.P.B. was anything but agreeable to him, though he made the best of it, for his misplaced irritation at what he called "Blavatsky worship" was not shared by the great majority of the European and American membership. In an excellent article, published in *Lucifer* at the time when H. P. Blavatsky was dangerously ill and did not see it, Mrs. Besant voiced an eloquent protest against the subversive actions of certain members in this connection. The following extract explains the situation:

Engraving by George L. Cower, F.T.S.

T. S. Headquarters, Adyar, Madras, 1887
with new Library at right, opened December 28, 1886

(1) Either she [H.P.B.] *is a messenger from the Masters, or else she is a fraud. . . .*

(2) In either case the Theosophical Society would have had no existence without her. . . .

(3) If she is a fraud, she is a woman of wonderful ability and learning, giving all the credit of these to some persons who do not exist. . . .

(4) If H.P.B. is a true messenger, opposition to her is opposition to the Masters, she being their only channel to the Western World. . . .

(5) If there are no Masters, the Theosophical Society is an absurdity, and there is no use in keeping it up.

– *Lucifer*, VII, 278–9, Dec. 1890

There is little to say about the last months of the messenger's life. She never gave up working except when her increasing weakness made it impossible. She gradually withdrew more into herself and, as Judge says, was obviously preparing for the great change. Yet she sat writing, writing, an almost uninterrupted stream of invaluable teachings and brilliant comments on the life around her. Her last article, "My Books," was hardly finished when she was seized with an attack of influenza which rapidly proved fatal. Worn out by heavy suffering, years of sickness, incessant toil; misunderstood and maligned by a prejudiced and uncomprehending world, and only partially appreciated by the majority of her friends, she passed away peacefully in her favorite armchair on May 8, 1891, at 19 Avenue Road, London. So went "Home," her duty done for that incarnation, one of those Servants of Humanity "whose strong hands hold back the awful cloud" and who "remain unselfish to the endless end." Her body was cremated and the ashes were divided between Adyar, New York, and London, the three main centers from which her activities had radiated light and hope upon a beclouded world.

An independent writer already cited, Victor B. Neuberg, sums up the magnificent accomplishment of this greatly misunderstood woman with right appreciation:

> The obscurantist children of the Dark did their damnedest to "dowse" the Lucifer of their age. By reason of a long and complicated miracle they failed. The long and complicated miracle was H.P.B.'s charmed life.
>
> Today the highest and clearest thought-atmosphere is enhued by the incalculably potent tinge brought to the western mind by H.P.B. and her circle.
>
> . . . we may find scores of societies, groups, cults, periodicals; all influenced, consciously, by the heritage of idea – the agelong wisdom – that H.P.B. restored to the West. The White Group that is said to hold the destinies of Europe in its "gift" chose the most improbable instrument conceivable because it was to prove the most efficient. . . . and the Intelligences that despatched H.P.B. as Messenger to her Age did not err. Her mission has been accomplished. She changed the current of European thought, directing it toward the sun.
>
> . . . But the very existence of the Path was forgotten in Europe until H.P.B. re-discovered it for herself, and announced her re-discovery to the West. – *The Aryan Path,* V, 277–8, May 1934

20

HER BOOKS

THE woman known as H. P. Blavatsky, the Masters' messenger of the nineteenth century, a wondrous Being in her essential Self, yet incarnate in a personality which was paradoxical in many ways, is a profoundly interesting study; but even she is of less importance than the message that is contained in her writings.

The order in which her books and articles appeared cannot be called accidental; a plan is plainly visible. *Isis Unveiled* came first, and it brought the idea that man is a far greater being than he dares to believe, and that he has marvelous powers and knowledge locked up within him of a nature hitherto unsuspected by Western psychologists. The existence of Adepts, living men who have evolved forth their latent powers, was made known to a skeptical generation; moreover, it was stated that *every* man could rise to godlike heights by his own efforts. This book also treated of the darker side of nature and humanity, and gave warning of the dangers and pitfalls in the evolutionary journey to the heights. It contained a very sketchy outline of the general principles of technical theosophy, leaving them to be worked out later.

Soon after the work was started in India, H. P. Blavatsky established *The Theosophist* magazine in which appeared more advanced teachings by herself and others, and the Oriental point of view was clearly stated by native scholars. *The Theosophist* was widely read by both Eastern and Western students and it formed that link of common understanding between them which makes for universal brotherhood.

In 1888 the time came for the appearance of her most important work, *The Secret Doctrine*, in which the philosophical and scientific teachings about the evolution of man and the universe were stated far more fully than in *Isis Unveiled.* Modern and ancient religions, sciences, and philosophies were analyzed and the ancient wisdom was traced and drawn forth from the tangle of confused presentations which have come down to us from antiquity.

The author intended *The Secret Doctrine* to be a far larger and more important work than *Isis Unveiled.* But even so, as she said, only

> the outline of a few fundamental truths from the Secret Doctrine of the Archaic ages is now permitted to see the light, after long millenniums of the most profound silence and secrecy. . . .
>
> One turn of the key, and no more, was given in "Isis." Much more is explained in these volumes.
>
> . . . the Secret Doctrine . . . contains all that can be given out to the world in this century [the nineteenth].
>
> — *S.D.*, I, xxii, xxxviii

According to H.P.B., the MS. of the first three volumes was ready early in 1888, and in the preface to the first volume she says: "The third volume is entirely ready; the fourth almost so." Dr. Archibald Keightley, a reliable theosophist, who had worked hard in preparing the MS. for the press, said:

> The third volume of "The Secret Doctrine" is in manuscript ready to be given to the printers. It will consist mainly of a series of sketches of the great occultists of all ages, and is a most wonderful and fascinating work. The fourth volume, which is to be largely

hints on the subject of practical occultism, has been outlined, but not yet written.

—*Theos.*, X, 597, July 1889

The third volume, however ("ready to be given to the printers"), was never published by H. P. Blavatsky, and the so-called third volume, published not long after her death, is a collection of leftover matter, or unfinished articles, found in her desk. Nothing at all is known of the "outline" of the fourth volume. In connection with the mystery of the disappearance of the third volume many contradictory statements have been made. The data and a full analysis are published in Dr. H. N. Stokes' *O. E. Library Critic.*

One of the most striking features of the Masters' teachings which she gave in *The Secret Doctrine* and elsewhere, and which are found in *The Mahatma Letters to A. P. Sinnett*, is the definite exposition of discoveries in natural sciences and, to a lesser degree, in archaeology, unsuspected when she wrote but now fully accepted. The subject is amply treated in theosophical literature. In several places H.P.B. spoke of the critical conditions at the end of the cycle terminating shortly before the close of the nineteenth century, and she specially mentions the year 1897 as a period of great significance. One of these references is particularly important and cannot be omitted, as it so fully supports her claim that she was in touch with sources of information inaccessible to scientists. In *The Secret Doctrine* (I, 612), she writes in regard to the mysteries of nature known to the Adepts and preserved in trust for future humanity:

Yet it is all there, and one by one facts and processes in Nature's workshops are permitted to find their way into the exact Sciences, while mysterious help is given to rare individuals in unravelling its arcana. It is at the close of great Cycles, in connection with racial development, that such events generally take place. We are at the very close of the cycle of 5,000 years of the present Aryan Kaliyuga; and between this time [1887–8] and 1897 there will be a large rent made in the Veil of Nature, and materialistic science will receive a death-blow.

Sir William Crookes, the famous chemist, was one of the "rare individuals" who received help from the Adepts.

H. P. Blavatsky passed away in 1891, but her prevision was confirmed to the very letter, although she did not live to know the new discoveries that led up to the great rent in nature's veil of which she speaks. Numerous scientific writers have pointed out that the year 1897 was the turning point of the new era of thought. Dr. W. C. D. Dampier-Whetham, F.R.S., in his authoritative *History of Science* makes much of this, as the reader will find on pp. 328, 383, 470, etc. He shows that the new physics became inevitable after Röntgen's announcement of the X-ray in 1895, and upon the amazing discovery of the divisibility of the atom – of subatomic particles or electrons.*

---

*In regard to the subatomic particles composing the atom which today have become little if anything more tangible than disembodied ghosts, wave-forms, notice what was taught in *The Secret Doctrine* long before science discovered the electron:

"The atom *is* elastic, *ergo,* the atom is divisible, and must consist of particles, or of *sub*-atoms. And these *sub*-atoms? They are either non-elastic, and in such case they represent no dynamic importance, or, they are *elastic* also; and in that case, they, too, are subject to divisibility. And thus *ad infinitum.* But infinite divisibility of atoms resolves matter into simple centres of force, *i.e.*, precludes the possibility of conceiving matter as an *objective* substance. . . .

"Accept the explanations and teachings of Occultism, and, the blind inertia of physical Science being replaced by the *intelligent active* Powers behind the veil of matter, motion and inertia become subservient to those Powers. It is on the doctrine of the illusive nature

Dr. Karl T. Compton, former president of the American Association for the Advancement of Science, in his address of December 1936, referred in the strongest possible language to the enormous importance of the revolution in the sciences which was brought about by the events of the few years preceding the climax in 1897 when the electron was discovered. He said:

> The history of science abounds with instances when a new concept or discovery has led to tremendous advances into vast new fields of knowledge and art whose very existence had hitherto been unsuspected. The discoveries of Galileo, Faraday and Pasteur are such instances. But, to my notion, no such instance has been so dramatic as the discovery of the electron, the tiniest thing in the universe, which within one generation has transformed a stagnant science of physics, a descriptive science of chemistry and a sterile science of astronomy into dynamically developing sciences fraught with intellectual adventure, interrelating interpretations and practical values. . . .
>
> In 1896, however, Zeeman tried the experiment of examining the spectrum of a light source placed in a strong magnetic field, . . . [and] in January, 1897, Lorentz showed that this experiment proved that light is caused by the oscillation of electric charges, . . . what was startling was Lorentz's proof that the Zeeman effect could only have been produced by electrified particles . . . Almost at once this conclusion was confirmed in a more dramatic and understandable way by J. J. Thomson . . . By measuring this curvature produced by a magnetic field of known strength . . . J. J. Thomson in 1897 first showed that cathode rays are negatively charged particles with a ratio of charge to mass nearly two thousand times that of hydrogen. He furthermore showed that these particles are of the same type, as

---

of matter, and the infinite divisibility of the atom, that the whole science of Occultism is built. It opens limitless horizons to *substance* informed by the divine breath of its soul in every possible state of tenuity, states still undreamt of by the most spiritually disposed chemists and physicists." — *S.D.*, I, 519–20

regards ratio of charge to mass, from whatever gas or cathode material they are produced. He therefore announced these particles, which he called "corpuscles," to be universal constituents of all substances. Thus was the electron discovered.

— *Science,* January 8, 1937

"Thus was the electron discovered" — according to Dr. Compton the most dramatic instance of transforming discovery in the history of science. It literally confirms the announcement in *The Secret Doctrine*, quoted above, that a great rent would be made in the "Veil of Nature" between 1888 and 1897, and that materialistic science would receive a deathblow. As Dr. Dampier-Whetham says, the old materialism was dead.

Dr. Compton refers to the important work done by Professor William Crookes, especially in regard to vacuum-tubes, and to the practical certainty that he would have discovered the X-ray if his attention had not been drawn in other directions just as he was almost touching it. As it was, his work was essential to the discovery of the electron.

H. P. Blavatsky claimed no credit for the teachings in her book, but only for the presentation and comments. In "My Books," dated only a few days before her passing, she closed her life's work with the words:

Nothing of that have I invented, but simply given it out as I have been taught; or as quoted by me in the *Secret Doctrine* (Vol. I p. 46 [xlvi]) from Montaigne: "I have here made only a nosegay of culled (Eastern) flowers, and have brought nothing of my own but the string that ties them."

Is any one of my helpers prepared to say that I have not paid the full price for the string? — *Lucifer,* VIII, 247, May 1891

In her impersonal presentation of theosophy, she made

no secret of her belief that the intuitive readers of *The Secret Doctrine* may find knowledge in it which she herself did not possess, as it came from higher sources than "poor, miserable" H. P. Blavatsky, as she calls herself. She was emphatic in stating that the book was not intended to give a final verdict on existence, but only to lead the student toward finding truth: "See in study a means of exercising and developing the mind never touched by other studies" (*Forum*, III, 257, Aug. 1932).

The Secret Doctrine was not, however, the final message of theosophy for the nineteenth century, for it was soon followed by the key to its spiritual interpretation, without which it would be hardly more than a profound scientific treatise on the evolution of man and the universe. This culmination of her teaching was reached with the publication in 1889 of *The Voice of the Silence*, an exquisite prose-poem. This little book reveals the true path leading to the mystical achievement of finding the Self, the inner god. It is the clearest expression of the central teaching of the theosophical movement – the way of attainment – for the individual and for the race. The deeper side of the *S.D.* cannot be understood without the spiritual illumination to be found by living the truths set forth in *The Voice of the Silence.*

Many persons ask for something *practical* when they come in contact with theosophy. For several years before the establishment of the Esoteric School, students of theosophy had been challenged to rise and take the kingdom of heaven by strength, to find the path to reality, to become conscious coworkers with nature, and to live *in* and *for* the world but not to be *of* it – in other words, to seek to tread the road of chelaship. In this little book the true way of life is taught in language of great poetical beauty and imagery. The selection of the aphorisms and the rendering into stately English are H. P. Blavatsky's own but, as she says:

> ". . . the *Voice of the Silence*, tiny book though it is, is simply becoming the Theosophists' bible.
>
> "They are grand aphorisms, indeed. I may say so, because you know I did not invent them! I only translated them from Telugu, the oldest South-Indian dialect. There are three treatises, about morals, and the moral principles of the Mongolian and Dravidian mystics." —*The Path*, X, 268, Dec. 1895

The high estimation in which the *Voice* is held by those qualified to judge is shown by the endorsement by the Tashi Lama of Tibet of a reprint of the original edition, published in China by Alice L. Cleather and Basil Crump. This high ecclesiastical authority states that H. P. Blavatsky gave the only true exposition in English of the "heart doctrine" of Mahāyāna Buddhism. In certain editions of the *Voice*, parts have unfortunately been omitted, but all authentic reprints contain the original teaching, also given by H.P.B. in her *Theosophical Glossary*, of the difference between the noble ideal of self-sacrifice of the Buddhas of Compassion and the spiritual selfishness of the Pratyeka-Buddhas. This is an important tenet in Mahāyāna Buddhism, as Dr. Evans-Wentz explains in his *Tibetan Yoga and Secret Doctrines*, pages 94, 144, 360.

William James, the eminent psychologist, discusses *The Voice of the Silence* in his *Varieties of Religious Experience* (420–1), and uses some passages to illustrate his belief that while the profounder mystical ranges of consciousness are best approached through music and not "conceptual speech," many mystical scriptures produce almost the same effect by seemingly self-contradictory or paradoxical phrases such as "the voice of Nāda, the Soundless Sound," used so effectively by H.P.B. and which, James says, "stir chords within you which music and language touch in common."

The archaic versions of spiritual realities such as H.P.B. translated into rhythmic phrases in the *Voice* spring from the fountainhead of wisdom, and strike the cosmic tones of the Music of the Spheres. Their rhythmic sweep of grandeur arouses a response which is beyond the range of the merely reasoning mind, at whose uttermost reaches begins the spiritual realm of the real man, who does not argue, but *knows*. William James says:

> There is a verge of the mind which these things haunt; and whispers therefrom mingle with the operations of our understanding, even as the waters of the infinite ocean send their waves to break among the pebbles that lie upon our shores.

In contrast to the devotional and mystical content of the *Voice*, her *Key to Theosophy*, also brought out in 1889, was a practical and timely textbook, treating principally of the theosophical movement, the nature of man's principles, reincarnation, karma, etc., while a large part is devoted to the application of theosophy to the affairs of the world – education, social reforms, duties of life, and the like.

About this time the instructive *Transactions of the Blavatsky Lodge* appeared. This consists of a stenographic report of the discussions in which H. P. Blavatsky explained certain difficult points in *The Secret Doctrine*. The spiritual-intellectual tone of these discussions, which covered profound philosophical and scientific topics, is in strong contrast with the aspect of the psycho-intellectual researches which Mr. Sinnett and his sympathizers were pursuing.

The Theosophical Glossary, *From the Caves and Jungles of Hindostan*, in English translation, *Nightmare Tales*, and *A Modern Panarion*, were published soon after her death. The *Collected Writings* of H. P. Blavatsky, now being published in successive volumes, will contain, it is expected, her entire literary output. Among these will be found her deeply instructive articles from *Lucifer*, one of which, "Psychic and Noetic Action,"* has been discussed by Professor C. E. M. Joad, the noted expositor of modern culture and philosophy. He refers incidentally to the contrasting philosophies of Kant and Hume, and shows that while H. P. Blavatsky's teaching agrees with Kant in regard to the dual nature of the soul and the existence of a continuing or unifying self, she was far more successful than any other thinker in refuting the objections against "spiritualized philosophy" brought by scientific materialism. The following quotation from Joad's tribute to her knowledge and insight indicates her true philosophic standing:

> It is interesting, by the way, to note how many of the novelties which have been put forward by philosophers in the twentieth century appear in her work. This is particularly true of the modern philosophical criticism of materialist science.
>
> . . . it is impossible not to feel the greatest respect for Madame Blavatsky's writings on this subject [the higher and lower selves]; of respect and, if the word may be permitted, of admiration. Writing when she did, she anticipated many ideas which, familiar today, were in the highest degree novel fifty years ago.
>
> —*The Aryan Path*, VIII, 202–3, May 1937

---

*[Available also with related articles in one volume under the title *Studies in Occultism*. —Ed.]

Novel? Yes, in the West, but brought to the West from the Orient by the self-sacrifice of the messenger of those guardians of the ancient wisdom who saw that the time had come to lift the veil of intellectual and spiritual knowledge a little higher in preparation for the new era that was at hand.

In 1925 *The Letters of H. P. Blavatsky to A. P. Sinnett* was brought out. It contains a certain amount of teaching not to be found elsewhere; but its main value lies in the revelation of her unshakable devotion to the great cause and to the Masters, in spite of the almost incredible sufferings, treacheries, misunderstandings, and slanders she had to endure.

WILLIAM Q. JUDGE and HENRY S. OLCOTT
San Francisco, October 1891

21

"KEEP THE LINK UNBROKEN"

THE last words of H. P. Blavatsky in regard to her work are said to have been: "Keep the link unbroken! Do not let my last incarnation be a failure." And notwithstanding many vicissitudes, crises, errors, and the defections of half-hearted members, the movement has not been a failure and unquestionably it has come to stay.

At the passing of H.P.B. the office of corresponding secretary, which she had reassumed after the near panic in India was over, was left vacant as a tribute to her memory. Instead of the depression that the enemies of theosophy imagined would be inevitable, the movement showed its innate vitality. The effect of H.P.B.'s departure from this plane was to arouse a tremendous determination to carry on her work with still greater success. A General Convention of the European Section was called, and as most of the leading members from the other sections, including the president and the vice-president, attended, it became practically a convention of the whole Society. The London Lodge, still under the direction of A. P. Sinnett, held aloof in its position as a quasi-independent body. Aside from this, a most fraternal and optimistic feeling prevailed, and when the members went away, the prospects were very bright. H. S. Olcott, W. Q. Judge, and Annie Besant stood out as the most capable and dedicated leaders in the Society at that time.

An important problem requiring immediate attention was the future of the Esoteric School. This should have been entirely confined to its own membership and settled within its own ranks, but unfortunate circumstances that arose later dragged the matter into public notice, and so a brief mention is necessary here. The most prominent persons in the School were W. Q. Judge and Mrs. Besant. Judge was one of the two remaining founders of the Society and had been for years the close and trusted friend of H.P.B., and, by appointing him her representative in America, she had given him the most responsible position, except her own, in the Esoteric School. Mrs. Besant was a new recruit, but she had quickly taken an active part in the School. H.P. B. wrote to W. Q. J. in March 1891, shortly before her passing, that Mrs. Besant by nature was "not psychic nor spiritual in the least – all intellect, and yet she hears Master's voice when alone, sees His Light, and recognizes his voice from that of *D*———." But her unselfish and courageous devotion to the service of suffering humanity had laid the foundation of this rapid progress *under the guiding hand of the Teacher.*

It was not surprising, then, when the question of the future management of the Esoteric School arose, and it was decided to carry it on along the lines laid down by H.P.B., that Mrs. Besant should have been regarded as a leading spirit in that department. To show the estimation in which she was held by H.P.B., the latter officially appointed her "Chief Secretary of the Inner Group and Recorder of the Teachings," shortly before she went to America to carry H. P. Blavatsky's Message to the American Convention in April 1891. When Mrs. Besant returned, the Teacher had passed away, and a new situation had to be met. There were no further teachings forthcoming from H.P.B., and so the position of Recorder had no duties attached.

Various candidates for leadership were vaguely indicated;

even the kindly and devoted Countess of Caithness was looked on favorably by the French lodges, but she could not have fulfilled the duties. W. Q. Judge naturally appeared to the Council and the leading members to be the fitted person to take the lead. Not only was he a cofounder of the Society with H. S. Olcott (who by then had dissociated himself from the E.S.), but he had the spiritual dedication, the theosophical knowledge, the long experience in the Society needed, as well as H.P.B.'s entire and unshakable trust. It has already been mentioned (p. 238) that she considered Judge the only person in whom she had "confidence enough not to have extracted from him a pledge." He had offered himself in Master's service even before the founding of the T. S. He also was the only person whom, so far as is known, she spoke of as being in close union with a high Adept, a nirmānakāya (p. 243).

But for his own voluntary act, Judge would have been given the sole management of the Esoteric School. However, when the decision as to the future arrangement had to be made, he produced and read to the responsible group in London a private letter from H.P.B. to him, written shortly before her death, which contained a passage referring to Annie Besant in high appreciation. This passage continues from the sentence quoted on page 276:

> "Judge, *she is a most wonderful woman*, my right hand, my successor, when I will be forced to leave you, my sole hope in England, as you are my sole hope in America."
>
> – *H.P.B. and the Present Crisis in the Theosophical Society*, 4

In view of this letter, and under a plan suggested by Judge, the managing group of representative members divided the control of the School between W. Q. Judge and Annie Besant, "the highest officials in the School for the present," as is recorded in the Minutes of the meeting. They were to be Co-Outer Heads, and it was expected that the work would be conducted according to H. P. Blavatsky's principles.

Judge's high sense of honor was never more conspicuous than on this occasion for, if he had not brought H.P.B.'s letter forward, he would have been given without question the highest position in the theosophical movement that the Council could offer. This action was in consonance with the impersonal nature of the man, which is shown throughout his entire career.

Some have since thought that H.P.B.'s reference to "successor" meant that Mrs. Besant was to be the sole Head of the School, but the members took it in the obvious meaning of the words – successor in leadership in England, working in close harmony with Judge as leader in America. Knowing H.P.B.'s high opinion of Judge, and also that he was unanimously supported by the Americans (by far the largest body of active workers in the T. S. at that time) the Council adopted a course that was an excellent working plan for the time being. That Mrs. Besant regarded Judge as better qualified than herself to carry on the Esoteric School, is shown by a quotation from a letter to *The Path*, written by Dr. Archibald Keightley:

In a letter dated July 2, 1891, Mrs. Besant says, writing to esotericists who did not wish to accept the co-headship of Mrs. Besant, the following:

"*If I could*, I would say to you, my dear ——, sign only to Mr. Judge. I should be quite content, for indeed there is no reason why you should have any confidence in me. *Only as They have put us together,* I have no power to stand aside." (Italics mine [A.K.].)

— *The Path,* X, 100, June 1895

The last sentence in the above letter refers to a written message found by her among her papers during the Council meeting, about the management of the School. It came from the Master M. and read: "Judge's plan is right." At that time and for about two years afterward, she was most insistent in her assurances that the conditions of its reception precluded any possibility of its being anything but a direct message from the Master, precipitated by occult means. In a statement dated July 14, 1893, signed by Constance Wachtmeister, G. R. S. Mead, Annie Besant, Laura M. Cooper, W. Wynn Westcott, and Alice Cleather — all of them members of the General Council who were present at the fateful meeting in July 1891 — the phenomenal reception of the message "Judge's plan is right" is described. It is stated to have contained a seal-impression recognized by the countess and others as identical with that found on letters received during H.P.B.'s lifetime. The statement concludes with a significant paragraph:

> The message was received as a most satisfactory sign of approval of the arrangement proposed, but that arrangement was in no sense arrived at in consequence of it, being, as above stated, based on H. P. Blavatsky's own letters and accepted as by her directions.
>
> — *Reply by William Q. Judge to Charges,* 22

In August 1893, Annie Besant and W. Q. Judge included the above statement in an E.S. circular, signed by their names alone. Mrs. Besant emphatically repeated to various members of the E.S. that it was absolutely impossible that there could be any mistake about the genuineness and phenomenal reception of the Master's message in question. However, shortly after her visit to America in September 1893, she entirely reversed her attitude toward Judge, and in a few months repudiated the authenticity of the message and charged him with having fabricated it. Yet even if Judge had been capable of anything dishonorable, such conduct would have been absurd because the decision of the Council had already been made. There was, however, a reason for this extraordinary and disastrous change in Mrs. Besant's point of view, which may become clear when certain events of the year 1893 are related.

A few words should be said here in regard to successorship in theosophical work. Colonel Olcott, in discussing the subject, said that H.P.B. mentioned, at different times, various persons as her successor, but as he found that nothing came from these suggestions he thought no more of them. Reasons could be given for the dropping out of such possible and, for a time, promising 'successors,' but in a spiritual enterprise like theosophy a true successor does not depend upon appointment or signed documents, but must bring the insignia of his office with him. The indiscriminating will ask for certificates, but the intuitive will recognize fitness when he sees it. It is worth recording, however, that Roger Hall, for one, states that shortly before her passing, H. P. Blavatsky personally told him that "W. Q. Judge was her favorite pupil and would worthily bear her mantle." She repeated this to him a little later, definitely saying that Judge was "her destined successor" (*Irish Theosophist*, III, 165, June 1895).

Soon after H.P.B.'s departure, numerous mediums claimed to receive communications from her, as she had expected and had provided against by positively stating that she would never communicate through such means. At least one psychic demanded to take her place on the strength of his 'messages'! W. Q. Judge and others showed the absurdity of these claims, and when the most importunate applicant for the post asserted that H.P.B. had "guaranteed" him the allegiance of the "higher spiritual intelligences and forces," Judge explained that no such guarantees were possible. The occult (not mediumistic) powers, the intellect, and other unique characteristics of a genius like H. P. Blavatsky cannot be guaranteed to anyone. In that sense any claim to successorship is preposterous and impossible. Speaking of the same claimant, Mr. Judge pointed out to him that he was not a member of the Society, and that he did not even accept its teachings! He wrote:

> Knowledge of and control over the higher potencies in Nature comes only by individual attainment through long discipline and conquest. . . . If a person moves on a lofty level, it is because he worked his way there. . . . When Mr. Foulke [the claimant-medium] produces a work like *Isis Unveiled* or *The Secret Doctrine*, he may be cited as H.P.B.'s intellectual peer; when he imparts such impulsion as does *The Voice of the Silence*, he may be recognized as her spiritual equal; when he adds to these an utter consecration to the work of the T. S. as his life-long mission, he may participate in such "succession" as the case admits. But it will not be through alleged precipitated pictures and imagined astral shapes. The effect of these on Theosophy, . . . may be stated in one word — nothing.
>
> — *Lucifer*, X, 82, Mar. 1892

Let there be no mistake about this. W. Q. Judge was referring to the outstanding fact that there could not be another leader of the same character and attainments as H. P. Blavatsky. Even Adepts of high rank have marked individualities, though they have far more consciousness of spiritual unity with all that exists than ordinary men. But, as she wrote in her "Preliminary Memorandum," while the "sluggards" who had neglected their opportunities would lose the chance of advancement in their present incarnation because of the approaching close of a great cycle in 1899, that did not mean that the Esoteric School would be closed and that there would be no successor to herself to protect it and to keep alive the spirit of the "original programme." Her own words are very significant:

> The writer of the present is old; her life is well-nigh worn out, and she may be summoned "home" any day and almost any hour. And if her place is even filled up, perchance by another worthier and more learned than herself, still *there remain but a few years* to the last hour of the term — namely, till December the 31st, 1899 . . . those who will not have reached a certain point of psychic and spiritual development, or that point from which begins the cycle of adeptship, by that day — those will advance no further than the knowledge already acquired . . . the sluggards will have to renounce every chance of advancement in their present incarnation . . .
>
> — *First Preliminary Memorandum*

However:

> As to the relations of the Masters to this Section, it may be further said, paradoxically, that with Them everything is possible and everything impossible. — Ibid.

In regard to the effect on the "sluggards" of this close of the first five thousand years of the kali-yuga cycle there has been much misunderstanding of H.P.B.'s words, and a few passages from an answer by G. de Purucker to a question on that subject must be quoted here. The questioner wonders if it is true, as asserted by some, that the Masters started a great movement, made "great promises, and then left it like a piece of drift-wood on the uncharted seas." This was not so, as Dr. de Purucker explains:

> H.P.B. points out that she is old, and that in consequence those who have been following her teachings, inner and outer, have but a relatively short time in which to profit by her presence amongst them; for during the last quarter of every century an especial impulse or effort is made by the Masters of Wisdom and Compassion to help the world, or rather humanity as a whole; and that this outpouring of a spiritual and intellectual impulse is a particularly important opportunity for esoteric students; and that they should not allow the remaining years of her presence with them to pass without straining every nerve to reach a certain point of psychic and spiritual development, i.e., that point from which *begins the cycle of adeptship.* Otherwise, she says, those who fail so to strive, will advance no farther than the knowledge already acquired. Such sluggards, she pointedly declares – and I repeat this word – such *sluggards* will have to forego all chance of advancing to chelaship in their present incarnation . . .
>
> The questioner will note that there is not one word in this paragraph, . . . supporting the grotesque and to me wicked idea that the Theosophical Society was left deserted when H.P.B. died, without spiritual guidance and without the direct link or connection with the Great Lodge. She does not say, nor has she ever said, that with her death the link would surely be broken. It is said that her final words were, before she drew her last breath in London: "Keep the link unbroken," which keeping could only be done by means of human hearts and minds devoted to the Cause which she ever so grandly served. – *Forum,* V, 230–1, April 1934

H. P. Blavatsky, then, fully envisaged the possibility of a competent successor who would be able to take charge of the central core of her work and who would carry the movement safely over the critical last hours of the term when the danger was greatest, owing to the confusion arising from the closing of the first five thousand years of the "dark age," kali-yuga. That, however, does not imply that another Blavatsky, with her exceptional endowments and unique character, would take her place, but it certainly indicates the probability that another chela of absolute devotion, impersonality, and considerable occult experience, was ready. More than one may have been available among the high Oriental chelas, such as Dāmodar, Gjual Khool, or others, but, as it happened, a qualified Western chela, William Q. Judge, was at hand. He had been personally trained by H. P. Blavatsky, was familiar with her plans, and the Master himself called him "my dear and loyal colleague." Not only did H.P.B. mention "successors," but Judge himself had no doubt that successorship was in order, as is shown, not only by his acceptance of the Co-Headship in 1891, but in his carrying out of a new arrangement made by the Master in 1894 for the administration of the Esoteric School.

Colonel Olcott, also, had no doubt that a successor to H. P. Blavatsky was coming immediately or at least very soon after her death, even though he did not know who it would be. Writing to Miss Francesca Arundale on February 9, 1885, just before Dāmodar went to Tibet and H.P.B. was sent by him and the rather weak-kneed councillors to Europe, he says:

> Damodar goes to Tibet for development and if she [H.P.B.] should die before his return I am to be the temporary link between the Masters and the T. S. These are His orders but I shall be a sorry substitute. However, let us hope I may not be called upon for that, but that they will keep her alive until her successor can be sent.
>
> – *Theos.*, LIII, 732, Sept. 1932

This "successor" would not be the Outer Head of the

Esoteric School, because the School was not started in 1885, but it would obviously be a high chela closely in touch with the Masters and through whom they could communicate with the members, and perhaps give further teaching. Dāmodar would possibly have been selected, as Olcott hints in this letter, but this was out of the question, as he did not return before H.P.B.'s death.

As already mentioned, the Council, in June 1891, placed the E.S. in the charge of Annie Besant and W. Q. Judge, with the approval of Master M. With certain adjustments, this arrangement was carried out for some years without difficulty. In 1894, however, the Master saw that a very critical time had arrived and that the movement was in danger of falling under ultraconservative Brahmanical influence and probably of being diverted from its true course. In view of this serious condition, he decided to reorganize the management of the School and to place it under the sole direction of W. Q. Judge.

In response, then, to the Master's orders, Judge issued a circular, dated November 3, 1894, in which he announced the change, saying (p. 12):

> I resume in the E.S.T. in full all the functions and powers given to me by H.P.B. ∴ and that came to me by orderly succession after her passing from this life, and declare myself the sole head of the E.S.T.

W. Q. Judge made it clear that although the Masters had adjusted the situation by this change, it was not because Annie Besant was personally ill-intentioned but because she had "simply gone for a while outside the line of her Guru (H.P.B. ∴), begun work with others, and fallen under their influence" (Ibid., 4).

Mrs. Besant, however, saw the matter in another light, and declined to admit the authenticity of the orders. Her refusal widened the breach in the Society, which had been insidiously started as early as 1892, a year before the World Parliament of Religions at Chicago, where she represented the European Section of the T. S. She withdrew from co-operation with Judge in the inner work, and carried on an esoteric body in her own way until her death.

22

THE CRISIS OF 1894–5

FOR many years W. Q. Judge's outstanding position as a theosophical leader had been widely recognized. The respect and confidence placed in him by the general membership of the Society was strongly demonstrated when the opportunity arose in 1892. Early in that year Colonel Olcott announced that he wished to resign the presidential office, giving as a reason that his health was failing. He indicated that he would be glad to devote his declining years to literary work for theosophy.

When the American Section met for its annual convention in April 1892, the members accepted, with sincere regret, Olcott's supposedly final resignation. At that time the election of a new president had to be conducted by each of the sections independently voting as a unit. The American Section, the first to vote, unanimously elected W. Q. Judge president of the Theosophical Society. This decision was, however, accompanied by the unanimous resolution, strongly supported by Judge, that Olcott should reconsider the situation and retain his office. A resolution was also passed urging the European Convention, which was to meet later, to associate itself with the Americans in requesting Olcott to remain president. As only three sections of the Society were then in existence, a majority in favor of this request would be assured if the Europeans accepted the American suggestion, however the Indian Section might vote. Judge cabled to Olcott the substance of the resolutions, and received an immediate reply saying that Olcott would "do anything that was just and fair," but must wait for further information by mail.

When, however, the European Section met in July 1892, many months after Olcott's announcement, the European members understood that his decision to resign was final, and they also elected W. Q. Judge president by unanimous vote. But, according to Colonel Olcott, this was done under a misunderstanding of the exact meaning of his words, and the outcome of this singular affair was that he withdrew his resignation and remained in office, saying that his health had greatly improved since his first statement. The Indian members were not, therefore, called on to vote, but it was understood that they would have chosen Judge if Olcott's resignation had been final. In officially announcing his willingness to remain president, he said:

> I declare William Q. Judge, Vice-President, my constitutional successor, and eligible for duty as such upon his relinquishment of any other office in the Society which he may hold at the time of my death.
> — *Theos.*, XIII, Suppl. xci, Sept. 1892

William Q. Judge, then, was recognized by the Society as a man worthy of its trust and of being its representative before the world; but his heart was not attracted by titles or personal prominence, and he was not willing to take the presidency so long as Olcott was able to perform the official duties. He had, however, the courage to take office when he was convinced that the welfare of the Society demanded the sacrifice. Writing to Dr. Franz Hartmann in May 1892, when the presidential succession was still unsettled, he says:

Thanks for your congratulatory letter. But – I am not yet Prest. of the T. S. . . .

For myself I would never wish this office as it is very troublesome and thankless, but H.P.B. – in whom I never lost faith – asked me to take it if O. went out or died. – *Forum*, IV, 132, Jan. 1933

Yet, about two years later, Judge was charged with using illegitimate means to satisfy the ambition to be president. His conduct under various circumstances, and his known character and the quality of his writings, show the absurdity of this charge. When the presidential office was actually within his grasp in 1892 he used his powerful influence with the American members to induce Olcott to withdraw his resignation. Judge's lack of personal ambition was on a par with that of H.P.B. Her attitude and that of all true spiritual leaders is shown by some interesting remarks which occur in a letter written by Judge to Olcott, dated Paris, April 30, 1884, when Judge was helping H.P.B. with *The Secret Doctrine*. He says there is a possibility of getting

a magnificent coadjutor, *if not a successor* to H.P.B. and one who has trained scientific methods of literary work, as well as psychical abilities of the kind that make H.P.B. so remarkable.

He thinks the Masters would let H. P. Blavatsky have her desire and 'vanish' if the person mentioned (Mrs. L. C. Holloway) would do, and says that while someone was extolling that lady:

H.P.B. leaned back and said, "*O my God, if I shall only find in her* A SUCCESSOR, *how gladly I will* PEG OUT!"

– *Theos.*, LIII, 202, Nov. 1931

Mrs. Holloway was found not properly qualified for the

position, however, for reasons which are given in the *Mahatma Letters,* pages 360, 368, etc., and H.P.B. had to suffer for six years before she was allowed to "peg out." Judge did not regard himself as a possible candidate, but the time came when conditions proved that he was the best fitted for leadership.

Although Olcott did not give up the duties of president in 1892, he found time for writing, and began to publish in *The Theosophist* his *Old Diary Leaves,* a lively, often gossipy, and semi-autobiographical narrative, chiefly notable for his picture of H. P. Blavatsky *as he saw her,* especially during the early days in New York when he and W. Q. Judge were in constant touch with her. Possibly from occasional lapses of memory or for other reasons, some positive errors are to be found, especially in the later volumes. His treatment of the other two cofounders of the T. S., H.P.B. and Judge, is not free from distortion in places, and a biased judgment is only too plain at times when he deals with occasions during which he was under severe emotional strain. It would be a serious mistake to rely upon his ill-advised comments in regard to the controversy that arose a few years after the passing of H. P. Blavatsky, the so-called Judge Case, and his attitude toward his Teacher's determined efforts to establish the foundation of the future school of the Mysteries is on the whole regrettable. As a successful man of affairs he gave all he had to the work, but he lacked the intuitive understanding of the esoteric and spiritual basis which makes it unique; yet his honesty and kindness of heart are undeniable, and he abandoned a promising world career to follow the call of the Masters. A comparison of his writings with those of W. Q. Judge shows why he could not penetrate deeply behind the sometimes uncouth personality which concealed the mystery of "H.P.B." When he published his first series of *Old Diary Leaves* in 1895 in book form he announced that it was intended "to prevent the creation of a Blavatsky sect," a notion that was taken advantage of by those who wished to minimize the esoteric trend of her work. These persons tried to turn the attention of the members toward certain Oriental teachings and practices at variance with the occult discipline.

Notwithstanding undercurrents of unrest, for more than two years after H.P.B. passed away the movement made great progress, especially in America and Europe, and the boast of its enemies that the Society would disappear with its founder proved vain. In 1893 an opportunity arose to take part in the Parliament of Religions held during the Chicago World's Fair. Distinguished representatives of Oriental religions were chosen from the ranks of the Theosophical Society, whose varied types well expressed its breadth of view and inclusive nature. Hewavitarna Dharmapāla, the famous resuscitator and teacher of Buddhism in Asia, came from Ceylon; and Professor G. N. Chakravarti, mentioned above in connection with the failure to defend H.P.B. in the Coulomb crisis, represented Brahmanism, bringing credentials from three Brahmanical Sabhās. W. Q. Judge organized the theosophical meetings and was one of the chief speakers for theosophy. He attracted great attention by his clear and logical presentation of its main principles. Annie Besant aroused much enthusiasm by her brilliant eloquence. The three days' sessions were attended by such large audiences that overflow meetings had to be arranged. Following this success the movement received a great impetus in America.

The official report of the theosophical proceedings alone fills a book of 195 pages.

Annie Besant was strongly impressed by the personality of the Brahmanical representative, G. N. Chakravarti, and for many years her opinions were colored by his point of view. W. Q. Judge watched his growing ascendancy over her mind with anxiety, feeling that it was not in harmony with H. P. Blavatsky's intense disapproval of the methods of what she called "religions of pomp and gold." He became more uneasy when, on Mrs. Besant's return to England with the party that included Mr. Chakravarti, she prepared to go to India on a long lecture-tour, and he warned her that it was not a propitious time to go. Before leaving, she spent a short time in London during which she saw a good deal of the Brahman, who left for India shortly before she and the Countess Wachtmeister started for the Orient. A vivid light is thrown upon this very critical time in the history of the T. S. by Dr. Archibald Keightley, a most reliable student under H.P.B. The following passage occurs in a long protest he made in defense of Mr. Judge during the crisis of 1895. After giving instances of Chakravarti's ability to throw a glamor over individuals or groups, he wrote:

> I lived at Headquarters [London] during Mr. Chakravarti's visit there and knew from Mrs. Besant, from him and from personal observation, of his frequent magnetisation of Mrs. Besant. He said that he did it to "coördinate her bodies for work to be done." To a physician and a student of occultism, the magnetisation of a woman advanced to the critical age of mid-life, a vegetarian, an ascetic, by a man, a meat-eater, one of full habit, large appetite and of another and dark race, is not wise. The latter magnetism will assuredly overcome the former, however excellent the intentions of both persons. And I

soon saw the mental effect of this in Mrs. Besant's entire change of view, in other matters besides those of H.P.B. and Mr. Judge.

—*The Path*, X, 99–100, June 1895

Only a few months before Mrs. Besant went to the Chicago Parliament of Religions, in August 1893, with a party which included G. N. Chakravarti and H. Dharmapāla, she made a solemn statement in the editorial pages of *Lucifer* about Mr. Judge, saying:

I want to place on record here my testimony to the splendid work done in America by the Vice-President of our Society, the General Secretary of the Section, WILLIAM Q. JUDGE. H.P.B. knew well what she was doing when she chose that strong quiet man to be her second self in America, to inspire all the workers there with the spirit of his intense devotion and unconquerable courage. In him is the rare conjunction of the business qualities of the skilful organizer, and the mystical insight of the Occultist — a combination, I often think, painful enough to its possessor with the shock of the two currents tossing the physical life into turbulence, but priceless in its utility to the movement. . . . he is its life and heart in the region where lie hidden the real sources of its energy. . . . our Brother's unshakable faith in the MASTERS and in Their care for the movement is a constant encouragement and inspiration to all who work with him.

—*Lucifer*, XII, 89–90, April 1893

In a few months her attitude began to change, and within two years she was demanding W. Q. Judge's expulsion from the Society on the grounds of questionable character.

It has been shown, in regard to Subba Row and other excellent theosophists who recognized H.P.B.'s occult relationship with the Masters, that their proud Brahmanical aversion against the release of an atom of their guarded secret knowledge to the "outcastes" was almost insurmountable. Only with the greatest reluctance did Subba Row consent to teach Hume and Sinnett some quite elementary philosophical points, although requested to by his Master. H.P.B. herself writes that much was given her for *The Secret Doctrine* which she never imagined would be allowed to pass the threshold of the Mystery schools. How greatly surprised and disturbed must some of the rigidly orthodox Brahmans of the temples have been. It would have indeed been strange if some of them had not tried to check the Theosophical Society or to capture it and divert its teachings, if they could not entirely suppress them.

Under the conditions described, it is not surprising that after the brilliant public success at Chicago, faint rumblings were heard of the most serious attempt since the Coulomb attack to weaken, if not to destroy the Society. It is now clear that the outward evidences of friction were only the effects of the clash of inner and very intense forces of which the general membership knew little or nothing. Even some of the most prominent members, Olcott not excepted, were confused as to the real issues and influences at work.

When Olcott wrote bitterly about the danger of creating "a Blavatsky sect" it was a sign that he had lost sight of her true position as the messenger of the Masters, and of her occult authority. Evidently her work was in danger of being undermined by subtle means. Vague charges of "dogmatism" and "worship" of H. P. Blavatsky were brought against unnamed persons by Colonel Olcott himself, as in the Foreword to his *Old Diary Leaves*, which was widely read. The following short extract from much more of a similar deplorable kind displays Olcott's disturbed condition:

The controlling impulse to prepare these papers was a desire to combat a growing tendency within the Society to deify Mme. Blavatsky, and to give her commonest literary productions a quasi-inspirational character. Her transparent faults were being blindly ignored, and the pinchbeck screen of pretended authority drawn between her actions and legitimate criticism. — *O. D. L.*, I, v

At the American Convention in 1892 when the president's resignation was being discussed, W. Q. Judge had brought forward a resolution which made plain the true position of the T. S. in regard to "authority," a position which still stands and will stand so long as the Society holds to H. P. Blavatsky's cherished "original programme." It runs:

Whereas, It is frequently asserted by those ignorant of the facts of the case and of the literature of the Society, that the T. S. or its leaders seek to enforce certain beliefs or interpretations upon its members, or to establish a credal interpretation of any of its philosophical propositions; therefore

Resolved, That the T. S., as such, has no creed, no formulated beliefs that could or should be enforced on any one inside or outside its ranks; that no doctrine can be declared as orthodox, and that no Theosophical Popery can exist without annulling the very basis of ethics and the foundations of truth upon which the whole Theosophical teachings rest; and in support of this resolution appeal is made to the entire literature of the Society, and the oft-repeated statements published wide-spread by H.P.B., Col. Olcott, Mr. Judge, and every other prominent writer and speaker upon the subject since the foundation of the Theosophical Society.
— *Report of 6th Convention, American Section*, April 1892, 23–4

Much foolish misapprehension has arisen on the subject of 'popery' in the Theosophical Society. Popery is not a synonym of leadership. It is properly used, as Judge uses it above, to express a tyranny of thought or opinion, the domination of some person, or some council claiming to speak with divine authority in regard to matters of faith and morals, and demanding obedience to such dogmas on pain of expulsion or worse. Such a mental tyranny is abhorrent to the first principles of theosophy. But leadership is entirely different. H.P.B. never dreamed of exercising a censorship or dictatorship of thought over her followers, but when the interests of her work were at stake she rightly took over the direction of the policy of the British and European sections as already described. She even threatened to leave the Society and start a new one! Since her time, changes have been made in the Constitution of the T. S., but the original principle of freedom of thought and expression remains unchanged.

In 1893, controversial articles began to appear in certain theosophical magazines, and it soon became clear that there was danger of serious disagreement. In this brief sketch it is not possible to enter into the complications which led to the disruption of the Society, but a hint has been given on a previous page as to one of the chief disintegrating influences.

In future, when all who took part in the struggle have passed away, the theosophical historian may feel called upon to publish a full account of the so-called Judge Case. There is plenty of documentary evidence, some not yet published; but earnest students surely would prefer that these "old, unhappy, far-off things" should be treated very briefly here, for the vital importance of W. Q. Judge's contribution to the success of the theosophical movement is now admitted by all well-informed theosophists.

On February 7, 1894, Olcott wrote Judge that charges were being circulated on his "alleged misuse" of "the Mahātmas' names and handwriting," and asked whether he would immediately retire from all his offices in the Society in view of these charges, leaving the president to make "a merely general public explanation"; or would he defend himself before a Judicial Committee. Judge must have been astonished at the apparent implication that he had no defense, for on March 10, 1894, he cabled in reply: "Charge absolutely false. You can take what proceedings you see fit; going London July."

On March 20, 1894, the president sent Judge a copy of "certain charges" and said that he would be "entitled to enjoy the full opportunity *to disprove* the charges brought against you." (Italics added.) Dispassionate observers have remarked that in American and English law the accused person is not expected to *dis*prove his guilt, but the prosecution has first to show that there is a *prima facie* case against him and then to prove it if possible. Olcott was a good lawyer, but he lays himself open to criticism in his approach to this case.

The eighth annual American Convention, San Francisco, April 1894, representing sixty-one active lodges, unanimously declared its confidence in the integrity and good faith of W. Q. Judge; and that the action of the president was uncalled for, and unconstitutional because it violated the neutrality of the Society in matters of belief. But this declaration was not accepted by the president and the proceedings continued. The Judicial Committee was appointed and met in London on July 10, 1894, W. Q. Judge being present and, as Colonel Olcott said, ready "to have the charges investigated and decided on their merits by any competent tribunal." But the tribunal must be *competent*.

The charges which had been brought by Annie Besant against Judge – grossly exaggerated by the enemies of the movement, and by sensational journalists, as she said – were concerned with very difficult problems in occultism which few theosophists even were qualified to decide; but it would be unfair to imagine that W. Q. J. wished or tried to evade a legitimate examination into the case. He claimed to have a complete answer to every point. He said:

> there will never be any objection from me to a proper investigation by a body of persons who know enough of Occultism as well as of Theosophy to understandingly inquire into these matters.
>
> – *Report of 8th Convention, American Section,* April 1894, 41

He strenuously objected to what is called "trial by newspaper" which so frequently entails a miscarriage of justice. In the course of his address to the convention he also declared that under the circumstances:

> The form which the whole matter has taken now compels me to say . . . that not only have I received direct communications from Masters during and since the life of H. P. Blavatsky, but that I have on certain occasions repeated such to certain persons for their own guidance, and also that I have guided some of my own work under suggestions from the same sources, though without mentioning the fact.
>
> – Ibid., 42

When the Judicial Committee considered the situation, it was found that as the charges were inextricably bound up with the belief in the existence of the Mahatmas, it was impossible to try them officially because of the absolute neutrality of the Society, as set forth in its Constitution. The Constitution was neutral upon that subject as upon all subjects except the belief in universal brotherhood. The American Convention had pointed this out in April, and the Judicial Committee fully admitted it. In an attempt to get round this difficulty an informal Jury of Honor without legal jurisdiction was suggested, but this plan was found unsatisfactory to all and was quickly abandoned. Finally Mrs. Besant and Mr. Judge made two Statements to the European Convention, then in session, which appeared to clear up the difficulties, and the matter was regarded by the members in general as being adjusted satisfactorily. The more deep-seated trouble – the obscure but very real rivalry between those who preferred H. P. Blavatsky's teaching and methods of spiritual discipline, and those who wished to follow other paths tending toward the psycho-intellectual, and perhaps hatha-yoga practices of the Orient, already mentioned in connection with Sinnett's early inclinations – was not openly discussed, as it could not be a matter of judicial decision but of individual preference.

It should be clearly understood that Annie Besant in her Statement told the Convention that the charges had been terribly exaggerated by unnamed persons and that in no way did she charge W. Q. Judge

> with forgery in the ordinary sense of the term, but with giving a misleading material form to messages received psychically from the Master in various ways, without acquainting the recipients with this fact. – *Lucifer*, XIV, 459–60, Aug. 1894

In regard to this charge, trifling as it was, being merely a matter of occult technique, it is worthwhile to quote a few sentences from the Mahatma K.H.:

> Another of our customs, when corresponding with the outside world, is to entrust a chela with the task of delivering the letter or any other message; and if not absolutely necessary – to never give it a thought. Very often our very letters – unless something very im-

portant and secret — are written in our handwritings by our chelas.
— *Mahatma Letters*, 296

> In noticing M's opinion of yourself [Sinnett] expressed in some of his letters — (you must not feel altogether so sure that because they are in *his* handwriting, they are written by him, though of course every word is sanctioned by him . . .) — Ibid., 232

Similar statements in regard to the material form in which the chelas reproduced the instructions from the Adepts are given by H. P. Blavatsky and others. It is evident that W. Q. Judge was following a procedure fully endorsed by the Masters, even if he did transcribe some telepathic messages received by him on certain occasions.

The Mahatma Letters to A. P. Sinnett, containing the above instructive quotations had not been published in 1894, though Mr. Sinnett had received the letters about ten years before. Sinnett took no part in Judge's defense, with which he had little or no sympathy, as might be expected from Sinnett's record and from his aloofness from H.P.B. in her latter years. Had the testimony of the Master as to methods of communication through chelas been presented to the Judicial Committee, the charge of "giving a misleading material form to messages received psychically from the Master" would have carried no weight.

The European Convention closed with the outward appearance of harmony, and the resolve to work unitedly for theosophy.

Unfortunately, this desirable condition did not last long. Grossly distorted reports and scurrilous articles about the recent difficulties appeared in sensational newspapers, written by enemies of theosophy, upon documentary information supplied by a suspended member of the E.S., who said he found it "intolerable" to be left in the position of "having brought charges without proving them." Within the Society sides were again taken. Mrs. Besant pressed her charges still more strongly, and Mr. Judge's defenders supported him with vigor. It soon became apparent that no satisfactory agreement could be reached between the contending parties. A temporary separation, at least, was the only way out of the difficulty. The final outcome was the decision of the American Section, the largest of the sections, to work henceforth as "The Theosophical Society in America" with complete independence, under the presidency of W. Q. Judge. This was effected with great enthusiasm at the Boston Convention on April 28–9, 1895, by a majority of 191 votes against 10.

A large number of the English lodges immediately took a similar course and formed "The Theosophical Society in England" under the same leadership. Many lodges and individual members in continental Europe and some of the Australians ultimately withdrew from the jurisdiction of Adyar, and affiliated with the new organizations that supported W. Q. Judge. The general feeling of the delegates was expressed in these words:

> The Unity of the Theosophical Movement does not depend upon singleness of organization, but upon similarity of work and aspiration; and in this we will "KEEP THE LINK UNBROKEN."
> — *Report of 9th Convention, American Section,* April 1895, 24

23

CARRYING THE MOVEMENT OVER INTO THE NEW CENTURY

THE ORIGINAL SOCIETY was now separated into two branches, a course which H.P.B. had herself been almost forced to adopt more than once as the only way to protect the work entrusted to her by the Masters. It is therefore necessary to touch on the fortunes of each division, but only in the briefest manner, because the main purpose of this book is not to give an extended picture of the theosophical movement so much as to present a concise outline of H. P. Blavatsky's career and her work as messenger and teacher.

On hearing of the decision of the American Section to continue its theosophical work without interference, Olcott issued an Executive Notice in which he recognized its "indisputable right" to do so, and proffered his best wishes for its success, saying that "a separation like the present one was far more prudent than the perpetuation of ill-feeling and disunity within our ranks by causes too well known to need special reference" (June 5, 1895). However, in the same Notice, he abrogated the Section charter, annulled those charters of branches which had voted for Judge and cancelled the diplomas of all Fellows who had elected to follow Judge's leadership. Yet two years before, on May 17, 1893, Olcott had written to Judge:

> If you want separate Theosophical Societies made out of Sections, have them by all means. I offered this years ago to H.P.B., and even to A.P.S. [Sinnett].
>
> —*Report, 9th Convention, American Section, 1895*, 23

Thus, as above stated, the original Theosophical Society was now divided into two autonomous branches, two sister societies, each thenceforth to work out its own destiny. The few lodges in America which had shown sympathy with Mrs. Besant and her views formed a new section recognizing Adyar as its headquarters. The entire Indian Section, a majority of the European, and most of the small Australian Section chose to follow Adyar. Mrs. Besant settled in India, where she devoted her tremendous energy to the development of the Adyar Society, temporarily depleted by the loss of support from the richer and more vigorous American Section and of so many active lodges and members in other countries.

For the remainder of his life Colonel Olcott worked indefatigably for Theosophy and Buddhism, making long and wearisome lecturing tours, establishing free schools for the "untouchables" and others, and constantly improving his headquarters at Adyar. Among his admirable contributions to human welfare and genuine scholarship, prominence must be given to the creation of an excellent Research Library at Adyar, now containing thousands of volumes and Oriental manuscripts. He died at Adyar in 1907, shortly after an accident on board ship. He was a good and unselfish man, as the Masters said, a very human man but not at all mystical, and he often misunderstood H.P.B. from ignorance of the occult orders under which she was acting, and which she could not reveal. She spoke and wrote very freely about his failings and his virtues to W. Q. Judge. Even during the times when Olcott was obstructing her plans and causing anxiety to those who could see his error, she was always just and kindly in her estimate of his character. For instance, in 1887, in writing to Judge, who was disturbed by certain of his activities, she says:

> You make too much of me & too little of him. He *is better than I am,* in many respects, for *I had* & he never had any training.
> . . . This is the *one priceless* quality in Olcott. FAITH in his Master, & no desire for reward; . . . —*Forum,* III, 225–6, July 1932

There can be no reasonable doubt that Olcott had occasional inner as well as some outer communication with his Master M. although, as he says, it was by no means continuous. At times he did need criticism and reproof from M. and K.H., yet they fully appreciated his record of devotion and unflagging energy.

Olcott had the unique task of building the material form, or vehicle, for the presentation of theosophy in the nineteenth century, and it is a wonder that he made so few mistakes. He had to blaze his way through unknown and difficult territory, confronted with obstacles and hampered with trials that would have made weaker and less determined men abandon the field in despair.

Annie Besant was elected president of the Theosophical Society (with headquarters at Adyar) in succession to H. S. Olcott, and she soon initiated certain changes in policy. One of the first was the recommendation that theosophists should enter more positively into other fields of activity – religious, social, philanthropic, etc. – in order to "theosophize" them. A department called the Theosophical Order of Service was organized to carry out this plan.

About the year 1906 a very severe crisis arose within the Adyar Theosophical Society, but fortunately it only affected other theosophists indirectly by the unfavorable publicity it gave to the movement in the eyes of the world. It was caused by the teachings of a prominent English member, C. W. Leadbeater, connected with the work in India in the early years, and later secretary of Sinnett's exclusive London Lodge, but living at Adyar in 1906. The trouble arose because he advocated certain methods of dealing with adolescent sex problems which were strongly objected to by many of the Adyar theosophists. Very trying complications ensued, and amid the clash of bitter controversy a large number of Adyar members resigned and several lodges disbanded. To prevent more serious disruption, Leadbeater withdrew from the Society. Mrs. Besant at that time spoke very strongly against his teachings on the subject mentioned, and Colonel Olcott, who also wholly disapproved of them, was greatly disturbed by the entire situation. After Olcott's death in 1907, it was announced that Mr. Leadbeater gave Mrs. Besant, the new president, an assurance that he would no longer continue the objectionable teachings, and on her recommendation the Council reinstated him as a member of the Society.

Another cause of anxiety and loss of membership arose from the opposition to Mrs. Besant's encouragement of the Liberal Catholic Church and the Co-Masonic Order, in both of which Mr. Leadbeater became strongly interested as a high official. Many theosophical workers considered such undertakings quite out of place in close association with the Theosophical Society, even though they were not actually affiliated with it. They thought the identification of many well-known members with those extraneous activities compromised the nonsectarian character of the Society, but Mrs. Besant's forceful personality and the weight of her authority carried the majority with her, though not without loss.

These and other side issues which caused such grave disturbances have been ascribed to the influence of the dominating personality of Leadbeater – a psychological problem which could be adequately treated only by a complete analysis of the voluminous data available.

Sincerely anxious to promote higher education in India, and to counteract the materialistic tendency of public secular education, Mrs. Besant started a High School and College at Benares in 1898. It was later handed over to the Hindu authorities and developed into the Benares Hindu University. Other valuable and extensive educational work has since been carried on in India, Ceylon, etc., under the auspices of the Adyar T. S. In 1918 Mrs. Besant organized the Indian Boy Scouts, she being appointed Honorary Commissioner of all India for the Boy Scouts Association.

In 1913 Mrs. Besant decided to enter the political field in order to promote the Dominion status of India within the British Empire. She founded several newspapers, and in 1917 she was elected president of the Indian National Congress. Although this activity was personal and not connected with the Theosophical Society (Adyar) as such, the public found it difficult to distinguish between her political and her theosophical work, owing to her prominence in both.

In 1911 Annie Besant organized the Order of the Star in the East to prepare for the coming of an expected "World Teacher." Jiddu Krishnamurti, a young Hindu boy, a protégé of Mrs. Besant and a pupil of Leadbeater, was appointed its head, and it was widely believed by Adyar theosophists that he would provide the physical vehicle for the incarnation of a very high Adept. Although this Order was not officially a part of the T. S., its leading members and, it is supposed, the majority of the fellowship, were Adyar theosophists, and again difficulties arose from those who feared that it would divert attention from theosophical work. Some years later, however, Krishnamurti dissolved his Order, although it had attained a large membership, and he has since devoted his activities to lecturing and writing. He has stated publicly that he is no longer a member of the Adyar Theosophical Society, or associated with it in any way.

Annie Besant was not only a most remarkable orator, lecturing throughout the world in the interest of her large Society and her other activities, but also an accomplished and prolific writer on theosophy and Indian social and political topics. After Mr. Judge's 1894 circular declaring his appointment as sole Outer Head of the Esoteric School she carried on a School of her own for those who preferred to follow her. She passed away at Adyar on September 20, 1933.

Dr. George S. Arundale, former vice-principal of the Benares Hindu College, was elected as her successor in the presidency of the Theosophical Society with headquarters at Adyar. His policy was marked by strict moderation and the desire to harmonize diverse points of view within his Society. He and Mrs. Arundale, a Hindu lady, actively promoted the artistic and cultural methods of introducing theosophy to the world, and he contributed considerably to theosophical literature, notably in regard to practical ethics and social betterment.*

At various times since the division into the two Theosophical Societies with international headquarters in America

*[Dr. Arundale passed away on August 11, 1945. Succeeding him as president of the T. S. (Adyar) have been C. Jinarājadāsa (1946–1953), N. Srī Ram (1953–1973), and John B. S. Coats (1973–). — Ed.]

and India, respectively, offshoots have branched out from each of them, with the result that today several other theosophical and some quasi-theosophical bodies are working independently under various names.

One of these active groups, The United Lodge of Theosophists, was established in Los Angeles, California, in 1909 by Robert Crosbie, who had been largely trained by William Q. Judge and Katherine Tingley, but who left the Theosophical Society, then headquartered at Point Loma, in 1904. It is announced in their Declaration that the U.L.T. "has no Constitution, no Bye-Laws, nor Officers," and that the only basis of association is "similarity of aim, purpose and teaching." The U.L.T. members publish the standard theosophical works of H. P. Blavatsky and W. Q. Judge, as well as magazines in which the technical and practical theosophy of H.P.B. and Judge are well presented.

The Independent Theosophical Society, and another small group, led by E. T. Hargrove (now dissolved) centered in New York, were derived from the original Society. There was also an "Independent T. S." in Australia. The "Blavatsky Association" in London was formed to perpetuate the memory and writings of H. P. Blavatsky. There are other (unattached) Theosophical Societies in Germany. Other associations and groups of students have been formed, such as Dr. Rudolf Steiner's Anthroposophical Society, originating as an offshoot from the Adyar Theosophical Society. These do not all employ the name theosophy, but they use its teachings to a considerable extent, interpreting them according to their own ideas, which may not always agree with the "Original Programme." The number of independent writers who have derived their inspiration directly or indirectly from H. P. Blavatsky's work is rapidly increasing.

It is not necessary here to refer to the unseemly counterfeits, the vulgar parodies which pervert the true teachings of occultism and exploit them for questionable purposes.

A brief sketch must now be given of the work done under W. Q. Judge and his successors. The growth of the American Section before the severance of the T. S. into two main bodies was so pronounced under Judge's masterly direction that it soon became the most active and vigorous of the three sections which constituted the Society. Unfortunately, Judge's health had been seriously undermined by the strain of the nearly three years' controversy, which accentuated the effects of a fever contracted in South America many years earlier. From the formation of the "Theosophical Society in America" in April 1895, until his death on March 21, 1896, he was struggling to carry on in spite of wasting disease and growing weakness; and although his voice completely failed he was able to write and thus continue to inspire the work of the Society till his death.

In 1890, shortly before her passing, H.P.B. emphasized the aphorism – "Ingratitude *is a crime in Occultism*" – by calling on the members to defend Judge against the attacks that had begun even during her lifetime. She called him "the Resuscitator of Theosophy in the United States" and "one of the three founders of the Theosophical Society, the only three who have remained as true as rock to the Cause."* By his great organizing ability and the inspiration of his example as well as his teaching, he had brought the American work

*E.S. *Instructions*, III, 1890.

to a high standard of devotion, harmony, and energy. Whenever trouble arose, he urged the members to concentrate on the spread of theosophy rather than to waste time wrangling on matters that would soon become a back number. The power of will that makes its way through any obstacle is shown in his early attempt to build an active center in New York. He hired a room for public meetings, and at first very few attended; sometimes he was the only person present. But whether any audience came or not, he would read from the *Bhagavad-Gītā*, and give his announced address. He had the faith that moves mountains, and by degrees helpers came; and the little seed grew into the large and important Aryan Lodge, the heart of the American work. He was an excellent speaker, and his lectures on the theosophical solution of the problems of life are masterpieces of clear exposition.

His books – though few – and his many articles in *The Path* are noteworthy for their practical good sense and their happy method of stating difficult mystical subjects in simple and attractive form. *The Ocean of Theosophy*, presenting briefly the teachings of the philosophy, and *Letters That Have Helped Me*, in which the first steps on the path of attainment are traced, are theosophical classics. W. Q. Judge possessed the true teacher's power of awakening the soul-life in others. A member who was asked if she had received psychic teachings from him replied: "I will tell you the kind of psychic teaching he gave me. It was this: 'Cast no one out of your heart.' " George W. Russell (Æ), the Irish poet and close friend of Judge, wrote on hearing of his passing:

> It was no surface tie which bound us to him. No one ever tried less than he to gain from men that adherence which comes from impressive manners. . . . Here was a hero out of the remote, antique,

giant ages come among us, wearing but on the surface the vesture of our little day. We, too, came out of that past, but in forgetfulness; he with memory and power soon regained.

—*Irish Theosophist,* IV, 123, April 1896

The last sentence refers to the record that when he was seven years old he had a mortal illness and was pronounced dead by the physician, but came to life in an inexplicable way and was found to be greatly changed, displaying knowledge and qualities of mind not evident before. He afterwards explained that the original ego occupying the Judge boy's body had abandoned it on its 'death,' and that he had been directed by his Master to enter it before the last spark of life had vanished. In consequence of this most unusual method of reincarnating, he brought over certain memories and aptitudes from his past.

Fortunately, the Society was not left without a guiding hand after his passing. About two years before his death he met a cultured New York lady busily engaged in philanthropic and similar activities. Her name was Katherine A. Tingley. She quickly recognized in W. Q. Judge one who was in perfect sympathy with her ideals and aspirations, and in theosophy a much larger field for her humanitarian zeal than that in which she had previously worked. Her years of labor among the poor and the criminal had convinced her that the true method of improving conditions had not been found, and that little permanent improvement was possible without a new system of education for the young. Her dream was to see what she called "schools of prevention" established which involved a change in character as the essential preliminary to any successful reformation. When she met W. Q. Judge she realized that theosophy contained the solution of the problem. She first saw him during a winter storm when she was working at the Do-Good Mission, the headquarters of an emergency relief society she had started. She was striving to feed several hundred starving women and children in a sudden crisis. Two days later Judge called upon her, and she writes:

> He told me he had read of my work among the poor, and had gone down there to see it for himself. He had found it, so far, practical and valuable, he said; but also had divined my discontent with it, and my hunger for something that would go much deeper – removing the causes of misery, and not merely relieving the effect.
>
> – *The Gods Await*, 79

During the last year or so of life still remaining to Judge, Katherine Tingley was able to give him valuable help and to relieve him of much labor. At the same time he was preparing her for the duties she would soon have to take up in the Society, especially those of the Outer Head of the Esoteric School. Only a few of the members, those closest to him, knew of her interest in theosophy, or of her association with him in theosophical work, until he had passed away; and in view of certain criticisms that were circulated after Judge's death, as to the fitness of an apparently new and unknown member to become leader of the Society, the following statement is quoted. It was made by Mrs. Archibald Keightley, a brilliant writer for theosophy and a close and trusted associate of W. Q. Judge, well known under her pen name of Jasper Niemand. She wrote:

> It is well known to members of the Inner Council in America and Europe that the present Outer Head [Mrs. Tingley] has for two years past assisted Mr. Judge in the *inner* work of the School as his associate and equal. Some of these Councillors were doing important work

under her directions, and by the order of Mr. Judge, for some time before he passed away. The present Outer Head had the entire confidence of Mr. Judge and has that of the Council. The Council, composed of members in America and Europe, is in entire harmony and unity on this point, and especially those members of it who were in close touch with H.P.B. during her lifetime. . . . For myself, I may say that as early as June, 1894, Mr. Judge told me of the standing of the present Outer Head in the School, . . . Of his appointment of the present Outer Head there is absolutely no doubt; and there is also no doubt of her entire ability to fill that appointment; or of her right to it; or that it came from and was directed by the Master.

—*The Search-Light*, I, 30, May 1898

W. Q. Judge left papers containing information confirming Mrs. Keightley's statement and expressing the very high estimation he had for Katherine Tingley.

At first, Katherine Tingley held no official post in the Society, though she was immediately called upon to direct its policies. In accordance with her wish, E. T. Hargrove of London was appointed president. He retained the office until September 1897, when he was succeeded by E. A. Neresheimer, a devoted member who had given great help to Judge during the strenuous years when he was building up the American Section.

In June 1896, Katherine Tingley set forth with a group of students on a lecture tour throughout the world, the first of many journeys. Her entire theosophical teaching was directed to the preservation of the philosophy as given by the Masters through H. P. Blavatsky. She protested against wanderings from the plainly defined theosophical course, either into identification with ecclesiasticism in any form or into the promotion of psychic, yoga, or other so-called occult practices, or other such side issues.

Katherine Tingley's world tour in 1896–7 attracted great attention, and many new centers of activity were started and connections made with influential persons. During this visit to the Orient she met certain Eastern occultists who are interested in the theosophical movement and, when in northern India, she was called to meet the Mahatma M. in the Himalayas just across the frontier near Darjeeling, where she received instructions about the special work she would be called on to do for the movement. An account of this interview with the Master in his natural body is given in her book *The Gods Await*. During a second world tour in 1903, in which G. de Purucker took part, she again met the Teacher, this time in Egypt.

Soon after the return of Katherine Tingley and her associates to New York in 1897, it was decided to move the headquarters from 144 Madison Avenue, New York, to California. A large estate had been purchased at Point Loma, San Diego, at her specific direction while on tour. In the same year the "International Brotherhood League" was organized as a means of bringing theosophy into public note through philanthropic work. This department carried on an extensive relief work in Cuba in 1898 after the Spanish-American War, and also among sick and wounded soldiers returning from the war. President McKinley authorized the use of government transportation to take KatherineTingley, her physicians and other workers to Cuba with large supplies of food, clothing, and medicines. This practical brotherhood work attracted wide attention and helped to make theosophy better known in America and, of course, in Cuba, where schools for children were established by the Society later on, when conditions had become more settled.

Not long after Katherine Tingley had become de facto director of the Society, opposition to her methods was shown in a few quarters. Warned by previous experience, the great majority of the members decided to take action which might guard the Society against the danger of further disruption. At the convention of the Theosophical Society in America in Chicago, on February 18, 1898, by an almost unanimous vote it became an integral part of the "Universal Brotherhood," established by Katherine Tingley, January 13, 1898. Under the new constitution the duties and responsibilities of the presidential office were greatly enlarged, the leader being given complete administrative authority for life over the business affairs and policy of the Society, with power to appoint a successor. Katherine Tingley was elected to fill the office. The T. S. in Europe, and the other sections and members that had followed W. Q. Judge, promptly affiliated with the Universal Brotherhood and united under its constitution. A limited number of individuals who disliked the extension of the principle of leadership dropped out of the organization, some continuing to work for theosophy in other ways.

Owing to the conditions prevailing within and without the T. S. when Katherine Tingley took the leadership she found the time opportune to introduce certain new activities. While she devoted much energy to the spread of the fundamental principle of universal brotherhood, by writing and lecturing in nontechnical but eloquent language which appealed to all who were seeking for the solutions of the practical problems of daily life, her plans comprehended the building up of the training center at Point Loma rather than the increase of the general membership. In fact, so strict was Katherine Tingley in her visioning of an ideal Theosophical Society devoted to essentially theosophic principles and practice, that as a preliminary to later expansion, since inaugurated, she finally closed a great many of the then existing lodges of the T. S.

With the establishment of a modern printing-press at Point Loma the output of literature was increased, and has never been interrupted. W. Q. Judge's *Path* – or *Theosophy*, as he renamed it shortly before his death – was enlarged later on and, under Katherine Tingley in 1911, became *The Theosophical Path*. New books and new editions of classical theosophical works are constantly being published.

Katherine Tingley passed away on July 11, 1929 on the historic island of Visingsö, Lake Vettern, Sweden, where for many years the Summer School for children and other theosophical activities were conducted. Sweden was always close to the heart of Katherine Tingley, and she visited that country on many of her lecture tours.

Theosophical work had started there a few years before H. P. Blavatsky's death, and in 1891, Colonel Olcott visited the then small but dedicated group at Stockholm, where he was graciously received as the official representative of the Society by the scholarly and philosophic King Oscar II. In later years Katherine Tingley and her party met King Oscar, who showed his appreciation of what the theosophical movement meant for the world at large. In 1907, shortly before his death, he granted her a long personal audience at Drottningholm Castle.

When Katherine Tingley died she left a united and harmonious Society and a well-knit, devoted body of students ready to support her successor, Dr. H. L. Gottfried de

Purucker, in carrying out the "Original Programme" of the Masters. His assumption of the leadership was enthusiastically received by members of the Universal Brotherhood and Theosophical Society throughout the world, and his declaration of the policy he proposed to adopt, in accordance with Katherine Tingley's wishes, was fully endorsed.

A few months after he assumed office, on December 5, 1929, a congress was convened at Point Loma, at which an amended constitution was unanimously adopted; also the name of the Society was shortened to what it had been in 1875, "The Theosophical Society."

In 1931 Dr. de Purucker made a lecture tour in Great Britain and the Continent, and while there participated in the H.P.B. Centennial Conference held in London on June 24 and chaired by A. Trevor Barker, president of the English Section of the Theosophical Society (Point Loma). This meeting, celebrating the hundredth anniversary of H. P. Blavatsky's birth, was well attended by leading representatives of the principal Theosophical Societies. A significant early feature of G. de Purucker's leadership was the promotion of fraternization among the separated portions of the theosophical movement.

G. de Purucker's literary output includes *Fundamentals of the Esoteric Philosophy*, a technical study of the basic principles of the cosmos and man; *The Esoteric Tradition*, dealing with theosophy in all its aspects, historical, religious, scientific and philosophical, with a special section on the Mystery schools. Among his shorter works are *Questions We All Ask*, an introductory series; *Man in Evolution*, a closely-reasoned refutation of the mechanistic interpretation of human origins; *Golden Precepts of Esotericism*, a devotional treatise for all who would set their feet on the path of spiritual attainment; and *Occult Glossary*, a Compendium of Oriental and Theosophical terms.*

In retrospect, it is seen that Dr. de Purucker's major contribution to the thought-consciousness of man consisted in the interpretation and elucidation of the spiritual principles of theosophy as outlined by H. P. Blavatsky and her teachers.

For more than forty-two years the international headquarters of the Theosophical Society was situated at Point Loma, California. In June 1942 Dr. de Purucker moved the headquarters to Covina, near Los Angeles.

He lived only a few months after carrying out this arduous undertaking, passing away suddenly on September 27th. The direction of the Society devolved for the time being upon the Cabinet as provided by Article VII, Section 7, of the Constitution. On October 20, 1945, the Cabinet selected as Leader Arthur L. Conger, who had joined the Society under William Q. Judge.†

---

*[Further volumes, derived from Dr. de Purucker's private and public lectures and writings, published posthumously are: *Messages to Conventions* (1943); *Wind of the Spirit* (1944); *Studies in Occult Philosophy* (1945); *The Dialogues of G. de Purucker* (1948); *Fountain-Source of Occultism* (1974). — Ed.]

†[In 1950–51 Colonel Conger moved the Society's international headquarters to its present location at Pasadena, California. — Ed.]

CHRONOLOGY

1831 H. P. Blavatsky born, August 11–12, about midnight (Russian style, July 31) at Ekaterinoslav, Ukraine, Russia.

1848 Traveled in western Europe with her father, Captain Peter Alexeyevich von Hahn.

1849 Married N. V. Blavatsky, Councillor of State, Vice-Governor of Erivan.

1849–50 Traveled in Turkey, Egypt, Greece, France, etc. Met Coptic Adept.

1851(?) Met the Mahatma Morya in London.

1851–8 Traveled in Canada, U.S.A., Mexico, India, Java, Tibet, South America, etc.

1858 Returned home to Russia.

1863–6 Traveled in the Caucasus, Mingrelia, Black Sea coast, Serbia, Italy, etc.

1868 Went to Tibet with her Master.

1870 Met the Master Hilarion (Illarion) in Greece. Shipwrecked near Spezzia (Spétsai).

1871 Attempted to start the *Société Spirite* at Cairo.

1872 Returned to her family at Odessa.

1873 Went to Paris for some months.

1873 July 7. Arrived in New York according to her Master's order.

1874 October. Met H. S. Olcott at Chittenden, Vermont, and W. Q. Judge soon after.

1875 April 3. Second marriage.

1875 Theosophical Society established.

1875 November 17. Presidential address delivered.

1877 *Isis Unveiled* published.

1878 Divorce obtained.

1878 May. Temporary amalgamation of T. S. with the Ārya Samāj, India.

1878 June. British T. S. established. Later called the London Lodge.

1878 July 8. H. P. Blavatsky became an American citizen.

1878 December 17. H.P.B. and Olcott leave New York for India.

1879 February 16. H.P.B. and Olcott, etc., reach Bombay, India.

1879 October. First number of *The Theosophist* issued.

1880 New Constitution of T. S. adopted at Bombay.

1880 May. H.P.B., Olcott, Dāmodar K. Māvalankar, etc., visit Ceylon.

1880 August. H.P.B. and Olcott go to Simla.

1881 Olcott writes *Buddhist Catechism.*

1882 H.P.B. dangerously ill. Is taken to Sikkim and restored to health by Masters.

1882 December 17. Headquarters transferred from Bombay to Madras (Adyar).

1882 First American Branch of Parent Society started at Rochester, N. Y.

1883 November. Olcott, Dāmodar, and Brown meet Mahatma Koot Hoomi at Lahore. Dāmodar visits Masters at āśrama near Jammu, Kashmir.

1884 American Board of Control established.

1884 February 20. H.P.B., Olcott, Mohini, etc., leave India for Europe. Visit Nice, Paris, London, Elberfeld.

1884 December. H.P.B., etc., return to Adyar.

1884–5 The "Coulomb Conspiracy."

1885 February 23. Dāmodar leaves Adyar, enters Tibet in April.

1885 March 31. H.P.B. leaves India for good.

1885–7 H.P.B. in Torre del Greco, Würzburg, and Ostend. Writing *The Secret Doctrine.*

1886 Sanskrit Library founded at Adyar.

1886 American Section organized. W. Q. Judge Secretary.

1887 H.P.B. settled in London. Blavatsky Lodge established. *Lucifer* started.

1888 *The Secret Doctrine* published. The Esoteric School founded.

1889 *The Voice of the Silence* and *The Key to Theosophy* published. Annie Besant joined T. S.

1890 European headquarters established at 19 Avenue Road, London.

1890 Death of Subba Row.

1891 May 8. Death of H.P.B. at 19 Avenue Road.

1893 Theosophical Congress at the World's Parliament of Religions, Chicago.

1894–5 The "Judge Case."

1895 April 28. "The Theosophical Society in America" established at Boston Convention. Judge elected President for life. Foreign National Sections and Lodges combine under him. H. S. Olcott continues as President of T. S. (Adyar) until his death on February 17, 1907. Annie Besant elected President. [See footnote, page 307, for chronology of presidents of the T. S. (Adyar) from 1907 on.]

1896 March 21. Death of W. Q. Judge.

1896 June 13. Katherine Tingley and party leave New York on lecture tour around the world.

1898 January 13. The Universal Brotherhood organization established by Katherine Tingley. February 18, the Chicago Convention of the T. S. adopts Constitution of the Universal Brotherhood.

1900 Headquarters of the "Universal Brotherhood and Theosophical Society" moved to Point Loma, California.

1929 July 29. Death of Katherine Tingley at Visingsö, Sweden. Succeeded by Dr. H. L. G. de Purucker as Leader.

December 5. Constitution of the "U.B. and T. S." amended and name of organization simplified to "The Theosophical Society."

1930 Fraternization among theosophical groups inaugurated by Dr. de Purucker.

1931 June 24. Joint celebration of H. P. Blavatsky's Centennial in London.

1942 June. International headquarters of the T. S. moved from Point Loma to Covina, California.

September 27. Death of G. de Purucker at Covina.

1942–45 Cabinet administers Society.

1945 October 20. Colonel Arthur L. Conger selected by Cabinet as Leader of T. S.

[1950–1 A. L. Conger moved the international headquarters of the Society from Covina to the Pasadena area.

1951 February 22. Death of Arthur L. Conger at Pasadena, succeeded by James A. Long.

1971 July 19. Grace F. Knoche assumed leadership upon death of James A. Long.]

BIBLIOGRAPHY

WORKS CITED IN TEXT:

Barker, A. Trevor, comp., *The Letters of H. P. Blavatsky to A. P. Sinnett*, T. Fisher Unwin Ltd., London, 1925; facsimile edition, Theosophical University Press, Pasadena, 1973.

———, comp., *The Mahatma Letters to A. P. Sinnett*, 2nd and revised edition, Rider & Co., London, 1926; facsimile edition, 1948.

Blavatsky, Helena P., *H. P. Blavatsky: Collected Writings*, compiled by Boris de Zirkoff, 11 vols. (1874–1889), Theosophical Publishing House, Wheaton, Madras, London, 1950–1973; in progress.

———, "A Few Questions to 'Hiraf***'," *Spiritual Scientist*, July 1875; reprinted in *Collected Writings*, I, 101–19.

———, *From the Caves and Jungles of Hindostan*, translated from the *Russkiy Vyestnik* (*Russian Messenger*), Theosophical Publishing Society, London, 1892; revised and expanded edition in preparation, Theosophical Publishing House, Wheaton, Madras, London.

———, *Isis Unveiled: A Master-Key to the Mysteries of Ancient and Modern Science and Theology*, 2 vols., J. W. Bouton, New York; Bernard Quaritch, London, 1877; reprint, Theosophical University Press, Pasadena, 1972.

———, *The Key to Theosophy, being a clear exposition, in the form of question and answer, of the Ethics, Science, and Philosophy for the study of which the Theosophical Society has been founded*, The Theosophical Publishing Co. Ltd., London, 1889; verbatim reprint with Glossary by H. P. Blavatsky, expanded index, Theosophical University Press, Pasadena, 1972.

———, *Letters from H. P. Blavatsky to the American Conventions: From the "Report of Proceedings" of Conventions of the American Section of the Theosophical Society, held at Chicago and Boston, 1888–1891*, Theosophical University Press, Pasadena.

———, *Nightmare Tales*, Theosophical Publishing Society, London, New York, Madras, 1892.

———, *The People of the Blue Mountains*, translated from *Au Pays des Montagnes Bleues*, Theosophical Press, Wheaton, 1930.

———, *Scrap-Books*, preserved in the archives of The Theosophical Society, Adyar, Madras, India.

———, *The Secret Doctrine: The Synthesis of Science, Religion, and Philosophy*, 2 vols., The Theosophical Publishing Co. Ltd., London, New York, Madras, 1888; verbatim reprint, Theosophical University Press, Pasadena, 1974.

———, *Studies in Occultism*, Theosophical University Press, Pasadena, 1973.

———, *The Theosophical Glossary* (posthumous), edited by G. R. S. Mead, The Theosophical Publishing Society, London, 1892; facsimile edition, The Theosophy Company, Los Angeles, 1966.

———, *Transactions of the Blavatsky Lodge of the Theosophical Society*, The Theosophical Publishing Society, London, 1890–1; reprint, Theosophical University Press, Pasadena, 1946.

———, trans., *The Voice of the Silence: being chosen fragments from the "Book of the Golden Precepts,"* The Theosophical Publishing Co. Ltd., London, New York, 1889; verbatim reprint, Theosophical University Press, Pasadena, 1971.

Blech, Charles, *Contribution à l'Histoire de la Société Théosophique en France*, Editions Adyar, Paris, 1933.

Boyd, Ernest A., *Ireland's Literary Renaissance*, John Lane Co., New York, 1916.

Butt, G. Baseden, *Madame Blavatsky*, David McKay Co., Philadelphia, 1925.

Carrithers, Walter A., Jr., "Madame Blavatsky: 'One of the World's Great Jokers,'" *Journal of the American Society for Psychical Research*, vol. LVI, July 1962, 131–39.

——— [pseudonym, Adlai E. Waterman], *Obituary: The "Hodgson Report" on Madame Blavatsky 1885–1960*, The Theosophical Publishing House, Madras, 1963.

Compton, Karl T., "The Electron: Its Intellectual and Social Significance," *Science*, vol. 85, January 8, 1937, 27–37.

Corson, Eugene R., *Some Unpublished Letters of Helena Petrovna Blavatsky, with an Introduction and Commentary*, Rider & Co., London (c. 1929).

Coues, Elliott, "Blavatsky Unveiled," *The Sun* (New York), July 20, 1890, 17.

Dampier-Whetham, W. C. D., *A History of Science: and its relations with philosophy & religion*, Cambridge University Press, London; Macmillan Co., New York, 1930.

Evans-Wentz, W. Y., *The Tibetan Book of the Dead: or The After-Death Experiences on the* Bardo *Plane, according to Lāma Kazi Dawa-Samdup's English Rendering*, Oxford University Press, London, 1927; 3rd edition, 1957.

———, *Tibetan Yoga and Secret Doctrines*, Oxford University Press, London, 1935; 2nd edition, 1958.

Garrett, John, *The Classical Dictionary of India*, Higginbotham & Co., Madras, 1871.

Hartmann, Franz, *Report of Observations, made during a nine months' stay at the Head-Quarters of the Theosophical Society at Adyar (Madras), India*, plus supplement, Scottish Press, Madras, 1884.

Hastings, Beatrice, *Defence of Madame Blavatsky*, 2 vols., The Hastings Press, Worthing, Sussex, 1937.

Hume, Allan O. ["H.X."], *Hints on Esoteric Theosophy, No. 1*, 2nd ed., The Theosophical Society, Calcutta, 1882 (pamphlet).

James, William, *The Varieties of Religious Experience: A Study in Human Nature* (Gifford Lectures 1901–02), Longmans, Green, and Co., New York, London and Bombay, 1902.

Jinarājadāsa, C., *Did Madame Blavatsky Forge the Mahatma Letters?*, Theosophical Publishing House, Madras, 1934.

———, ed., *The Golden Book of the Theosophical Society, A brief History of the Society's growth from 1875–1925*, Theosophical Publishing House, Madras, 1925.

———, comp., *Letters from the Masters of the Wisdom 1881–1888*, Theosophical Publishing House, Madras, 1919; 5th edition, 1964; *Second Series*, 1925; 2nd edition, 1973.

Judge, William Q., *The Bhagavad Gita* [Recension], The Path, New York; The Theosophical Publishing Society, London, 1890; *Bhagavad-Gita combined with his Essays on the Gita*, Theosophical University Press, Pasadena, 1969.

———, "The Esoteric She: The Late Madame Blavatsky – A Sketch of her Career," *The Sun* (New York), September 26, 1892; reprint, *The Theosophical Forum*, vol. XVIII, May 1941, 377–80.

———, "Madame Blavatsky in India. A Reply to Moncure D. Conway," *The Arena*, vol. V, March 1892, 472–80.

———, *The Ocean of Theosophy*, The Path, New York; Theosophical Publishing Society, London, 1893; reprint, Theosophical University Press, Pasadena, 1973.

———, *Letters That Have Helped Me*, compiled by Jasper Niemand [Julia Campbell Ver Planck], The Path, New York, 1891; *Vol. II*, compiled by Thomas Green and Jasper Niemand, Thos. Green, Radlett, Herts, 1905; reprint, 2 vols. in one, Theosophical University Press, Pasadena, 1953.

———, ed., *Oriental Department Papers*, New York, 1891–1897.

———, *Practical Occultism: From the Private Letters of William Q. Judge*, edited by Arthur L. Conger, Theosophical University Press, Pasadena, 1951.

———, *Reply by William Q. Judge to Charges of misuse of Mahatmas' names and handwritings*, April 29, 1895 (pamphlet).

Keightley, Julia Campbell Ver Planck, quoted in "By Thy Words ——— ——— ———," *The Search-Light*, vol. I, May 1898, 30.

Kingsford, Anna, and Maitland, Edward, *The Perfect Way, or the Finding of Christ*, Field & Tuer, London, 1882; revised and enlarged, 1887.

Kingsland, William, *The Real H. P. Blavatsky: A Study in Theosophy, and a Memoir of a Great Soul*, John M. Watkins, London, 1928.

Light (London), July 31, 1931, editorial.

Mead, G. R. S., ed., *Five Years of Theosophy: Mystical, Philosophical, Theosophical and Scientific Essays Selected from "The Theosophist,"* 2nd and revised edition, Theosophical Publishing Society, London, New York, Madras, 1894.

Morgan, H. R., "*Reply to a Report of an Examination by J. D. B. Gribble,* M.C.S. *into the Blavatsky Correspondence,*" 2nd edition, "Observer" Press, Ootacamund, 1884.

Navaratne, Gamini, "Henry Steel Olcott: The Only Foreigner on our Roll of National Heroes," *The Times of Ceylon* (Colombo), December 8, 1967.

Olcott, Henry S., *A Buddhist Catechism: According to the Sinhalese Canon*, orig. ed., 1881; 45th ed., Quest Book Miniature, Theosophical Publishing House, Wheaton, Madras, London, 1970.

———, *A Historical Retrospect, 1875–1896, of the Theosophical Society: Extract from the Twenty-first Anniversary Address of the President-Founder of the Society*, Published by the Society, Madras, 1896 (pamphlet).

———, *Old Diary Leaves: The True Story of The Theosophical Society*, G. P. Putnam's Sons, New York and London, Madras, 1895; 2nd–4th Series, Theosophical Publishing Society, London, Madras, 1900–1910; 5th–6th Series, Theosophical Publishing House, Madras, 1932–1935.

———, *People From the Other World*, American Publishing Co., Hartford, 1875.

Patterson, George, "The Collapse of Koot Hoomi," *Christian College Magazine* (Madras), September, October 1884.

Purucker, Gottfried de, *The Dialogues of G. de Purucker*, edited by Arthur L. Conger, 3 vols., Theosophical University Press, Pasadena, 1948.

———, *The Esoteric Tradition*, 2nd edition, Theosophical University Press, Pasadena, 1940; facsimile reprint, 1973.

———, *Fountain-Source of Occultism*, edited by Grace F. Knoche, Theosophical University Press, Pasadena, 1974.

———, *Fundamentals of the Esoteric Philosophy*, edited by A. Trevor Barker, Rider and Co., London; David McKay Co., Philadelphia, 1932; reprint, Theosophical University Press, Pasadena, 1947.

———, *Golden Precepts of Esotericism*, 2nd edition, Theosophical University Press, Point Loma, 1935; 3rd and revised edition, edited by Helen Todd and W. Emmett Small, Point Loma Publications, San Diego, 1971.

———, *Man in Evolution*, Theosophical University Press, Pasadena, 1941.

———, *Messages to Conventions and Other Writings*, Theosophical University Press, Pasadena, 1943.

———, *Occult Glossary: A Compendium of Oriental and Theosophical Terms*, Rider & Co., London, 1933; reprint, Theosophical University Press, Pasadena, 1972.

———, *Questions We All Ask*, 4 vols., Theosophical University Press, Pasadena, 1947.

———, *Studies in Occult Philosophy*, compiled by Helen Savage and W. Emmett Small, Theosophical University Press, Pasadena, 1945; reprint, 1973.

———, *Wind of the Spirit*, Theosophical University Press, Covina, 1944; 2nd edition compiled by W. Emmett Small and Helen Todd, Point Loma Publications, San Diego, 1971.

Le Rappel, ["The Buddhist Mission to Europe"], Paris, 1884.

Row, T. Subba, *Notes on the Bhagavad-Gita*, Theosophical University Press, Point Loma, 1934.

The Sun (New York), Editorial retraction of Coues' charges against H. P. Blavatsky, September 26, 1892; reprinted in *The Path*, vol. VII, 249.

Sinnett, Alfred P., *Esoteric Buddhism*, 6th American ed., Houghton, Mifflin and Co., Boston and New York, 1912; new edition (revised), Theosophical Publishing House Ltd., London, Madras, Wheaton, 1972; reprint of 5th annotated edition (Secret Doctrine Reference Series), Wizards Bookshelf, Minneapolis, 1973.

———, ed., *Incidents in the Life of Madame Blavatsky: Compiled from Information supplied by her Relatives and Friends*, George Redway, London, 1886.

———, *The Occult World*, 6th American from the Fourth English Edition, Houghton, Mifflin and Co., Boston, New York, 1889; 9th edition, Theosophical Publishing House Ltd., London, 1969.

———, *The "Occult World Phenomena," and the Society for Psychical Research*, George Redway, London, 1886 (pamphlet).

Society for Psychical Research, "Report on Phenomena connected with Theosophy," *Proceedings of the Society for Psychical Research*, vol. III, December 1885, 201–400.

Solovyoff, Vladimir, Review of *The Key to Theosophy*, by H. P. Blavatsky, *Russkoye Obozreniye*, August 1890.

Solovyoff, Vsevolod, "A Letter to the Editor," *Rebus*, July 1, 1884; quoted in Sinnett's *Incidents in the Life of Madame Blavatsky*, 273.

The Theosophical Society, *The Theosophical Society: Its Origin,*

Plan and Aims, Printed for the Information of Correspondents, 1878 (circular).

The Theosophical Society, American Section, *Report of Proceedings, Second Annual Convention of the Theosophical Society, American Section, April 22–3, 1888*, Chicago; *Fifth Convention, April 26–7, 1891*, Boston; *Sixth Convention, April 24–5, 1892*, Chicago; *Eighth Convention, April 22–3, 1894*, San Francisco; *Ninth Convention, April 28–9, 1895*, Boston.

———, *The Theosophical Congress held by the Theosophical Society at the Parliament of Religions, World's Fair of 1893, at Chicago, Ill., September 15, 16, 17, Report of Proceedings and Documents*, American Section Headquarters T.S., New York, 1893.

The Theosophical Society, European Section, *Report of Proceedings, First Annual Convention, The Theosophical Society in Europe*, London, July 9–10, 1891.

Tingley, Katherine, *The Gods Await*, Aryan Theosophical Press, Point Loma, 1926.

Vania, K. F., *Madame H. P. Blavatsky: Her occult phenomena and the Society for Psychical Research*, Sat Publishing Co., Bombay, 1951.

Wachtmeister, Constance, *H. P. B. and the Present Crisis in the Theosophical Society*, Privately Printed (c. 1895).

———, Letter to the Editor, *The Occult Word* (Rochester), July 1886.

———, and others, *Reminiscences of H. P. Blavatsky and "The Secret Doctrine,"* Theosophical Publishing Society, London, New York, Madras, 1893.

Wilson, H. H., trans., *The Vishnu Purāna*, 5 vols. plus Index, Trübner & Co., London, 1864–77.

Wittgenstein, Emil von Sayn-, Letter to the Editor, *The Spiritualist* (London), June 18, 1878.

THEOSOPHICAL PERIODICALS CITED IN TEXT (passim):

The Aryan Path, Bombay.

The Canadian Theosophist, Toronto.

The Irish Theosophist, Dublin.

Lucifer, London.

O. E. Library Critic, Washington, D.C.

The Path, New York.

The Theosophical Forum, New York.

The Theosophical Forum, Point Loma.

The Theosophical Path, Point Loma.

Theosophical Quarterly, New York.

The Theosophist, Bombay, Madras.

The Vahan, London.

World Theosophy, Los Angeles.

ADDITIONAL READING:

Barborka, Geoffrey A., *H. P. Blavatsky, Tibet and Tulku*, Theosophical Publishing House, Madras, Wheaton, London, 1969.

———, *The Mahatmas and Their Letters*, Theosophical Publishing House, Madras, London, Wheaton, 1973.

Besant, Annie, *H. P. Blavatsky and the Masters of the Wisdom*, Theosophical Publishing Society, London, 1907 (pamphlet); reprint, Theosophical Publishing House, Los Angeles, 1918.

Blavatsky, Helena P., *H. P. B. Speaks*, 2 vols., edited by C. Jinarājadāsa, Theosophical Publishing House, Madras, 1950–51.

Conger, Margaret, *Combined Chronology: for use with The Mahatma Letters to A. P. Sinnett and The Letters of H. P. Blavatsky to A. P. Sinnett,* Washington D.C., 1939; reprint, with First Letter of K.H. to A. O. Hume and View of the Chohan on the T. S., Theosophical University Press, Pasadena, 1973.

Eek, Sven, comp., *Dāmodar: and the Pioneers of the Theosophical Movement,* Theosophical Publishing House, Madras, 1965.

———, and de Zirkoff, Boris, compilers, *William Quan Judge: 1851–1896, The Life of a Theosophical Pioneer and some of his Outstanding Articles,* Theosophical Publishing House, Wheaton, Madras, London, 1969.

Hanson, Virginia, ed., *H. P. Blavatsky and The Secret Doctrine: Commentaries and Her Contributions to World Thought,* Quest Book paperback, Theosophical Publishing House, Wheaton, Madras, London, 1971.

Holt, Elizabeth G. K., "A Reminiscence of H. P. Blavatsky in 1873," *The Theosophist,* vol. LIII, December 1931, 257–66.

Keightley, Archibald, "Reminiscences of H. P. Blavatsky," *Theosophical Quarterly,* vol. VIII, October 1910, 109–22.

Keightley, Bertram, *Reminiscences of H. P. B.,* Theosophical Publishing House, Madras, 1931.

Kingsland, William, *The Physics of The Secret Doctrine,* Theosophical Publishing Society, London, 1910.

Kuhn, Alvin Boyd, *Theosophy: A Modern Revival of Ancient Wisdom,* Henry Holt and Co., New York, 1930.

Linton, George E., and Hanson, Virginia, eds., *Readers Guide to The Mahatma Letters to A. P. Sinnett,* Theosophical Publishing House, Madras, Wheaton, London, 1972.

Murphet, Howard, *Hammer on the Mountain: Life of Henry Steel Olcott (1832–1907),* Theosophical Publishing House, Wheaton, Madras, London, 1972.

———, *When Daylight Comes: A Biography of Helena Petrovna Blavatsky*, Theosophical Publishing House, Wheaton, Madras, London, 1975.

Müller, F. Max, *Theosophy or Psychological Religion* (Gifford Lectures 1892), Longmans, Green and Co., London, New York, 1893.

Neff, Mary K., *The "Brothers" of Madame Blavatsky*, Theosophical Publishing House, Madras, 1932.

———, comp., *Personal Memoirs of H. P. Blavatsky*, E. P. Dutton & Co., New York, 1937; reprint, Quest Book paperback, Theosophical Publishing House, Wheaton, Madras, London, 1971.

Psaltis, Lina, comp., *Dynamics of the Psychic World: Comments by H. P. Blavatsky on Magic, Mediumship, Psychism, and the Powers of the Spirit*, Quest Book paperback, Theosophical Publishing House, Wheaton, Madras, London, 1972.

Purucker, Gottfried de, *H. P. Blavatsky: The Mystery*, in collaboration with Katherine Tingley, Point Loma Publications, San Diego, 1974.

The Theosophical Society, *H. P. B.: In Memory of Helena Petrovna Blavatsky*, by Some of Her Pupils, Theosophical Publishing Society, London, New York, Madras, 1891; 2nd edition, The Blavatsky Association, John M. Watkins, London, 1931.

Tingley, Katherine, *Helena Petrovna Blavatsky: Foundress of the Original Theosophical Society in New York, 1875*, Aryan Theosophical Press, Point Loma, 1921.

Zhelihovsky (also Jelihovsky), Vera P., "Helena P. Blavatsky: Biographical Sketch," *Russkoye Obozreniye*, vol. VI, November, December 1891; translation, *Lucifer*, vols. XV–XVI, November 1894 – April 1895.

Index

INDEX